FROM SUBJECTS TO SUBJECTIVITIES

QUALITATIVE STUDIES IN PSYCHOLOGY

This series showcases the power and possibility of qualitative work in psychology. Books feature detailed and vivid accounts of qualitative psychology research using a variety of methods, including participant observation and field work, discursive and textual analyses, and critical cultural history. They probe vital issues of theory, implementation, representation, and ethics that qualitative workers confront. The series mission is to enlarge and refine the repertoire of qualitative approaches to psychology.

GENERAL EDITORS
Michelle Fine and Jeanne Marecek

Everyday Courage:
The Lives and Stories of Urban Teenagers
by Niobe Way

Negotiating Consent in Psychotherapy
by Patrick O'Neill

Voted Out:
The Psychological Consequences of Anti-Gay Politics
by Glenda M. Russell

Inner City Kids:
Adolescents Confront Life and Violence in an Urban Community
by Alice McIntyre

Flirting with Danger:
Young Women's Reflections on Sexuality and Domination
by Lynn M. Phillips

From Subjects to Subjectivities:
A Handbook of Interpretive and Participatory Methods
edited by Deborah L. Tolman and Mary Brydon-Miller

FROM SUBJECTS TO SUBJECTIVITIES

A Handbook of Interpretive and
Participatory Methods

Edited by

DEBORAH L. TOLMAN AND
MARY BRYDON-MILLER

New York University Press
New York and London

NEW YORK UNIVERSITY PRESS
New York and London

Library of Congress Cataloging-in-Publication Data
From subjects to subjectivities : a handbook of interpretive and
participatory methods / edited by Deborah L. Tolman and
Mary Brydon-Miller.
p.   cm. — (Qualitative studies in psychology)
Includes bibliographical references and index.
ISBN 0-8147-8258-2 (alk. paper) —
ISBN 0-8147-8259-0 (pbk. : alk. paper)
1. Psychology—Research—Methodology. 2. Qualitative research.
I. Tolman, Deborah L. II. Brydon-Miller, Mary. III. Series.
BF76.5 .F76 2000
150'.7'2—dc21   00-010743

New York University Press books are printed on acid-free paper,
and their binding materials are chosen for strength and durability.

Manufactured in the United States of America

10   9   8   7   6   5   4   3   2   1

Contents

■ ■ ■ ■

Acknowledgments

This book had its origins in a special issue of the *Journal of Social Issues* entitled "Transforming Psychology: Interpretive and Participatory Action Research Methods." Daniel Perlman, the editor who shepherded our proposal through, and Phyllis Katz, the editor who published the volume, took a chance on producing a very unusual issue of this journal. We are grateful to the contributors for their willingness to be innovative and committed in their work, as well as concise in presenting it. We want to thank Jennifer Hammer, our editor; Michelle Fine and Jeanne Marecek, who edit the Qualitative Studies in Psychology series; and New York University Press for supporting and sharing our vision. We are also grateful to Susan Bailey, director of the Center for Research on Women, whose support of this project has made it possible. Most especially, we want to thank Renée Spencer, who agreed cheerfully, as is her wont, to the onerous tasks of keeping track of wayward papers, compiling the manuscript in compliance with rules of style unfamiliar to psychologists, and offering her very astute insight on everything from how the book should be organized to editorial suggestions that strengthened our own chapters.

We each have some personal acknowledgements as well:

Mary: I would like to thank my husband, Bronwyn Williams, for all of his work on making this volume possible, and my children, Griffith and

Rhys, who provide equal parts inspiration and comic relief. I would also like to acknowledge Paulo Freire, Myles Horton, and especially my father, Dr. John G. Miller, for teaching me the power of intellectual rigor combined with compassion.

Deborah: I would like to thank my husband, Luis Ubiñas, and my two sons, Max and Ben, for sharing me with my work and this book. I am grateful to Michelle Porche, Myra Rosen, and Darce Costello, who kept the other ship(s) afloat in the final hours of this book. I would also like to thank Carol Gilligan and Michelle Fine, who have always encouraged me to push the envelope on methods.

Contextualizing Interpretive and Participatory Methods

Part I

1

■ ■ ■ ■ ■ ■ ■ ■ ■

Interpretive and Participatory Research Methods

Moving toward Subjectivities

Deborah L. Tolman and Mary Brydon-Miller

RECENT YEARS HAVE SEEN an expansion of interpretive and participatory methods in the field of psychology. However, little guidance is available for aspiring adventurers in these labor-intensive and often emotionally exhausting approaches to the production of psychological knowledge. This book represents an attempt to fill that gap.

While all of the contributors are psychologists, the title *From Subjects to Subjectivities* reflects our realization and hope that this book will be useful for researchers working in all domains of social science. We anchor the book in psychology. Although psychology has not been on the forefront in embracing such methods, psychologists have been using them. Thus, while we write explicitly as psychologists about the transformative potential these methods offer within psychology, we are keenly aware that the elements of transformation we articulate here have comparable implications for other disciplines.

One of the goals of this volume is to examine the ways in which the field of psychology contributes to processes of personal and social transformation. Transformation can take many shapes. It may be found in the developing awareness of an adolescent girl of the power and source of her experiences of anger, and the entirely new way a researcher listening to her comes to understand anger, girls, women, and herself. Or it may be seen in the efforts of Guatemalan Mayan people to rebuild their communities through the lives of their children. Or it may be seen in new ways of looking at mental illness and the ability of those who are challenged by it to redefine our basic notions of effective treatment.

Transformation is always in some way personal, political, and psychological. The interpretive and participatory methods presented in this volume are bridged by the ways in which each embeds transformation. The psychologists whose work is included here use a variety of methods and approaches, yet they all share a perspective that links psychology with the politics of real people's lives and a commitment to achieving positive social change. These psychologists are dedicated to a vision of fuller and more fulfilling lives for all people, especially those who are oppressed psychologically and politically, and to a society that supports the ability to lead such lives. The theoretical and methodological choices reflected in their work underscore this stance. For this work to flourish, however, we need transformation within the field of psychology. One of our goals is to bring to light the ways in which participatory and interpretive methods are already contributing to psychology and to provide a diverse set of models for researchers of how they might adopt such methods into their work.

Pick up any book about participatory and qualitative methodologies in the social sciences and you will find yourself in the midst of an interdisciplinary exchange of ideas and conversations that generally includes, in order of their preponderance, sociologists, anthropologists, more sociologists, and a sprinkling of psychologists. One can expect various disciplines to be represented in volumes about pursuits of knowledge that share a concern about the subjectivity of participants, a commitment to research that has implications beyond publication in peer-reviewed journals, and an acknowledgment of the relationships between researchers and participants. However, as psychologists, we have been mindful and somewhat puzzled by the sparse representation of psychology in such endeavors.

Demanding the dismantling of disciplinary boundaries in social science research is perhaps a requisite postmodern stance for practitioners of qualitative and participatory methods, in which case the discipline of such researchers becomes a moot point. We are a bit uneasy with this impulse to meld, however, in part because the particular type of knowledge that is the stuff of psychology seems at risk of being left out of the mix. This volume provides an opportunity for a growing group of psychologists to speak about what we know: that psychology matters to the body of knowledge being built by qualitative and participatory research, and that it matters to

psychology that psychologists are using these methods to produce important, complex, socially useful, politically powerful, and potentially disruptive knowledge about human psyches, processes, behaviors, and relationships.

We could leave it at that and provide a straightforward "how-to" for researchers wishing to broaden their methodological repertoires. This path would be the easiest, surely, and the least contentious. However, we would be remiss not to mention the elephant in the room. Positivism is still the dominant paradigm organizing the discipline of psychology. The goals of discovering knowable truths by attaining objectivity, eliminating bias and subjectivity, quantifying constructs in measurable units, and achieving the ability to predict and control are at the heart of a positivistic practice of psychological research. This epistemology has been operationalized in psychology through experimental, survey, and other quantitative methodologies.

The epistemological underpinnings of interpretive and participatory action methods fundamentally challenge these assumptions. These methods are relational in that they acknowledge and actively involve the relationships between researchers and participants, as well as their respective subjectivities. They are also primarily qualitative, using various forms of interview, ethnographic, and social action strategies to generate data that are systematically analyzed in the forms in which they are produced. Researchers using these methods reject the possibility of a neutral stance; thus, rather than attempting to eliminate bias, we explore and embrace the role of subjectivity in psychological research. Embedded in these methods is the importance of trust and relationship between researchers and participants; such work is anchored by the goals of understanding the experiences of others and working collaboratively with them to generate social change and knowledge that is useful to the participants as well as to psychologists.

These epistemological and methodological differences create a tension that is apparent throughout this volume and within psychology at large. When psychologists recognize interpretive and participatory action methods as credible, certain questions are raised: What is "good" psychological research? How do we square or live with the epistemological contradictions between methods that reflect a positivist stance and more interpretive, action-oriented methods grounded in poststructural epistemologies? What are the implications for a primarily positivist psychology in acknowledging the legitimacy of interpretive and participatory methods? Some contributors to this volume would reject traditional experimental and survey methods as defined by the tenets of positivism, along with the assumptions of positivism, arguing that, in a poststructural light, positivism is no longer an acceptable or appropriate foundation for research in psychology. Others argue for a more inclusive approach in which various methods and epistemologies are understood as making distinct valid contributions to the field. The debate is not resolved here, but we hope that by articulating this tension, we can initiate a much-needed civilized discussion concerning the underlying philosophical justifications for our methodological choices. The potential transformations of the discipline of psychology, then, are embodied in this book.

The book is divided into four parts. Part I considers the place of interpretive and participatory methods in the field of psychology. Vita Rabinowitz and Susan Weseen (chapter 2) recount how fundamentally different views about the nature of reality have shaped the QQD—that is, the quantitative-qualitative debates—concerning various approaches to research. Rather than focus on the divide, they identify challenges to and suggest directions for methodological diversity that will yield "a more meaningful, promising, and socially responsible psychological science." Jeanne Marecek, Michelle Fine, and Louise Kidder (chapter 3) uncover the real legacy of qualitative methods in social psychology and relate the experience of "working between two worlds." The authors discuss from overtly personal perspectives the attractions and challenges of engaging in qualitative research, with evidence of both a rich history and a vibrant future for such work.

Part II provides three epistemological alternatives to the positivist model now dominant in the field. Mark L. Tappan (chapter 4) begins by examining the contribution of theoretical hermeneutics, in particular the work of Wilhelm Dilthey, to the development of interpretive psychology. Drawing on his own work and that of others in the field, Tappan clarifies the distinction between explanatory and descriptive models of psychological phenomena and outlines the unique contribution that can be made by interpretive methods. Feminist theory has richly and significantly altered the landscape of these methods in the field of psychology. Jill Morawski (chapter 5) discusses the way in which feminism underpins widely applicable methodologies for psychological research. Mary Brydon-Miller (chapter 6) reviews the basic assumptions of Participatory Action Research, highlighting the role of critical theory as an alternative to positivism. In particular, she articulates the advantages of this framework, as manifested in participatory methods, in contributing to social change in both developing and developed nations.

Part III, the most extensive part of the book, provides a number of examples of studies using interpretive and participatory research methods. The first three chapters in the Interpretive Methods section offer exemplars of a specific interpretive method called the "Listening Guide." Pioneered by Lyn Brown, Carol Gilligan, Elizabeth Debold, Deborah L. Tolman, and others at the Harvard Project on Women's Psychology and Girls' Development (see Brown et al. 1991; Brown and Gilligan 1992; Brown, Tolman, and Debold forthcoming), the Listening Guide is distinguished as a systematic and rigorous approach to specifically psychological interpretation. This method is premised on the role of narrative in organizing human experience and recognizes that there are multiple layers of meaning in experiential narratives, which are (most often) co-constructed in various interview contexts. It is especially sensitive to the relational nature of research and how researchers can and must negotiate their own and their participants' subjectivities in collecting and analyzing interview data.

Each of the three chapters emphasizes and explicates different features and implications of the Listening Guide method; together, they form a kind of primer for how this method can be utilized for making interpretations. The Listening Guide is a very flexible method that can be applied to many types of narrative data, and each author illustrates how this method can be useful in answering distinct research questions on different topics.

The work of Lyn Mikel Brown (chapter 7) is grounded in her ongoing interactions with white working-class girls in rural Maine; videotapes of the girls' group work provide the data for her interpretive analysis of the impact of culturally dominant definitions of femininity on girls' daily lives. Illustrating a new and important use of the Listening Guide, Brown offers the compelling account she is able to construct of the meanings these girls make of their lives and of their feelings about themselves and their feminine identities.

Niobe Way (chapter 8) demonstrates how a feminist research method can be used as a powerful tool for examining the experience of adolescent boys. Like atoms in the Heisenberg theory, these boys display very different characteristics, depending on the nature of the questions and the quality of the interactions they have with the researchers, giving weight to the complex nature of human lives and interactions.

Deborah L. Tolman (chapter 9) illustrates the use of the Listening Guide as a strategy for an in-depth case analysis of one young woman's struggles with her sexuality. Tolman describes how she developed specific "voices"—an erotic voice and a voice of the body—for which to listen in the stories and descriptions offered by this high school adolescent in response to questions inviting her to describe her experiences with her own sexuality. Tolman notes an absence of "an erotic voice" in this girl's stories and gathers evidence to establish that the girl experiences herself as a sexual object and organizes her sexuality in terms of romance conventions that deny her sexual subjectivity.

Sandra J. Jones (chapter 10) offers an example of a different interpretive method—the use of narrative analysis informed by grounded theory. Moving from the sociolinguistic focus that is more common in narrative analysis toward a more psychological approach, she narrates from her own subjective working-class position how she learns from analyzing a working-class academic woman's narratives the specific ways in which class consciousness becomes a part of her identity in childhood and remains entrenched in adulthood, even as she moves into the upper middle class as an adult.

Larry Davidson and his colleagues (chapter 11) incorporate both interpretive and participatory methods in working with individuals diagnosed with schizophrenia. By integrating both of the methodologies embraced in this book, this chapter serves as a bridge from chapters on interpretive exemplars to chapters on participatory action, as well as an exemplar for how the two can work in tandem. Davidson and colleagues demonstrate the strength of interpretive methods in clarifying the different world views and priorities of individuals faced with the demands of deinstitutionalization. They pair this analysis with evidence of how real change can be achieved through participatory methods that take into account the motivations and desires of community members and allow for community collaboration in the effective support of deinstitutionalized individuals.

M. Brinton Lykes chapter 12), whose continuing commitment to working with the Mayan people of Guatemala has given her a rich understanding of the ways in which culture and tradition can be made an integral part of processes of individual and social healing, discusses how she has used participatory research methods to advance these goals.

S. Darius Tandon, James Kelly, and Lynne Mock (chapter 13) describe their work looking at leadership development within a grassroots organization. They illustrate how their ability to offer their research skills informs their collaboration with this group and enables a significant contribution to local development efforts, clarifying for other researchers how they can be part of, without dominating, a critical community process.

Niva Piran (chapter 14) reports on a participatory action research project with adolescent girls attending a residential dancing school. She describes how these young women were able, through groups she facilitated, to develop and act upon a critical consciousness about their negative feelings about their bodies and how others treated them. These interactions led to a lower rate of eating disorders that more didactic approaches fail to achieve.

Cynthia J. Chataway (chapter 15) discusses some of the difficulties of using participatory methods, particularly when the researcher comes from outside a community to provide technical support in the form of research. Based on her work with a Mohawk community in Quebec, she illustrates some of the vulnerabilities a participatory researcher must accept when engaging in a process defined by and under the control of members of that community.

In Part IV we consider the road that lies ahead for interpretive and participatory methods in psychology. Among other things, this vision requires a critical view of these research methods. The United Kingdom has a longer and more well-established history of using interpretive methods. Based on that history, Erica Burman (chapter 16) analyzes the "progressive features" that are attributed to these methods, detailing how qualitative or interpretive methods have been misused and misunderstood within qualitative endeavors, while urging avoidance of evaluating qualitative efforts by quantitative standards. Drawing on her experience teaching participatory action research in South Africa, Patricia Maguire (chapter 17) suggests ways in which our pedagogy must change to reflect the values and practices of interpretive and participatory research methods. The challenge will be to be as creative and courageous in restructuring our classrooms as we have been in our communities.

Michael Billig (chapter 18) describes how discursive psychologists have approached such psychological processes as thinking, remembering, and forgetting by examining the practice of talk to understand the use of emotions in social interactions. He offers examples of his own extension of discursive analysis into unconscious processes, which he argues are required to produce the skills necessary for repression. From the perspective of senior feminist scholars, Abigail J. Stewart and Stephanie A. Shields (chapter 19) consider gatekeeping practices "that are alive and well in psychology" and are often used against qualitative researchers. They join their knotty experiences with those of other senior feminists whom they surveyed about how they engage in challenging the status quo from within when it comes to reviewing junior feminists' work for jobs, tenure, and publication.

In the concluding chapter, we turn our attention to how we can coax psychology out of its practice of silencing the reality that these methods are an effective means of producing new and socially significant knowledge. We consider some changes that can be made in the accepted practices of our discipline that would facilitate the integration of new methods into psychology.

Each of the authors in this volume has chosen in one way or another to take on the challenge of engaging in research that displaces the social construction of research participants as subjects (which, we all know, has really meant objects) of research. Moving from "subjects" to "subjectivities" to signify the organizing principles of our research practices acknowledges that as researchers with subjectivities of our own, we can connect with and relate to people whose subjectivities expand our notion of what constitutes psychological knowledge. This shift necessitates interpretive and participatory methodologies, among other qualitative methods, that have made unique and exciting contributions to our field.

It is our hope that this book will serve as an irresistible invitation to many of our readers to join in this work.

References

Brown, L., E. Debold, M. Tappan, and C. Gilligan. 1991. Reading narratives of conflict for self and moral voice: A relational method. In *Handbook of moral behavior and development: Theory, research and application*, eds. W. Kurtines, and J. Gewirtz. Hillsdale, NJ: Lawrence Erlbaum.

Brown, L., and C. Gilligan. 1992. *Meeting at the crossroads: Women's psychology and girls' development*. Cambridge, MA: Harvard University Press.

Brown, L., D. Tolman, and E. Debold. Forthcoming. *A guide to interpreting narratives of psychological experience*. New York: New York University Press.

2

■   ■   ■   ■   ■   ■   ■   ■   ■

Power, Politics, and the Qualitative/ Quantitative Debates in Psychology

Vita Carulli Rabinowitz and Susan Weseen

THE DEBATE ABOUT THE VALUE and use of qualitative and quantitative research methods has swirled within and around psychology for well over two decades. Until recently, the qualitative/quantitative debate, by now so familiar in some quarters that it is known as the QQD, raged mostly in areas related to, but outside of, psychology. It appeared in applied areas such as education, public health, and program evaluation, which are historically interdisciplinary and self-conscious about research methods. Within psychology, the debate erupted on the margins, in areas such as the psychology of women and gender, where awareness of unequal power relationships among groups (including the researcher and the researched) forced a critical analysis of the research process, and especially of the historically dominant quantitative paradigm.

As the lines that divide basic and applied research, as well as the subfields of psychology, become blurred, and as the face of the discipline changes with respect to the gender, race/ethnicity, social class, and sexual orientation of its practitioners, variations on the QQD are now erupting in mainstream psychology (e.g., Gergen 1991; Slife and Williams 1997). This development, we argue, presents intriguing opportunities for the armchair philosophers among us, offering possibilities for rethinking our methods and the underlying conceptual models of individual and social processes they represent, as well as for adding new research tools to our repertoire. But if the divisiveness in evaluation research (Sechrest 1992; Lincoln and Guba 1992; Sechrest, Babcock, and Smith 1992; Reichardt and Rallis 1994) is any guide, the QQD portends decidedly mixed consequences for on-the-ground researchers, who, in the wake of methodological pluralism, may be increasingly uncertain not only about how to conceptualize and study problems, but also about psychology's integrity and status as an intellectual discipline. Some argue that a new "pragmatism" has taken hold of most social science disciplines, and that multiple methods are used as a matter of course (Tashakkori and Teddlie 1998). In psychology, however, nontraditional methods are still viewed with skepticism, and the terms "qualitative" and "quantitative" remain placeholders for different commitments, philosophies, and positions. Like many other problematic dichotomies, the qualitative/quantitative divide has taken on a life of its own.

In this chapter, we attempt to break some of the deadlocks in the debate as it is usually cast. We resist the temptation to follow the usual trajectory of QQD pieces that begins with a note about how nice it is that we have raised our epistemological/methodological consciousness and aired our concerns, continues with a discussion of how sorry it is that the debate has gotten nasty (or esoteric or repetitive), and concludes with a call to stop arguing and use multiple methods. For twenty years, this seemingly reasonable argument has failed to move hearts and minds—or research—as many obviously feel that it should, and exasperation is increasingly apparent on both sides (Sechrest 1992; Lincoln and Guba 1992; Denzin and Lincoln 1994b; Sechrest and Sidani 1995). Instead, we attempt to illuminate the darker corners of the QQD—issues that are glossed over or completely overlooked in most discussions to date, in part because they reveal deep social, political, and personal tensions among and within all researchers.

World (View) Wars or Mere Tools in the Toolbox?

Qualitative and quantitative methods have been variously defined, and in these differing conceptualizations we can see through to the heart of the debate. From the quantitative camp, Reichardt and Cook (1979) draw a simple distinction on the level of research techniques, with no consideration of the theoretical underpinnings of methodological choices:

> By quantitative methods, researchers have come to mean the technique of randomized experiments, quasi-experiments, paper and pencil "objective tests," multivariate statistical analyses, sample surveys, and the like. In contrast, qualitative methods include ethnography, case studies, in-depth interviews, and participant observation. (7)

On the qualitative side, Denzin and Lincoln (1994b) see a deeper chasm and speak of differing sensibilities between the two approaches:

> Qualitative researchers stress the socially constructed nature of reality, the intimate relationship between the researcher and what is studied, and the situational constraints that shape inquiry. Such researchers emphasize the value-laden nature of inquiry. . . . In contrast, quantitative studies emphasize the measurement and analysis of causal relationships between variables, not processes. Inquiry is purported to be within a value-free framework. (4)

Not all qualitative researchers would endorse this definition of their work, but Denzin and Lincoln's description characterizes an important strain of qualitative research that takes a critical stance toward power relationships embedded in much traditional research.

As the differing definitions of the two approaches suggest, a central issue in the QQD from its inception has been whether quantitative and qualitative approaches represent inherently different and irreconcilable world views, or simply different strategies at the disposal of any broadly educated, well-equipped researcher. The literature on the QQD in various areas suggests that, at least until now, qualitative and quantitative researchers may have taken different positions on this issue. Qualitative researchers were more likely, implicitly or explicitly, to subscribe to the notion that methods reflect paradigms or world views. In fact, it is from the qualitative side that the discussion of meta-issues such as world view, paradigm, epistemology, and ideology usually emanates (e.g., Rorty 1982; Guba 1996; Denzin and Lincoln 1994b). More traditional scientists have tended to be silent on these issues, preferring to talk "nuts and bolts" at the level of particular research methods (e.g., Reichardt and Rallis 1994).

As we see it, a common model for the entries from the qualitative side of the debate ties the use of qualitative methods to postmodern sensibilities, pairing a stinging critique of quantitative approaches (and the assumptions about truth, reality, and knowledge that they appear to embody) with an embrace of a broad range of more and less systematic interpretative approaches, ranging from grounded theory to—in extreme cases—fictionalized accounts of data (see Denzin and Lincoln 1994b; Harris 1997). Many qualitative researchers see a place for some quantification or use of experimental methods or statistical analyses (e.g., Kidder and Fine 1987), but some do not (e.g., Keller 1985). Quantitative researchers often resist the notion that methods reflect "world views" or paradigms—indeed, they avoid such terms—and instead argue for the idea that each method has assets and liabilities in particular contexts. Many of the quantitative entries in the QQD painstakingly list the errors, misunderstandings, and excesses of the critics of "logical positivism," claim that of course everyone knows that positivism is dead, and wonder why we can't all get along (Reichardt and Cook 1979; Reichardt and Rallis 1994; Shadish 1995; Sechrest and Sidani 1995).

It is not clear that the relationship between epistemology and method can be resolved by an appeal to essential definitions of qualitative and quantitative research. People have used and will continue to use these terms as proxies for a host of other terms with which they are correlated, such as "inductive" and "deductive," "hypothesis-generating" and "hypothesis-testing," "passive-observational" and "experimental," and "constructivist" and "positivist." Perhaps instead of asking about a logical correspondence between world view and practicing methodologies, we need to examine the psychological, as well as the social and political, correspondences between the two. Rhoda Unger (1983) has tracked down and reviewed the undeservedly obscure empirical (mostly quantitative) literature documenting the impact of people's values and backgrounds on the kind of research they do and the results they report. A challenge for psychologists is to uncover the variables that are related to different constructions of meaning for qualitative and quantitative researchers. Such correspondences are in fact likely to change over time. Indeed, there was a time in psychology when qualitative and quantitative methods were more easily combined than they are today. Famous experimental social psychologists such as Solomon Asch, Stanley Milgram, and Leon Festinger combined both approaches in some of their most famous works, although the qualitative aspects of the pieces tend to get lost in textbook accounts of their work, as well as in the minds of many instructors and researchers (Friend, Rafferty, and Bramel 1990; Kidder and Fine 1997).

Methodological Pluralism, Integrating Methods, and the "Suffocating Consensus"

Many discussions of research methodology note that methodological pluralism is the hallmark of good science; that in the natural (hard) sciences, which use a variety of qualitative and quantitative methods, such debates do not rage in the same way; and that social sciences such as sociology and anthropology have long ago resolved these debates in favor of "triangulation"—the use of multiple methods to converge on a solution to a puzzle (Shadish 1995; Sechrest and Sidani 1995; Kidder and Fine 1987; Krantz 1995). Historically, psychology has been perched uncomfortably between the natural sciences, to which it has aspired, and the other, less "experimental" social sciences, which it has spurned. Possibly because it seeks scientific status but cannot take it for granted, and, in the eyes of some, appears to have so much to lose (in status and funding) in its embrace of less quantitative methods, psychology is especially and perhaps uniquely challenged by the QQD.

In the literature on the debate, methodological pluralism is rarely problematized by either side; rather, it is seen as a way of exploiting the assets and neutralizing the liabilities of all methods (Jick 1979). Researchers are advised to use multiple methods wherever possible—to "become bicultural" (Kidder and Fine 1987). But specific ways of thinking about how to integrate methods and manage diverse forms of data have only recently begun receiving serious attention (see, e.g., Hedrick 1994; Tashakkori and Teddlie 1998; Crawford and Kimmel 1999). These efforts have emerged in the face of pervasive resistance to integrating qualitative and quantitative methods in mainstream research outlets in anything but the most primitive and patronizing ways, as when quantitative researchers spice up their numbers with a few quotes, or qualitative researchers add qualifiers such as "many" or "most." Questions about which methods work well together and which work against each other, the sequencing of qualitative and quantitative data collection in authentic attempts at integration, and the articulation of quantitative and qualitative story lines have yet to receive adequate attention in psychology.

Are Qualitative Methods (Ever) Scientific? Are They (Even) Valid?

At the heart of the QQD is the question of whether qualitative methods are scientific or valid. This question automatically places qualitative psychologists on the defensive, compelling them to meet standards of validity (and reliability and generalizability) about which they may have serious reservations. As with questions about the correspondence between epistemology and method, questions of whether qualitative research is scientific or valid are unlikely to be satisfactorily resolved at the philosophical level by appeals to a particular definition of science. This is not to say that such discussions are uninteresting or useless. Certainly if one's definition of science includes dispassionate, disinterested, unbiased observation, then practically no research on either side is scientific, because description is always evaluative and always comes from a particular point of view, with a particular purpose in mind (Unger 1983). If one prefers to define science more simply, as systematic empiricism, then one can probably classify some but not all qualitative work as scientific. (Of course, some qualitative researchers do not seek to be scientific but are more interested in seeking methodological alternatives that reopen links to the humanities [e.g., Eisner 1991]). We argue that there is no definition of science that clears this up neatly: the devil is in the details. For instance, the terms "systematic," "reliable," and "valid" are themselves slippery, and their meanings can be, and are, endlessly debated.

Obviously, much of psychology is not scientific, at least not according to typical definitions of the term. And it has long been recognized that the respected traditions of clinical and developmental psychology, among others, include much work that is not experimental or quantitative, indeed, not even demonstrably "systematic." Yet few would argue that the works of Freud, Erikson, Piaget, or Maslow have not enriched the field. In this connection Kidder and Fine (1997) recently "outed" the important early qualitative work of such noted experimentalists as John Dollard and Leon Festinger. Despite its early roots as a discipline that embraced both approaches, since mid-century, psychology has turned to science with a vengeance. Notwithstanding the many great contributions that "unscientific" work has made to psychology, science has gained a currency and credibility in our field that borders on the fanatical.

This stance on the "science question" has led some on the quantitative side to doubt whether qualitative methods even represent a legitimate research style by which one can adequately describe and explain processes and relationships, including causal relationships (Filstead 1979; Haack 1996). But to other quantitative researchers, much qualitative work is vulnerable to criticism on grounds of bias or arbitrariness, not because its approaches are inherently invalid, but because specific information is lacking about the principles that have guided selections of, for example, the sample of research participants, what questions were asked of participants, and how data were analyzed and interpreted.

In our view, it is too seldom noted that quantitative researchers have at their disposal shorthand ways of referring to problems and solutions regularly encountered in their research that have no parallel in qualitative research. For example, noting that there was random assignment to groups, that variables were held constant, and that differences between groups were not "significant" communicates a wealth of information to experimentalists. This shorthand is not available in the same way to qualitative researchers.

Presentations of qualitative work are often considerably longer than quantitative reports, and would be longer still if all decisions and descriptors were articulated. Space considerations may seem mundane, but they are very real. In reports on qualitative work, development of theory and presentation of results compete with method for journal space in a way that they do not in quantitative reports.

Moreover, the very shorthand that enables quantitative researchers to convey so much with so little text also enables them to hide mistakes, problems, and even outright fraud behind the conventions of traditional science writing. On-the-ground quantitative researchers know, for instance, that the strict requirements of random assignment to group and random selection from a population are often not met, double-blind procedures break down, numerical outliers are sometimes dropped from analyses, important confounds are not discussed, and measures and analyses that do not "work out" are not always reported. In their excellent book on the problems of fraud and deceit in science, Broad and Wade (1982) state that if scientists were permitted to express themselves naturally in describing their work instead of relying on the literary conventions of scientific reporting, beliefs in the objectivity, rationality, and universality of science would vanish instantly.

Mistakes, problems and "data massaging" are harder to hide in qualitative research, because there is less presumption of objectivity, and the dearth of conventions specifying how to report procedures and analyses confers less protection. Louise Kidder (1996) notes that qualitative research can look unsystematic and disorderly because procedures for fieldwork are not often set out in advance. But, she argues, there is a logic of induction—certainly at least a psychology of induction—and an order not imposed at the beginning emerges by the end. As qualitative methods gain wider acceptance, this order may have to be better articulated. In this connection, we note that in the first edition of the excellent and highly regarded *Handbook of Qualitative Research* (Denzin and Lincoln 1994a), only half of the thirty-six chapters discuss specific methods and strategies of collecting and analyzing data. Undoubtedly, this is in part because the field is still being defined in ways that demand epistemological, political, and ethical discussion. Further, it is the very nature of qualitative work that much of it is interpretive, so that such hard and fast rules are not likely to apply. Nonetheless, this lack of specific information can leave researchers, particularly those in the early stages of learning their craft, without clear guidelines as to how to evaluate and conduct qualitative research (Jaffe et al. 1999).

Power and Politics: The High Road and the Low Road of the QQD

When we survey the terrain usually covered in the debate, we discern a high road and a low road. When the debate takes the high road, we encounter issues at the abstract, philosophical level. Here we find logical arguments about whether there is a necessary correspondence between "world view" and methodology. As we have just seen, traditionalists question whether qualitative methods qualify as science, good research, or even psychology. Qualitative researchers counter that the search for causal variables is epistemologically misguided and obscures the complex, dynamic nature of reality (Denzin and Lincoln 1994b; Richardson 1994), that quantitative methodology is inherently sexist, racist, and heterosexist (Herek et al. 1991; Landrine, Klonoff, and Brown-Collins 1992), and, despite its claims to objectivity, is just as biased as qualitative research.

As important as the philosophical level is and will continue to be to the QQD, the debate is probably not resolvable on that level, nor are the philosophical arguments as useful and generative as they might be. But they dominate debate because, as abstruse as the philosophical dimension can get, it is infinitely easier to discuss in the scholarly literature than are the political, social, and personal dimensions of the debate.

The low road of the debate, however, is pervaded by long-standing prejudices and animosities that go largely unmentioned in public forums. One of the aims of this section is to illuminate these "dirty" secrets, so often glossed over or denied in the debates about methodology.

The low road of the debate has played out for years in the classrooms and hallways of academia and, more recently, on electronic mail and the Internet. Since the early 1990s, it has burst forth in the scholarly literature as well (Sechrest 1992; Lincoln and Guba 1992; Sechrest, Babcock, and Smith 1992; Reichardt and Rallis 1994). Here, the debate is often reduced to snide remarks and name-calling that cannot be easily dismissed as harmless fun. It too closely resembles the stereotyping, prejudice, and discrimination that so many of us deplore in other guises. And it costs people jobs, grants, and countless other opportunities.

One of the fascinating and disturbing peculiarities of this debate is that the terms "qualitative" and "quantitative" have become hopelessly mired in such stereotypes and caricatures, virtually foreclosing the possibility of genuine conversation. Qualitative researchers are often characterized as everything from trendy, left-wing, and politically correct to untrustworthy, soft-headed, hypocritical, and exhibitionist. They are criticized for a supposed lack of interest in truth, reality, reason, and anything else that stands in the way of advancing their social agenda or promoting their own careers. Their "unscientific" research is often ridiculed as predictably biased and ultimately worthless. On the other hand, much of the critique of quantitative research rails against "logical positivism" and "positivists," even though those terms are rarely defined, poorly understood, and probably not applicable to anyone alive today. These terms have become code words for a host of ills allegedly associated with the quantitative paradigm:

that quantitative researchers as a group are uninterested in theory, understanding, context, getting close to the data, and respecting the integrity of research participants, or even that they are sexist, racist, homophobic, and so on.

The QQD has become conflated with larger "culture wars" raging throughout academia, where practitioners of traditional science and cultural studies have clashed over the social construction of scientific knowledge, and even the legitimacy of scientific research. Until recently, it was the upstart critics of science who were on the relentless attack. In an important sense, the pursuit of qualitative research (at least research that falls within the critical tradition) committed the researcher to a sustained critique of the reigning quantitative paradigm (Denzin and Lincoln 1994b).

Surely the immense project of interrogating an enterprise as prestigious and successful as modern science profits from, if it does not in fact require, an unequivocally negative stance toward the biases and shortcomings of the privileged quantitative paradigm. Our reading of the QQD literatures suggests that the qualitative side appears to want to preserve the distinctions among methods (cf. Denzin and Lincoln 1994b), while the quantitative side seeks to minimize them (cf. Reichardt and Cook 1979; Sechrest and Sidani 1995). Some qualitative authors have seemed almost "separatist" in their rejection of the "other" method, whereas quantitative researchers in print have seemed, at least superficially, more welcoming of multiple methods.

In our view, what may come across as intemperance on the qualitative side and what may pass for moderation on the quantitative side is the product of profoundly unequal power relations between the two camps in psychology. In large part, jobs, contracts, grants, journal space, and other forms of professional power and prestige have rested and continue to rest in the hands of traditional scientists. Until recently, at least, quantitative researchers have had the luxury of ignoring or lightly dismissing what some see as their querulous qualitative peers.

But the contempt in which postmodern sensibilities and the critique of science (and the qualitative research paradigm associated with those sensibilities and that critique) are held by many quantitative researchers is hardly a secret. Denigrated as hip revisionists or leftist academics, critics of science, especially from within the social sciences, are coming under increasingly harsh attack in public forums, from a conference entitled "The Flight from Reason and Rationality" at the New York Academy of Sciences (June 1995), to a front-page article in the *New York Times* ("Postmodern Gravity Deconstructed, Slyly," May 18, 1996). Despite inroads made by the critics of science, traditional science still commands great respect throughout academia and society, and traditional scientists form a large and powerful fraternity. Science has started kicking back, and it is kicking back hard.

There is increasing evidence that doctoral students in psychology are intrigued and excited by the vast array of methodological choices available to them today, but are also concerned about the implications that the use of different methods—especially qualitative methods—might have for the scholarship they generate and the professional opportunities they will be afforded (Rabinowitz and Weseen 1997; Jaffe et al. 1999). For established researchers with tenure and full professorships, the choice of research topics and methods, or the label of "feminist" or "social constructionist," may not be so consequential. But for those who are less entrenched, the choices can seem critical indeed. Of course, federal funding agencies increasingly support qualitative research, and qualitative researchers hold positions in elite institutions. But, in choosing their methods, many young researchers still seem to feel that they are also choosing between being branded "neanderthals" on the quantitative side or "flakes" on the qualitative side, largely because of the political and social divisions in our field (Rabinowitz and Weseen 1997).

Obviously, psychologists in the early stages of their careers should not have to fear that their choice of legitimate research approaches could lock them out of the opportunity to have rewarding professional careers. The difficulties of conducting research on "your own kind" notwithstanding, we see a need for a resuscitation of the call for a vigorous psychology of science (Campbell 1963, 1989). This could include, for example, the study of stereotyping, in-group and out-group bias, and discrimination in our own backyard, including not only perceptions of qualitative and quantitative researchers, but also those who are labeled by virtue of their political commitments or other personal or social characteristics. Only in this way will we develop an understanding of the psychological, social, and political underpinnings of our field.

A Possible Future for the QQD in Psychology

As two nonphilosophers, we have experienced in writing this chapter how immensely enjoyable it is to think and write about epistemological issues. For the most part, such writing is in fact easier than planning research and collecting and analyzing data. As others have noted, it is always easier to discuss metatheoretical issues than it is to change the practice of a discipline (Morawski 1986), and it is easier to advance a plausible, conceptually coherent vision than it is to grapple with unyielding and unwieldy realities (Dippo 1994). Our concern is that the relentless disembodied philosophical critique of both qualitative and quantitative methods in psychology will deepen the divide between those at the poles and have a paralyzing effect on those in the middle, who are susceptible to arguments from both sides. Indeed, Fine and Weis (1996) have noted that some veteran scholars who write about the dilemmas posed by the debate have virtually stopped doing research. Clearly, we would be wise to contemplate how the upstart debate in psychology can inform, promote, and liberate empirical research, instead of merely reproducing the swollen "QQD industry" that so many have found abstract, sterile, and polarizing.

An interesting paradox haunts the current debate on the use of qualitative and quantitative methods: The more public respect there is for the use of qualitative methods, and the more common the call is for the integration of qualitative and quantitative methods, the more bitter the tone of many debaters becomes. As we have noted, several prominent qualitative researchers have essentially adopted separatist positions and treat quantitative methods as relics of a historical moment whose time, mercifully, has past. Frustrated to see their "good will," in the form of calls for tolerance and integration, denied, some quantitative researchers have come to sound exasperated and dismissive. Sechrest and Sidani recently wrote:

> Qualitative researchers, particularly those who rely on ethnographic, ethnomethodological, hermeneutic, and other predominantly cognitive strategies may be aware of the by now large body of evidence that shows conclusively how difficult it is to get accurate information about what is in people's minds and how difficult it is to detect and deal with the cognitive biases of both respondents and the processors of those responses. If they are aware, however, they rarely attend to the problems in any explicit way. (1995, 80)

Quantitative researchers cannot themselves boast a strong record of applying what is known about participants'—and especially researchers'—cognitive biases and distortions to improve the trustworthiness of their own research. It is easy to turn Sechrest and Sidani's (1995) criticism around and ask of traditional social scientists why they have not better used the vast stores of scientifically gathered information about cognition, motivation, and social processes in science to examine critically the processes of scientific inquiry and the products of their fields. For example, a quick perusal of the recently published *Social Psychology: A Handbook of Basic Principles* (Higgins and Kruglanski 1996) finds superb chapters on such topics as the cognitive and motivational processes involved in hypothesis testing; the steps that people follow in generating and affirming particular explanations for events; the social psychology of decision-making; automaticity in thinking, feeling, and evaluating; and the meaning of social identification. All of these topics are highly relevant to the practice of psychology and science generally, and all should be scrutinized by those concerned with the validity of scientific findings.

Sechrest and Sidani's words further suggest that quantitative researchers are more critical of their own methods than qualitative researchers are of theirs. Like some quantitative researchers, some qualitative researchers have been highly self-critical, but qualitative and quantitative researchers have questioned themselves in different and highly selective ways. From the quantitative camp, self-scrutiny tends to focus on the nuts and bolts of method and relatively little on epistemology and ethics. From the qualitative camp the self-criticisms are more likely to be focused on epistemological and ethical issues. A central challenge for adherents of the quantitative paradigm is to be more self-conscious about their epistemology and ethics, just as for adherents of the qualitative paradigm the challenge is to be more explicit about their methods.

As we have attempted to show, the QQD raises many points where epistemological and methodological issues border on psychological ones. These include the cognitive biases and blind spots of researchers, the motivational psychology of scientists, personality and science, and the psychological description of the criteria of evidence used by scientists. We see a clear need for investigations in which researchers "study the studiers" in the tradition of participatory action research (Brydon-Miller 1993; Slife and Williams 1997). Beyond this, if we are going to have the honest conversation about methods that both sides claim to want, we must also acknowledge the power disparities in our field and how those disparities affect the way people think and behave. We must be especially aware of the debate this problem poses for students as they struggle to learn their trade and make sense of the social and political forces that shape the professional lives of their mentors and will come to shape their own (see Rabinowitz and Weseen 1997).

Finally, we reiterate our conviction that issues surrounding this debate demand reconceptualization and empirical study. We want to move the debate from the armchair, where we have all become so comfortable, to the trenches of concrete experience, where we are all less safe. It may not be enough to declare, as some have recently, that the "paradigm wars are over" (e.g., Tashakkori and Teddlie 1998, 5), that most research questions are best answered with "mixed method" or "mixed model" research designs, and that, logically, there is no reason why we cannot easily combine research methods. In fact, the evidence suggests that most researchers do not combine research methods, and we need to question why this is so: practically, why it is so difficult to obtain the training, support, time, and resources to use both methods skillfully; socially, why it may be unwise to express interest in the "wrong" method; and psychologically, why it may be hard to commit wholeheartedly to two distinct modes of inquiry. Beyond individual struggles, the methodological choices with which people grapple are community struggles, with important implications for graduate training and the socialization of psychologists, as well as the long-standing debates on what counts as knowledge in psychology.

References

Broad, W., and N. Wade. 1982. *Betrayers of the truth: Fraud and deceit in the halls of science.* New York: Simon and Schuster.

Brydon-Miller, M. L. 1993. Breaking down barriers: Accessibility self-advocacy in the disabled community. In *Voices of change: Participatory research in the United States and Canada,* eds. P. Park, M. L. Brydon-Miller, B. Hall, and T. Jackson, 125–143. Westport, CT: Bergin and Garvey.

Campbell, D. T. 1963. Social attitudes and other acquired behavioral dispositions. In *Psychology: A study of a science,* vol. 6, *Investigations of man as socius,* ed. S. Koch, 94–172. New York: McGraw-Hill.

———. 1989. Fragments of the fragile history of psychological epistemology and theory of science. In *Psychology of science: Contributions to metascience*, eds. B. Gholson, W. R. Shadish, R. A. Neimeyer, and A. C. Houts, 21–46. Cambridge: Cambridge University Press.

Crawford, M., and E. Kimmel, eds. 1999. Innovations in feminist research. *Psychology of Women Quarterly* 23 (1,2): 1–456.

Denzin, N., and Y. S. Lincoln, eds. 1994a. *Handbook of qualitative research*, 1-17. Thousand Oaks, CA: Sage.

————. 1994b. Introduction: Entering the field of qualitative research. In *Handbook of qualitative research*, eds. N. R. Denzin and Y. S. Lincoln, 1–17. Thousand Oaks, CA: Sage.

Dippo, D. 1994. Distance and relation reconsidered: Tensions in the ethnographic text. In *Power and method: Political activism and educational research*, ed. A. Gitlin, 203-216. New York: Routledge.

Eisner, E. 1991. *The enlightened eye: Qualitative inquiry and the enhancement of educational practices*. New York: Macmillan.

Filstead, W. J. 1979. Qualitative methods: A needed perspective in evaluation research. In *Qualitative and quantitative methods in evaluation research*, eds. T. D. Cook and C. S. Reichardt, 33–48. Newbury Park, CA: Sage.

Fine, M., and L. Weis. 1996. Writing the "wrongs" of fieldwork: Confronting our own research/writing dilemmas in urban ethnographies. *Qualitative Inquiry* 2:251–274.

Friend, R., Y. Rafferty, and D. Bramel. 1990. A puzzling misinterpretation of the Asch "conformity" study. *European Journal of Social Psychology* 20:29–44.

Gergen, K. J. 1991. *The saturated self: Dilemmas of identity in contemporary life*. New York: Basic Books.

Guba, E. G. 1996. What happened to me on the road to Damascus. In *From positivism to interpretivism and beyond: Tales of transformation in educational and social research: The mind-body connection*, eds. L. Heshusius, and K. Ballard, 43–49. New York: Teachers College Press.

Haack, S. 1996. Toward a sober sociology of knowledge. In *The flight from science and reason*, eds. P. R. Gross, N. Levitt, and M. W. Lewis, 259–273. *Annals of the New York Academy of Sciences* 775.

Harris, B. 1997. Repoliticizing the history of psychology. In *Handbook of critical psychology: An introduction*, eds. D. R. Fox and I. Prilletensky, 21–33. Thousand Oaks, CA: Sage.

Hedrick, T. E. 1994. The quantitative-qualitative debate: Possibilities for integration. In *The qualitative-quantitative debate: New perspectives*, eds. C. Reichardt and S. F. Rallis, 45–52. San Francisco: Jossey-Bass.

Herek, G. M., D. C. Kimmel, H. Amaro, and G. B. Melton. 1991. Avoiding heterosexist bias in psychological research. *American Psychologist* 46:957–972.

Higgins, E. T., and A. W. Kruglanski, eds. 1996. *Social psychology: A handbook of basic principles*. New York: Guilford.

Jaffe, S., K. C. Kling, E. A. Plant, M. Sloan, and J. S. Hyde. 1999. The view from down here: Feminist graduate students consider innovative methodologies. *Psychology of Women Quarterly* 23:423–430.

Jick, T. D. 1979. Mixing qualitative and quantitative methods: Triangulation in action. *Administrative Science Quarterly* 24:602–610.

Keller, E. F. 1985. *Reflections on gender and science.* New Haven, CT: Yale University Press.

Kidder, L. H. 1996. *Reversing the order and rewriting the rules with qualitative methods.* Paper presented at the meeting of the International Congress of Psychology, Montreal.

Kidder, L. H., and M. Fine. 1987. Qualitative and quantitative methods: When stories converge. In *Multiple methods in program evaluation: New Directions for Program Evaluation*, no. 35, eds. M. M. Mark and R. L. Shotland, 57–75. San Francisco: Jossey-Bass.

———. 1997. Qualitative inquiry in psychology: A radical tradition. In *Handbook of critical psychology: An introduction*, eds. D. R. Fox and I. Prilletensky, 34-50. Thousand Oaks, CA: Sage.

Krantz, D. L. 1995. Sustaining vs. resolving the quantitative-qualitative debate. *Evaluation and Program Planning* 18:89–96.

Landrine, H., E. A. Klonoff, and A. Brown-Collins. 1992. Cultural diversity and methodology in feminist psychology. *Psychology of Women Quarterly* 16:145–163.

Lincoln, Y. S., and E. G. Guba. 1992. In response to Lee Sechrest's 1991 AERA presidential address: "Roots: Back to our first generations," February 1991, 1–7. *Evaluation Practice* 13:165–169.

Morawski, J. G. 1986. Contextual discipline: The unmaking and remaking of sociality. In *Contextualism and understanding in behavioral science: Implications for research and theory*, eds. R. L. Rosnow and M. Georgoudi, 47–66. New York: Praeger.

Rabinowitz, V. C., and S. Weseen. 1997. Elu(ci)d(at)ing epistemological impasses: Re-viewing the qualitative/quantitative debates in psychology. *Journal of Social Issues* 53:605–630.

Reichardt, C. S., and T. D. Cook. 1979. Beyond qualitative and quantitative methods. In *Qualitative and quantitative methods in evaluation research*, eds. T. D. Cook and C. S. Reichardt, 7–32. Newbury Park, CA: Sage.

Reichardt, C. S., and S. F. Rallis. 1994. The relationship between the qualitative and quantitative research traditions. In *The qualitative-quantitative debate: New perspectives*, eds. C. Reichardt and S. F. Rallis, 5–12. San Francisco: Jossey-Bass.

Richardson, L. 1994. Writing: A method of inquiry. In *Handbook of qualitative research*, eds. N. K. Denzin and Y. S. Lincoln, 516–529. Thousand Oaks, CA: Sage.

Rorty, R. 1982. *Consequences of pragmatism (Essays: 1972–1980).* Minneapolis: University of Minnesota Press.

Sechrest, L. 1992. Roots: Back to our first generations. *Evaluation Practice* 13:1–7.

Sechrest, L., J. Babcock, and B. Smith. 1992. An invitation to methodological pluralism. *Evaluation Practice* 14:227–235.

Sechrest, L., and S. Sidani. 1995. Quantitative and qualitative methods: Is there an alternative? *Evaluation and Program Planning* 18:77–87.

Shadish, W. R. 1995. The quantitative/qualitative debate: "DeKuhnifying" the conceptual context. *Evaluation and Program Planning* 18:47–49.

Slife, B. D., and R. N. Williams. 1997. Toward a theoretical psychology: Should a subdiscipline be formally recognized? *American Psychologist* 52:117–129.

Tashakkori, A., and C. Teddlie. 1998. *Mixed methodology: Combining qualitative and quantitative approaches.* Applied Social Research Methods Series, vol. 46. Thousand Oaks, CA: Sage.

Unger, R. K. 1983. Through the looking glass: No wonderland yet! (The reciprocal relationship between methodology and models of reality). *Psychology of Women Quarterly* 8:9–32.

3

■　　■　　■　　■　　■　　■　　■　　■　　■

Working between Two Worlds
Qualitative Methods and Psychology

Jeanne Marecek, Michelle Fine, and Louise Kidder

THE HEART OF A QUALITATIVE STANCE is the desire to make sense of lived experience. All three of us were originally trained in experimental and quantitative methods; we came to a qualitative stance by working in places where cultural difference squarely confronted us: in Sri Lanka, India, and Japan and in urban schools in the United States. In these settings, we had little choice but to work inductively. The ways that people understood their world and moved about in it were foreign to us as outsiders. We learned to use perplexing encounters, strained interactions, and the inevitable faux pas as peepholes into worlds different from our own. We were led to a qualitative stance by our need to understand experiences that were different from our own, and lives that moved to music we didn't hear.

Qualitative Inquiry and Social Issues:
Reclaiming a History

Although such methods are currently relegated to the margins of social psychology in the United States, several classic studies used field-based qualitative approaches. In the 1930s, John Dollard conducted field-based, qualitative work on race and class relations. A researcher in the psychology department at Yale, Dollard went south to learn how race operated within the social life of a town he called "Southerntown." He was a participant-observer and an outsider, a northern white psychologist naive about southern race relations. He recognized that his naiveté necessitated that he be educated by his data:

> This social sharing was of two degrees and involved two roles: there was first the casual participation possible as a "Yankee down here studying Negroes" and second the more intensive participation and the more specific role of the life history taker. . . . The primary research instrument would seem to be the observing human intelligence trying to make sense of the experience; and the experience was full of problems and uncertainty in fact. Perhaps it does not compare well with more objective-seeming instruments, such as a previously prepared set of questions but as to this question the reader can judge for himself. It has the value of offering to perception the actual, natural human contact with all of the real feelings present and unguarded. (1937, 18)

At the heart of Dollard's work is his qualitative stance: His desire to make sense of "human contact with all of the real feelings present and unguarded." Although Dollard headed south with a research agenda, his field of variables was not specified in advance. He could gather data that moved across the terrain of racial, political, and economic hierarchies of the South.

In the 1950s, Muzafer and Carolyn Sherif and their coworkers immersed themselves in the rivalries of boys at a summer camp (Sherif et al. 1961). Leon Festinger, Henry Riecken, and Stanley Schacter (1956) infiltrated a doomsday sect to observe what happens when prophecies fail. Philip Zimbardo and his students examined de-individuation in a mock prison (Zimbardo et al. 1975). David Rosenhan (1973) and a group of colleagues and students entered a mental hospital by feigning hallucinations. All these researchers explicated nuances and textures of real life. They explored their biases and worried about ethics and relationships in the field. Nonetheless, no one doubted that they were doing psychological research.

A qualitative stance invites broad-based inquiry into spaces that are undocumented in other studies. Unlike a hypothetico-deductive stance, in which a fixed set of hypotheses constrains the field of investigation, a qualitative stance allows researchers to pry open territory about which they have only vague hunches. Instead of specifying at the outset the variables whose main effects and interactions will be tracked, qualitative workers begin with a period of exploration and immersion. They enter the field without structured questionnaires, predetermined variables, or research designs; only later do they narrow their focus. Propelled by a desire to know what is unknown, to unravel mysteries, to be surprised and jostled by what turns up, qualitative researchers embark on an intellectual adventure without a map or even a clear destination. This way of working requires giving up control, going along for the ride, not always having hold of the steering wheel—and still taking good notes.

Qualitative Work and "Bias"

When we peer into the cubbyholes and crevices where qualitative work in psychology has been stuffed, we find researchers admitting and apologizing for their "biases." Reflecting on his experiences as a pseudopatient, David Rosenhan wrote in *Science* about how stunned he was by the depths of depersonalization provoked by his short stay:

> Neither anecdotal nor "hard" data can convey the overwhelming sense of powerlessness which invades the individual as he is continually exposed to the depersonalization of the psychiatric hospital. . . .
>
> I and the other pseudopatients in the psychiatric setting had distinctively negative reactions. We do not pretend to describe the subjective experiences of true patients. Theirs may be different from ours, particularly with the passage of time and the necessary process of adaptation to one's environment. But we can and do speak to the relatively more objective indicators of treatment within the hospital. It would be a mistake and a very unfortunate one to consider that what happened to us derived from malice or stupidity on the part of the staff. Quite the contrary, our overwhelming impression of them was of people who really cared, who were committed, and who were uncommonly intelligent. Where they failed, as they sometimes did painfully, it would be more accurate to attribute those failures to the environment in which they, too, found themselves than to personal callousness. (1973, 265, 268)

Rosenhan is here confessing what he calls an "overwhelming impression." His personal experience dramatizes the power of institutional arrangements over both the good will of the staff and the sanity of the residents. Without his self-reflective experience as participant and observer inside the institution, Rosenhan's work would have lacked the passion and much of the evidence that makes it so compelling.

Self-reflection and acknowledgment of subjectivity are now intrinsic to scholarship in many intellectual domains, but they have not yet become so in psychology. Yet critical self-reflection is not a new idea in social psychology. Nearly fifty years ago, the Sherifs had this to say:

> The research man [*sic*] has his own group identifications. We have noted that every group represents a point of view as it stands in relation to other groups. Every group has its own explicit or implicit premises as to the nature of human relations, as to the directions that the values and goals of group relations should take. From the outset, research and generalizations are doomed to be deflections or mere justifications of the point of view and premises of the group or groups with which one identifies himself, if one does not start his work by clear, deliberate recognition and neutralizing of his personal involvement in these issues. If this painful process of deliberate recognition and neutralizing of one's own personal involvements is not achieved, his autism will greatly influence his design of the study and his collection and treatment of data. (1953, 11)

This acknowledgment of personal involvements was largely forgotten in the ensuing decades, as was the injunction that researchers reflect on their positions and allegiances. Instead, we psychologists came to trust that proper scientific methods would protect us from our "autisms." Further, we came to believe that such methods would yield what Donna Haraway (1988) called the "god's-eye view of reality," a view uninfluenced by the vantage point of onlooker. However, denying the biases inherent in the privileged position of a researcher does not negate them.

Qualitative Work: On Listening and Words

A psychology concerned with social life should attend to people's words and their meaning (Billig 1994). Social relations are constituted and managed through language. As the medium of social negotiations about truth and reality, language thus determines what we see and know. When researchers restrict participants to speaking only in our terms, we lose access to theirs. When researchers use structured attitude scales, inventories, and tests, the respondents' standpoints are located on dimensions of the researchers' making.

In contrast, a qualitative stance involves listening to and theorizing about what emerges when people use their own words to make sense of their lived experience. It requires paying attention to the lexicon participants use and to the interpretive repertoire upon which they draw (Potter and Wetherell 1987); it involves interpreting silences, gaps in a narrative, or the absence of a language for certain things (Visweswaran 1994). By working with people's own words, we hope to bring into social psychology's purview rich stories of relationships, struggles, despair, and engagements.

Our own projects illustrate how people use words to connect to, reproduce, resist, and transform the contexts in which they live. Jeanne Marecek and Diane Kravetz, in their study of feminist therapists, have asked how feminist therapists' identities and ideas about their work have shifted under the pressures of the antifeminist backlash of the 1990s (Marecek and Kravetz 1998a). Only two of the eighty-nine therapists they interviewed could label themselves publicly as feminist therapists, although many said that they had openly embraced that title in the past. Some took pains to conceal their feminist identity even from clients in ongoing therapy. Nonetheless, feminism remained central to their work and their personal identities. Some managed this tension between the public and private by discursively erasing the boundary between feminist therapy and therapy in general, equating feminist ideals with norms of "good mental health" and "common sense" and feminist therapy with "just good therapy." As one therapist said, "I can't imagine that anyone could be an effective healthy therapist without being a feminist therapist." Some demarcated themselves as feminists who were exempt from the objectionable stereotypes of feminists with statements like "*I* don't stuff it down people's throats," "*I'*m pretty gentle," and "I *like* men" (Marecek and Kravetz 1998b). This rhetorical strategy is double-edged, inadvertently lending credence to the very stereotypes it seems to challenge.

Susan Condor (1986) described her discontent with work that surveyed nonfeminist or right-wing women merely to reaffirm the obvious: that "they" were not "us." She implored feminist researchers to engage with qualitative methods, to listen to the words of participants. She challenged feminist colleagues to dare to learn how right-wing women made sense of the world. We extend and broaden Condor's challenge: Dare we learn how those who are not "us"—who are impoverished, or mentally ill, or urban teenagers, or even just nonpsychologists—make sense of the world? And do we dare learn how they are "us"?

Working as a rape crisis volunteer, Michelle Fine (1983) met a young African-American woman, Altamese, who had been gang raped. They spent many hours talking in the hospital. Michelle describes their encounter in retrospect: "I realize now that I was trying to talk her into ways of coping. I doused her with all that I as a feminist counselor, white academic, and social psychologist, believed would be good for her: Report them, tell your social worker, let your family know, don't keep it in. . . ."

At some point, Altamese had enough of Michelle's advice and let her know that she would not press charges, nor would she let her family know what happened. In her community, an African-American neighborhood in North Philadelphia, the police might not believe her. If she told her brothers, they might go out and kill the perpetrators. Telling a therapist might help briefly, but she would still carry the pain inside. When Michelle stopped talking and listened to Altamese's story, she could hear her way of making sense of and surviving in a world where neither the justice system nor the streets were trustworthy; where protecting her mother, brothers, and children was more important than abstract notions of justice. Michele could have measured Altamese's degree of learned helplessness, her attributional biases, or her external locus of control. Instead, she listened and was thereby able to hear how racism, poverty, and personal and cultural circumstances made a profound difference in her and Altamese's responses to a gang rape.

When researchers listen with close attention to what respondents say, the respondents become active agents, the creators of the worlds they inhabit and the interpreters of their experiences. And as researchers become witnesses, bringing their knowledge of theory and their interpretive methods to participants' stories, they too become active agents.

Qualitative Work: From the Ground Up

Qualitative approaches are less formulaic than orthodox psychology methods. Researchers may alter their approach and even their initial hypotheses upon discovering that something else works better. For instance, when Louise Kidder (1992) began interviewing Japanese students who were "returnees," she asked students who had lived outside of Japan to talk about what it was like to live abroad and to return to Japan. She began with a series of open-ended questions in a structured interview schedule. No sooner had she begun than she discovered that it was much more effective to let the students talk without interruption. Their stories centered on what it was like to return to Japan and find they were no longer considered "really" Japanese. Their body language and attitudes marked them as "returnees." Listening to these stories, Louise began to discern the requirements for "being Japanese."

For conventionally trained psychologists, switching to a qualitative stance can induce vertigo; many of the usual methodological props are pulled away. Qualitative researchers search through transcripts or field notes for the glimmer of a pattern instead of coding structured data sets. They pore over what other psychologists might consider "error variance" and "uncodable" responses, awaiting inspiration and serendipitous realizations.

The practices of qualitative work stand in sharp contrast to those we were taught in graduate school. We learned to defer data collection until we had clearly specified our hypotheses, operationalized our variables, pilot-tested our measures, and specified our coding and analytic strategies. We maintained tight control over research outcomes, strictly limiting what participants could do or say. Structured interviews and questionnaires provided predetermined options for responding, typically phrased in a standard format stripped of nuance and local meaning (e.g., Agree, Somewhat Agree, Neither Agree nor Disagree . . .). Our participants could register experiences that we researchers were not ready to hear only by scribbling in the margins of a questionnaire, amending a question before answering it, or using the option marked "Other: _____" Typically such efforts at communication were ignored or even considered "uncodable."

We learned to stand at a safe distance from those we studied, running them through procedures designed to extract data from them. Research was not a shared, intersubjective activity. This stance is akin to what Robert Stolorow calls "the theory of the isolated mind" (Atwood and Stolorow 1984). Such a stance makes it hard to learn the participants' point of view, as Joyce Ladner notes:

> The relationship between researcher and his subjects, by definition, resembles that of the oppressor and the oppressed, because it is the oppressor who defines the problem, the nature of the research, and to some extent, the quality of interaction between him and his subjects. . . . This inability to understand and research the fundamental problem—neocolonialism—prevents most social researchers from being able accurately to observe and analyze Black life and culture and the impact that racism and oppression have on Blacks. (1971, vii)

Qualitative Research: Social Life and Power

Michel Foucault (1980) has observed that modern societies regulate their citizens without brute force, relying instead on self-discipline and self-surveillance. Power in these circumstances is diffuse; it operates "from below," flowing through social relations, knowledge structures, and regimes of truth that justify existing hierarchies. To grasp how power from below operates, we need to listen to the negotiated narratives of power that flow through streets and gutters; to situate our research in mundane conversations and practices; to see how people are situated in and by institutional contexts, and how they maneuver to resituate themselves (Guinier, Fine, and Balin 1997; Smith 1987).

During a sojourn in India, Louise (Kidder, forthcoming) studied expatriates' conversations with one another about their domestic servants. She noted that expatriates occupied the elevated status of "masters," enjoying a status and benefits that exceeded what they experienced back home. Instead of making Indian friends and learning Indian ways of living, they became part of an expatriate subculture and found their friends among others like themselves. As wealthy, white foreigners, they occupied the outsider's position of privilege and power. But being relatively unacquainted with Indian culture and society, they were also dependent on domestic servants for cultural knowledge and daily living skills. The relationship of master to servant was not simply hierarchical; power and dependency were intertwined. As Albert Memmi says, "[t]he dominant person isn't always the least dependent one" (1984, 8). An American woman's story illustrates her family's dependence on their Indian cook:

> We discovered that we were poisoning [my husband] right in our own kitchen. I wasn't getting sick at all, but he had something all the time. . . . Finally, we realized that he was eating sandwiches and I wasn't—and it must have been the mayonnaise that [the cook] was making. I don't know if it was a batch of bad eggs or what, but that was doing it. He was getting poisoned in our own house! (Kidder 1997, 164)

Jeanne's work in Sri Lanka has concerned that country's dramatic upsurge in suicide deaths. Among Sri Lankans, interpersonal conflicts often trigger suicidal acts, particularly when loss of honor, face, status, or respect is at stake. As a social practice, suicidal acts serve to reestablish one's rightful place in the hierarchy or to redress a grievance by pointing the finger of blame toward those who are at fault. (Marecek 1997). In one project, Jeanne studied news reports of official inquiries into suicide deaths, asking how these reports reasserted interpretive authority over the death (Marecek 1995). Among other things, she found that if suicide victims were in subordinate positions, the news reports emphasized their emotional state, especially the culturally disapproved emotions of anger and desire for revenge. The instigating actions of higher-status individuals (e.g., beatings by one's husband; coercion or extortion by a petty government officer) were mentioned perfunctorily and put aside. In contrast, if the victim was the higher-status party, the texts emphasized the instigating actions of the other (e.g., a daughter who eloped; a drunken son; a disobedient wife) or impersonal societal forces (e.g., poverty; unemployment). For higher-status victims, emotional state was not a focus. Thus, the news reports worked to concentrate moral opprobrium on lower-status parties and deflect it from higher-status ones.

In the United States, Louise studied the negotiation of meaning between a hypnotist and her subjects (Kidder 1972). Enrolled as a participant in a hypnosis workshop, Louise recorded not only the hypnotic inductions but also the arguments that ensued when participants said such things as "I don't think I was really in a trance." Her analyses focused on how the hypnotist and doubting participants negotiated what hypnosis is and what makes someone a good or bad hypnotic subject. The frameworks for Louise's analysis—attribution and social learning theory—come from the heart of social psychology. She explored the process by which the hypnotist and the workshop participants allocated blame when someone failed to go into trance. She also documented how the hypnotist meted out praise to compliant participants and punishment to doubters. Louise's work illuminated both the power of language to define participants' reality and how that discursive power was not evenly distributed in that social situation.

Rigorous qualitative research involves attention to context, meanings, and power relations in data collection and analysis. Qualitative researchers situate words, discourses, persons, relations, and groups within local, societal, and sometimes global contexts. Such an approach enables a study of power relations that more conventional psychological methods of study, such as individual-difference testing or laboratory experimentation, preclude.

Qualitative Work and Ethical Shadows

In conversations that swirl around qualitative work, issues of ethics and responsibility surface that go far beyond the formal American Psychological Association (APA) ethical guidelines. Why is qualitative work the lightning rod for such concerns? We contend that it is time for all psychologists to talk seriously about why we do the work we do, whom we choose as our participants, and at which constituencies our work is aimed. Are we willing to engage the variety of standpoints that exist in any single context? How much do our own standpoints shape which stories we are told, which ones we are able to hear, which ones we take to be data, and which ones we don't? What are the ethics of studying "down" and thus, deliberately or not, replicating a focus on people too often held responsible for social-structural decay? Whether we study "down" or "up," what are the ethics of telling or not telling participants what we are really up to? To what extent do we anticipate the political and ethical implications of our work? Do we have an obligation to do so? In an interview, Kenneth Clark reflected on ethical concerns that he and Mamie Clark had about their research on black children's self-images:

> "We were really disturbed by our findings," Kenneth Clark recalls, "and we
> sat on them for a number of years. What was surprising was the degree to

which the children suffered from self-rejection, with its truncating effect on their personalities, and the earliness of the corrosive awareness of color. I don't think we quite realized the extent of the cruelty of racism and how hard it hit. . . . Some of these children, particularly in the North, were reduced to crying when presented with the [black] dolls and asked to identify with them. They looked at me as if I were the devil for putting them in this predicament. Let me tell you, it was a traumatic experience for me as well." (Kluger 1975, quoted in Cross 1991, 29)

Clark worried about the impact of his research on the children and on the community in general. His research methods were not qualitative, but his ethical concerns—expressed in the interview, but not in his research text—are ones that often emerge in qualitative work.

The ethical issues that surface in qualitative research go beyond preserving the rights of individual participants. They are not put to rest by scrupulous adherence to procedures for informed consent, anonymity, and confidentiality. Participants in qualitative studies may demand to know "who owns the data?" This is an ethical question that participants in laboratory studies do not think to ask. Whose interpretation counts? Who has veto power? What will happen to the relationships that were formed during the research? What are the researcher's obligations after the data are collected? Can the data be used against the participants? Will the data be used on their behalf? Do researchers have an obligation to protect the communities and social groups they study, or just to guard certain rights of individuals? Such questions reveal how much ethical terrain is uncharted by APA guidelines and institutional review boards. It is qualitative researchers who are wrestling with such ethical dilemmas, but the dilemmas are present in much psychological research, regardless of the researcher's methodological commitments.

Conclusion

Our enthusiasm for qualitative work notwithstanding, we sometimes have crises of identity and loyalty: Are we still psychologists? What is at stake in that identity? Apart from its methods, what is psychology? Why is the disciplinary boundary now drawn where it is? Should one be drawn at all?

We have a sense of urgency in asking why psychology in the United

States lags so far behind our international and interdisciplinary colleagues in developing qualitative methods. As John Richardson notes,

> There is a great deal of scope for psychologists in North America to catch up with their counterparts in the UK and with their compatriots in the other social sciences in terms of their understanding and appreciation of qualitative research methods. (1996, 8)

We do not claim that qualitative methods are new or radical or necessarily progressive. We do not claim that qualitative work is the only emancipatory approach or that such work always yields emancipatory results. Any research strategy can be used for emancipatory or repressive ends. Our goal here has been to give evidence of a rich history of and vibrant future for qualitative work in psychology. In doing so, we hope we have laid a strong bridge on which psychologists can walk between worlds.

References

Atwood, G., and R. Stolorow. 1984. *Structures of subjectivity: Explorations in psychoanalytic phenomenology.* Hillsdale, NJ: Analytic Press.

Billig, M. 1994. Repopulating the depopulated pages of social psychology. *Theory and Psychology* 4:307–335.

Condor, S. 1986. Sex role beliefs and "traditional" women: Feminist and intergroup perspectives. In *Feminist social psychology: Developing theory and practice,* ed. S. Wilkinson, 97–118. Philadelphia: Open University Press, 1986.

Cross, W. E., Jr. 1991. *Shades of black: Diversity in African-American identity.* Philadelphia: Temple University Press.

Dollard, J. 1937. *Caste and class in a southern town.* Garden City, NY: Doubleday.

Festinger, L., H. Riecken, and S. Schacter. 1956. *When prophecy fails.* Minneapolis: University of Minnesota Press.

Fine, M. 1983. Coping with rape: Critical perspectives on consciousness. *Imagination, Cognition, and Personality: A Scientific Study of Consciousness* 3:249–264.

Foucault, M. 1980. *Power/Knowledge: Selected interviews and other writings, 1972–77,* ed. C. Gordon. New York: Pantheon.

Guinier, L., M. Fine, and J. Balin. 1997. *Becoming gentlemen: Women, law school, and institutional change.* Boston: Beacon Press.

Haraway, D. 1988. Situated knowledges: The science question in feminism and the privilege of partial perspective. *Feminist Studies* 14:579–599.

Kidder, L. H. 1972. On becoming hypnotized: How skeptics become convinced: A case of attitude change? *Journal of Abnormal Psychology* 80:317–322.

———. 1992. Requirements for being "Japanese": Stories of returnees. *International Journal of Intercultural Relations* 16:383–393.

———. 1997. Colonial remnants: Assumptions of privilege. In *Off White: Readings on Race, Power and Society*, eds. M. Fine, L. Weis, L. C. Powell, and L. M. Wong, 158–166. New York: Routledge.

———. Forthcoming. Dependents in the master's house: When rock dulls scissors. In *Home and hegemony: Domestic service and identity politics in South and Southeast Asia*, eds. S. Dickey and K. M. Adams. Ann Arbor: University of Michigan Press.

Ladner, J. A. 1971. *Tomorrow's tomorrow: The Black woman*. Garden City, NY: Doubleday.

Marecek, J. 1995. *Textualizing suicide: Newspaper narratives of suicide in Sri Lanka*. Paper presented at the Fifth International Sri Lanka Studies Conference, Durham, New Hampshire.

———. 1997. *Wild justice: Meritorious and condemned suicides in Sri Lanka*. Paper presented at the Sixth International Sri Lanka Studies Conference, Kandy, Sri Lanka.

Marecek, J., and D. Kravetz. 1998a. Power and agency in feminist therapy. In *Contemporary feminist psychotherapies: Reflections on theory and practice*, eds. C. Heenan and I. B. Seu, 13–29. London: Sage.

———. 1998b. Putting politics into practice: Feminist therapy as feminist praxis. *Women and Therapy* 21:17–36.

Memmi, A. 1984. *Dependence*. Boston: Beacon Press.

Potter, J., and M. Wetherell. 1987. *Discourse and social psychology: Beyond attitudes and behavior*. London: Sage.

Richardson, J. T. E., ed. 1996. *Handbook of qualitative research methods for psychology and the social sciences*. Leicester, UK: BPS Books.

Rosenhan, D. 1973. Being sane in insane places. *Science* 179:250–258.

Sherif, M., O. J. Harvey, B. J. White, W. R. Hood, and C. W. Sherif. 1961. *Intergroup conflict and cooperation: The robbers' cave experiment*. Norman, OK: University Book Exchange.

Sherif, M., and C. W. Sherif. 1953. *Groups in harmony and tension: An integration of studies on intergroup relations*. New York: Harper and Brothers.

Smith, D. E. 1987. *The everyday world as problematic: A feminist sociology*. Toronto: University of Toronto Press.

Visweswaran, K. 1994. *Fictions of feminist ethnography*. Minneapolis: University of Minnesota Press.

Zimbardo, P., C. Haney, W. C. Banks, and D. Jaffe. 1975. The psychology of imprisonment: Privation, power, and pathology. In *Theory and research in abnormal psychology*, eds. D. Rosenhan and P. London, 271–287. New York: Holt, Rinehart, and Winston.

Theoretical Perspectives

Some Underpinnings of Interpretive
and Participatory Methods

Part II

4

■　　■　　■　　■　　■　　■　　■　　■　　■

Interpretive Psychology

Stories, Circles, and Understanding Lived Experience

Mark B. Tappan

MY AIM IN THIS CHAPTER is provide an overview of an "interpretive" or "hermeneutic" approach to psychological research. Historically, hermeneutics has focused almost exclusively on interpreting literary and religious texts (see Bleicher 1980; Howard 1982; Palmer 1969); in recent years, however, there has been a significant turn toward what has been called "interpretive social science" (see Rabinow and Sullivan 1979). Although psychology has been somewhat slower than other disciplines (e.g., anthropology) to make this hermeneutic turn, the last decade or so has nevertheless witnessed a growing interest in interpretive approaches to psychological inquiry (see Bruner 1986, 1990; Burman 1996; Freeman 1984, 1985, 1993; Gergen 1994; Gilligan 1982; Honey 1987; Messer, Sass, and Woolfolk 1988; Mishler 1986; Packer 1985, 1994; Packer and Addison 1989; Polkinghorne 1988; Sarbin 1986; Tappan and Brown 1992; Tappan and Packer 1991). Needless to say, this book represents an important addition to this growing list.

While there are a number of sources to which I could turn to explicate the theoretical underpinnings of interpretive psychology, I have chosen to focus on the work of one major figure, Wilhelm Dilthey. Dilthey, who was primarily a philosopher and literary historian, is generally recognized as the "father" of the modern hermeneutic enterprise in the human sciences (Howard 1982). His aim was to develop a broad theoretical framework for the study of human existence and experience. This led him to focus his attention not only on philosophy, history, and literary studies, but also on the developing fields of psychology, sociology, economics, and social anthropology—the so-called "human sciences." He was particularly interested in the methodologies employed by these disciplines in their respective forms of inquiry, and he sought to address a number of important questions—the most important of which was whether or not these disciplines could use the successful methods of the physical sciences, in spite of the differences between social and physical processes.

Dilthey concluded, ultimately, that the human world was significantly different from the natural world, and that different methods were required for studying the former. As human beings, unlike atoms, stones, and flowers, or even insects and rats, we reflect on what we do. We interpret the situations in which we find ourselves; we set goals and plan for the future; we communicate with each other; we adopt conventions and follow traditions. Consequently, we cannot study human beings without taking these processes of reflection and self-interpretation into account. Moreover, in the human disciplines, because we study ourselves and our fellows, there is not only an immediacy of insight, but we must also take into account the dangers of bias and prejudice. *Hermeneutics*, the deliberate and systematic methodology of interpretation, was the solution Dilthey proposed to address these challenges.

In the first section, I summarize Dilthey's vision of hermeneutics and consider his conception of the so-called "hermeneutic circle," which characterizes the complex dynamics involved in the process of interpretation. In the second section I consider the vexing problem of how to evaluate the "validity" of interpretive accounts. In the concluding section I consider some of the ethical implications of adopting a hermeneutic approach to psychological research. In particular, I suggest that the process of interpretation is, inescapably, a relational enterprise. Consequently, I argue that interpreters must be aware of the power that they hold to shape the understanding of others' lived experience.

Interpretive Psychology: Dilthey's Legacy

Dilthey ([1900] 1976) argues that hermeneutics, the art and practice of textual exegesis or interpretation, is the methodology most appropriate for understanding "recorded expressions" of human existence and experience. The relationships among experience, expression, and understanding are key to Dilthey's conception of hermeneutics (see Palmer 1969) and how it functions as the methodological basis for the human sciences. Let me, therefore, briefly examine what Dilthey has to say about each of these three terms.

"Lived experience" is, for Dilthey, the primary, first-order category that captures an individual's immediate, concrete "experience as such." It is, in other words, an act of consciousness itself; it is something that is lived in and lived through; it is the attitude taken toward life as it is lived in the moment (Palmer 1969). As such, it also consists of a primary unity of thinking, feeling, and acting. Dilthey ([1894] 1977) suggests, in fact, that the "structure of psychic life," and hence the nature of "lived experience," consists of three indissociable psychological dimensions: cognition, emotion, and volition (see Tappan 1990). It is, moreover, in the context of an immediate lived experience that these three psychological dimensions engage and interact—as one simultaneously thinks, feels, and acts.

Dilthey clearly assumed that lived experience is a private, subjective phenomenon that, in its primary and unitary form, cannot be described or analyzed from the "outside." Consequently, if an experience is to be understood and interpreted, it first must be expressed. "Expression" is the term Dilthey ([1910] 1977) used to capture the move from lived experience to the symbolic representation of that experience, in the form of language (spoken or written), music, or visual images. Such a move is necessary, he claimed, because others cannot gain access to one's subjective lived experience unless it is expressed in some way. An "expression," however, is not simply a spontaneous overflow of powerful feelings. Rather, it is something far more encompassing—an "expression of life" or, more specifically, an "expression of lived experience." An expression, therefore, can be a story, a poem, a painting, a film, a dance, a piece of music, an interview narrative—anything that expresses the lived experience of human beings.

Dilthey's ultimate goal was to find a way to interpret such expressions in order to understand other persons. This, in fact, was Dilthey's dream for hermeneutics as the foundation for the human studies: "to study individual human beings and particular forms of human existence scientifically," at the same time acknowledging that "while the systematic human studies derive general laws and comprehensive patterns from the objective apprehension of the unique they still rest on understanding and interpretation" (Dilthey [1900] 1976, 247). Consequently, Dilthey wanted to develop a method for obtaining "objectively valid" interpretations of unique expressions of human experience.

"Understanding" is the term Dilthey used to refer to this process of interpretation; it designates the process by which the interpreter grasps or gains access to the "mind" or "spirit" of another (Palmer 1969). More specifically, for Dilthey, in understanding one grasps the cognitive, affective, and conative dimensions of the other's "psychic life" as they are revealed in a particular expression of lived experience:

> There is a special connection between [the expression of lived experience], the life from which it sprang, and the understanding which it brings about. The expression can indeed contain more of the psychic nexus than any introspection can reveal. It raises life out of depths which are unilluminated by consciousness; but at the same time it lies in the nature of lived experience that the relationship between this expression and the spiritual or human meaning which is expressed in it can only very approximately be taken as a basis for understanding. (Dilthey [1910] 1977, 124)

Because of their complexity, understanding the meaning of such expressions of lived experience is quite difficult. Consequently, said Dilthey, we must turn to systematic methods of interpretation (i.e., hermeneutics) in order to understand their meaning.

"Interpretation" thus begins with a fixed textual expression of lived experience, for example, a tape-recorded interview narrative (see Mishler 1986). Once such a text is fixed in a form in which it can be carefully studied and analyzed, it can then be interpreted. Although, for Dilthey, this process of interpretation and exegesis clearly entailed turning a "special personal giftedness" for understanding into a permanent "technique" that can serve as the foundation of the human studies, it nevertheless is also a process based on common sense:

> Exegesis or interpretation would be impossible if the expressions of life were utterly alien. It would be unnecessary if there were nothing alien in them.

Thus exegesis lies between these two extreme opposites. It is requisite in every case where there is something alien which the art of understanding is to assimilate. ([1910] 1977, 143)

Furthermore, Dilthey argued, the process of understanding is fundamentally inductive. That is, it is not a process by which a general law is deduced from an incomplete series of instances. Rather, it is a process by which a particular interpretation is derived from a series of instances, which then serves to unify those instances as parts of a larger whole. As such, the interpreter necessarily enters what Dilthey called the "hermeneutic circle":

Here we encounter the general difficulty of all interpretation. The whole of a work must be understood from individual words and their combination, but full understanding of an individual part presupposes understanding of the whole. . . . [Thus] the whole must be understood in terms of its individual parts, individual parts in terms of the whole. . . . Such a comparative procedure allows one to understand every individual work, indeed, every individual sentence, more profoundly than we did before. So understanding of the whole, and of the parts, are interdependent. (Dilthey [1900] 1976, 259–262)

This suggests, finally, that interpretation must take as its starting point the historical and psychological reality of the lived experience of both the subject whose expression of experience is being interpreted and the interpreter herself. And it is here that the work of those who followed Dilthey in exploring and articulating hermeneutic principles—specifically Martin Heidegger ([1927] 1962), Hans-Georg Gadamer (1975), Paul Ricoeur (1979), and Charles Taylor (1979)—becomes most salient.

An interpreter who ignores the historicality of the subject's lived experience, and thus applies atemporal categories to a particular experience, can only with irony claim to be "objective," because she has from the start distorted the experience she is trying to understand. Furthermore, the interpreter must acknowledge that the reality of the hermeneutic circle means there is no such thing as nonpositional understanding. An interpreter understands by constant reference to her own perspective, which shapes her understanding of the world based on her expectations, preconceptions, biases, and assumptions. These, in turn, are based upon her life-style, life-experiences, culture, and tradition. Her methodological task, therefore, is not to immerse herself completely in the experience of the subject (which, needless to say, is impossible). Rather, it is to search for ways in which she can interact with the text in order to increase her understanding of the subject's experience, based, at least in part, on her own experience (see also Palmer 1969).

Validity in Interpretation

Perhaps the most vexing problem facing interpretive psychologists is the question of how to evaluate a particular interpretive account. Although I cannot construct a fully developed answer to this question within the parameters of this chapter, let me nevertheless sketch out an initial response to this very important concern.

Hermeneutic approaches, including the qualitative methods discussed in this volume, typically eschew the strict subject-object dichotomy between the knower and the known that is characteristic of traditional empiricist and rationalist approaches to psychological inquiry, with their striving for "objectivity" and a detached point of view. As such, hermeneutic approaches also do not subscribe to a "correspondence theory of truth," which assumes that the truth of a particular theoretical statement is determined by the degree to which it corresponds to the hard and fast "facts" of reality. According to this theory, the ultimate goal of any science is to provide accurate (or, at the very least, "falsifiable") descriptions and explanations of an independent reality (see Packer 1985; Packer and Addison 1989). Hermeneutic approaches, on the other hand, view the knower and the known as fundamentally interrelated. They assume that any interpretation necessarily involves a circularity of understanding—a hermeneutic circle—in which the interpreter's perspective and understanding initially shapes his interpretation of a given phenomenon, but that interpretation is open to revision and elaboration as it interacts with the phenomenon in question, and as the perspective and understanding of the interpreter, including his biases and blind-spots, are revealed and evaluated (Packer and Addison 1989).

Traditionally, those addressing questions about how interpretive accounts can be evaluated have done so from the standpoint of concerns about "validity." Although, from a hermeneutic perspective, such concerns about "validity in interpretation" (see Hirsch 1967) often tacitly assume a correspondence theory of truth (i.e., they reflect a search for a way to evaluate a given interpretation in terms of fixed norms and standards), it is possible to evaluate an interpretive account based on different assumptions and criteria (Packer and Addison 1989). Let me briefly sketch out one such perspective—one that focuses on "interpretive agreement" within the context of an "interpretive community" (see Tappan and Brown 1992).

This perspective is informed primarily by the work of Stanley Fish (1980). Fish argues that what an interpreter does when she interprets a text is not to construe or detect its "true" meaning, but to construct or produce its meaning, based on her response to that text. This view that meaning is made, not found, does not lead inexorably to subjectivism and relativism, because the means by which meaning is made are social and conventional, and thus are limited by the institution or community of which the interpreter is a part. There is no such thing as an isolated individual working alone to interpret a text in some unique and idiosyncratic manner: "We do not do these things because we cannot do them, because the mental operations we can perform are limited by the institutions in which we are already embedded" (331). In other words, the "interpretive community" of which a particular interpreter is a member is ultimately responsible for the kinds of interpretations she produces:

> If the [interpreter] is conceived of not as an independent entity but as a social construct whose operations are delimited by the systems of intelligibility that inform it, then the meanings it confers on texts are not its own but have their source in the interpretive community (or communities) of which it is a function. Moreover, these meanings will be neither subjective nor objective, at least in the terms assumed by those who argue within the traditional framework: they will not be objective because they will always have been a product of a point of view rather than having been simply "read off"; and they will not be subjective because that point of view will always be social or institutional. Or, by the same reasoning one could say that they are both subjective and objective: they are subjective because they inhere in a particular point of view and are therefore not universal; and they are objective because the point of view that delivers them is public and conventional rather than individual or unique. (335–336)

Fish's work suggests that the effort to attain "interpretive agreement" among members of an interpretive community should replace the quest for objectively valid interpretations as the primary aim of interpretive inquiry.

If a text does not have one true meaning, but rather different meanings according to the interpretive communities that construct them, then achieving agreement within communities is the ultimate goal: "The fact of agreement, rather than being a proof of the stability of objects, is a testimony to the power of an interpretive community to constitute the objects upon which its members (also and simultaneously constituted) can then agree" (338). In other words, interpretive agreement holds the only key to evaluating the "truth" or "validity" of any given interpretation of what a text means: if the members of an interpretive community agree on what a text means, based on their jointly shared biases, assumptions, prejudices, and values, then that interpretation is considered to be "true" or "valid"—unless and until a new interpretation is offered that the members of that community agree is better (see Tappan and Brown 1992; Uebersax 1988).

With these considerations in mind, how might the interpretations of an interpretive psychologist be evaluated? An interpretation can be evaluated, ultimately, only when an interpretive community can be formed that shares the biases, assumptions, and prejudices of the interpreter. When such a community is formed, our interpretations can and must be considered, in an attempt to reach agreement. Such an attempt will necessarily involve debate, discussion, and even disagreement—how could it be otherwise in a domain in which meanings are made, not found? Yet such a process also ultimately has its own rewards: the opportunity for insight and enlightenment is increased enormously when different voices and perspectives are joined together in a common effort of understanding.

Conclusion

I have sought to offer a brief overview of the hermeneutic or interpretive approach to psychological inquiry. Following Dilthey's lead I have outlined the basic parameters of the interpretive process, explored the hermeneutic circle, considered the problem of how to evaluate interpretive accounts, and suggested that a conception of interpretive agreement, within an interpretive community, might yield a more useful approach to evaluation than traditional concerns about reliability and validity.

In conclusion, I turn to a set of complex ethical issues raised by a focus on the interpretive process. In so doing I follow Robert Scholes (1989), who suggests that we must develop what he calls an "ethic of reading,"

based on an understanding that the interpretive process is never value-neu-
tral, but always consists of value-judgments grounded in the interpreter's
own ethical and political commitments:

> An ethic of reading . . . require[s] us to connect what is represented in the
> text with what we see in the world—in a manner that is ethical because it
> is political and political because it is ethical. This is a crucial point. The
> notion of textuality reminds us that we do nothing in isolation from oth-
> ers. We are always connected, woven together, textualized—and therefore
> politicized. This is why there can be no ethics of reading that is free of po-
> litical concerns. (154)

Scholes also argues that reading/interpreting is fundamentally a dialectical activity in which the impulse to understand a text and the impulse to
connect that text to the reader's/interpreter's life experiences stand in an
ongoing dynamic tension, and it is this tension that drives the interpretive
process. He emphasizes, however, that both of these impulses require critical and creative skills:

> Reading is always, at once, the effort to comprehend and the effort to
> incorporate. I must invent the author, invent his or her intentions, using
> the evidence I can find to stimulate my creative process. . . . I must also
> incorporate the text I am reading in my own textual repertory—a
> process that is not so much like putting a book on a shelf as like wiring a
> new component in an electronic system, where connections must be
> made in the right places. (9)

This dialectic becomes, in fact, another version of Dilthey's "hermeneutic
circle": In order to understand a text the reader must make a creative connection between that text and the context of his own life experiences, and
yet to make such a connection the reader must understand that text in its
own terms.

It seems to me that a similar dialectic exists in any genuine relationship
between two human beings. That is, one dimension of any relationship is
the impulse to understand the other in her own terms, to try to see the
world through her eyes, and to appreciate the truth of her experiences.
The other dimension is the impulse to bring one's own experiences into
the relationship, to share one's own perspective, and thus to respond to
the other by trying to connect one's own life to hers. Both impulses are

powerful ones, and in any given relationship they are not always equally balanced—that is, some people spend more energy trying to understand and appreciate the experiences of others than they do offering and expressing their own thoughts and feelings, while others spend more energy seeking connections between their experiences and the experiences of others (and incorporating the experiences of others into their own) than they do simply trying to understand the experiences of others in their own terms. In the end, however, if a relationship is authentic, genuine, and mutual, both dimensions will be manifest, and a healthy tension between them will be maintained (see Tappan and Brown 1992).

I would argue, therefore, that the process of interpretation itself is essentially a relational activity. The activity of relationship entails both the impulse to comprehend and the impulse to respond and connect—impulses that are central to the process of interpretation. Attempting to understand the intended meaning of a text, in the author's own terms—while perhaps never fully possible—is a crucial dimension of the process of interpretation, just as attempting to understand the other in his own terms is an important aspect of any relationship. Bringing the values, biases, and assumptions shared by oneself and one's interpretive community to one's interpretation of a text is also an inescapable and undeniable aspect of the process of interpretation, just as connecting one's own experiences and perspective to those of another is also an important aspect of a genuine relationship.

In the end, however, the interpretive psychologist must acknowledge that, even in the context of a relationship with another person, based on an autobiographical or interview text that represents a person's lived experience, the temptation to violate the symmetry of that relationship and to assume ultimate power to interpret another's experience will be everpresent, by virtue of the prestige, status, and authority afforded to psychologists (and other academic researchers) in our culture at this time (Tappan and Brown 1992). What we must seek to do as readers, interpreters, researchers, and psychologists, therefore, as we come into relationship with those we study (the participants in our research projects), is to be constantly aware of our power to define the right, the good, the best, the ideal; to become accountable to the power of naming, and thus to try not to violate, unwittingly, the humanity of those whose lives we hope to understand.

References

Bleicher, J. 1980. *Contemporary hermeneutics*. London: Routledge and Kegan Paul.

Bruner, J. 1986. *Actual minds, possible worlds*. Cambridge, MA: Harvard University Press.

———. 1990. *Acts of meaning*. Cambridge, MA: Harvard University Press.

Burman, E. 1996. Continuities and discontinuities in interpretive and textual approaches to developmental psychology. *Human Development* 39:330–345.

Dilthey, W. [1910] 1976. The construction of the historical world. In *W. Dilthey: Selected writings*, ed. and trans. H. Rickman, 170–245. Cambridge: Cambridge University Press.

———. [1900] 1976. The development of hermeneutics. In *W. Dilthey: Selected writings*, ed. and trans. H. Rickman, 246–263. Cambridge: Cambridge University Press.

———. [1894] 1977. Ideas concerning a descriptive and analytic psychology. In *W. Dilthey: Descriptive psychology and historical understanding*, trans. R. Zaner and K. Heiges, 21–120. The Hague: Martinus Nijhoff.

———. [1910] 1977. The understanding of other persons and their expressions of life. In *W. Dilthey: Descriptive psychology and historical understanding*, trans. R. Zaner and K. Heiges, 121–144. The Hague: Martinus Nijhoff.

Fish, S. 1980. *Is there a text in this class? The authority of interpretive communities*. Cambridge, MA: Harvard University Press.

Freeman, M. 1984. History, narrative, and life-span developmental knowledge. *Human Development* 27:1–19.

———. 1985. Paul Ricoeur on interpretation: The model of the text and the idea of development. *Human Development* 28:295–312.

———. 1993. *Rewriting the self: History, memory, narrative*. London: Routledge.

Gadamer, H.-G. 1975. *Truth and method*. New York: Crossroad.

Gergen, K. 1994. *Realities and relationships: Soundings in social construction*. Cambridge, MA: Harvard University Press.

Gilligan, C. 1982. *In a different voice: Psychological theory and women's development*. Cambridge, MA: Harvard University Press.

Heidegger, M. [1927] 1962. *Being and time*. Trans. J. Macquarrie and E. Robinson. New York: Harper and Row.

Hirsch, E. D. 1967. *Validity in interpretation*. New Haven, CT: Yale University Press.

Honey, M. 1987. The interview as text: Hermeneutics considered as a model for analyzing the clinically informed research interview. *Human Development* 30:69–82.

Howard, R. 1982. *Three faces of hermeneutics*. Berkeley: University of California Press.

Messer, S., L. Sass, and R. Woolfolk, eds. 1988. *Hermeneutics and psychological theory: Interpretive perspectives on personality, psychotherapy, and psychopathology.* New Brunswick, NJ: Rutgers University Press.

Mishler, E. G. 1986. *Research interviewing: Context and narrative.* Cambridge, MA: Harvard University Press.

Packer, M. 1985. Hermeneutic inquiry in the study of human conduct. *American Psychologist* 40:1081–1093.

———. 1994. Cultural work on the kindergarten playground: Articulating the ground of play. *Human Development* 37:259–276.

Packer, M., and R. Addison. 1989. Evaluating an interpretive account. In *Entering the circle: Hermeneutic investigation in psychology,* eds. M. Packer and R. Addison. Albany: State University of New York Press.

Palmer, R. 1969. *Hermeneutics.* Evanston, IL: Northwestern University Press.

Polkinghorne, D. 1988. *Narrative knowing and the human sciences.* Albany: State University of New York Press.

Rabinow, P., and W. Sullivan. 1979. The interpretive turn: Emergence of an approach. In *Interpretive social science: A reader,* eds. P. Rabinow and W. Sullivan, 1–21. Berkeley: University of California Press.

Ricoeur, P. 1979. The model of the text: Meaningful action considered as a text. In *Interpretive social science: A reader,* eds. P. Rabinow and W. Sullivan, 73–102. Berkeley: University of California Press.

Sarbin, T. 1986. The narrative as a root metaphor for psychology. In *Narrative psychology: The storied nature of human conduct,* ed. T. Sarbin, 3–21. New York: Praeger.

Scholes, R. 1989. *Protocols of reading.* New Haven, CT: Yale University Press.

Tappan, M. 1990. Hermeneutics and moral development: Interpreting narrative representations of moral experience. *Developmental Review* 10:239–265.

Tappan, M., and L. Brown. 1992. Hermeneutics and developmental psychology: Toward an ethic of interpretation. In *The role of values in psychology and human development,* eds. W. Kurtines, M. Azmitia, and J. Gewirtz, 105–130. New York: John Wiley and Sons.

Tappan, M., and M. Packer, eds. 1991. *Narrative and storytelling: Implications for understanding moral development.* San Francisco: Jossey-Bass.

Taylor, C. 1979. Interpretation and the sciences of man. In *Interpretive social science: A reader,* eds. P. Rabinow and W. Sullivan, 25–72. Berkeley: University of California Press.

Uebersax, J. 1988. Validity inferences from interobserver agreement. *Psychological Bulletin* 104:405–416.

5

■   ■   ■   ■   ■   ■   ■   ■   ■

Feminist Research Methods

Bringing Culture to Science

Jill Morawski

WHAT ARE FEMINIST RESEARCH METHODS? What would a list of them look like? We could begin to answer these questions with a basic definition of feminism: a belief that gender is a primary category of experience (and, therefore, of analysis) and an attendant commitment to remedying the disadvantages of women. Applying this elemental definition to psychology, we then could locate a large number of methods that accommodate gender as a central analytic category. For any particular method to be feminist, it would have to be not only applicable to observing or measuring gender but also "gender-fair" or absent of unacknowledged gender meanings. Such a list would be substantial and would conjoin some otherwise highly distinguishable research practices. This inductive approach to defining feminist research methods, however, collapses together some significant efforts on the part of feminist researchers. It also underplays the problems of gender in science in order to extend accountability to the practice of science.

In order to capture the exciting and occasionally controversial inquiries that attend feminist work in science, I begin this chapter by examining the idea of feminist science. Feminism is often seen as inimical to science; in such stereotypical contrasts, science often is taken to be isomorphic with positivism—a reductive, quantitative, and value-free or apolitical conception of science. Such analyses ultimately cast feminist methods as antagonist, marginal, or otherwise opposing science (and sometimes each other). A more complete picture requires comprehending science as a culture sustained by particular yet changing practices, including feminist work.

Not all feminist psychologists subscribe to this cultural understanding of science, and the second part of the chapter considers feminist research that ensues from a more conventional view of science as an abstract set of rules. This view, often called feminist empiricism, "argues that sexism and androcentrism are social biases correctable by stricter adherence to the existing methodological norms of scientific inquiry" (Harding 1986, 24).

Others who venture into feminist science, influenced by feminist scholarship across the disciplines, are wary of the notion that scientific norms are free of gender dynamics. These studies proceed by examining the culture of science itself. In the third section of this chapter I draw upon feminist reappraisals of objectivity and subjectivity to illustrate these other feminist revisions of scientific methods. I then conclude by considering the future of feminist methods in psychology.

The Science of Feminism

In textbooks as well as popular accounts, science often is taken as a set of prescriptions or precise rules of procedure, violations of which render a research project invalid or nonscientific. However, studies of science as early as those of Fleck ([1935] 1979) and Kuhn (1962) upturned such idealist, reified accounts, revealing instead how science is constituted through historically bound, shifting practices. What counts as rules of evidence is not pre-given, but results from debates that often have political implications. The rise of particular kinds of methods, such as statistics, is governed by larger social needs and interests (Porter 1995).

Within psychology, methodological norms such as operationalism (Leahey 1980), statistical inference (Gigerenzer 1991), debriefing (Harris 1988), aggregate sampling (Danziger 1990), and validity (Cronbach 1988; Hornstein 1988) were designed and promoted to resolve not just technical problems but political ones as well. Other matters of scientific techniques such as experimental artifacts (Suls and Rosnow 1988), experimenter characteristics (Morawski 1997), and language (Lamb 1991; Lopes 1991), go unresolved for long periods, and correcting them risks further revealing the cultural dynamics of psychological inquiry.

Once it is understood that science is not rule-bound, but is constituted through a complex set of sustained, consensual practices, then concepts such as objectivity, reality, validity, and representation are revealed to be the *results* of scientific work, and not unproblematic *preconditions* of that work. Science no longer can be taken to be independent of its practitioners, their actions, their aspirations, and their culture; nor is it always separate from the actions of nonscientific actors or institutions. In brief, a contextualized view enables and demands an appreciation of science as a cultural activity and moves us beyond complying with so-called abstract methodological norms to appraise the complex practices of science, including practices that test or contest those presumed norms.

Contemporary feminism has entered the culture of science with an agenda that includes more than the routine study of gender experience. Feminist science, in all its variants, entails multiple strategies to revise or transform the dominant practices of science that have been found to be androcentric or sexist. Primed with evidence of systematic bias in scientific representations of reality and of women's experiences as marginal participants in science, feminist scholars have excavated sexism in science. Sandra Harding (1986) has categorized these efforts into five distinguishable programs: studies of inequities surrounding women's participation in science; studies of sexist misuse of scientific knowledge; analyses of sexist bias in research; interrogations of linguistic and/or textual biases in science; and explorations of alternative gender-fair or feminist epistemologies.

However distinct these programs, and however varied the methodologies or theories employed in them, they share a belief captured in Virginia Woolf's observation that "science, it would seem, is not sexless; she is a man, a father, and infected too" (1938, 139). Beginning with this shared belief, which acknowledges the connections between science and social relations, feminist scientists elect different strategies to change what Donna Haraway (1986) calls the "narrative field" of science. They collectively, if sometimes tacitly, hold that the boundaries between the scientific analyst and the rest of the world are permeable, and that the links between scientific practice and other political actions are substantive and foundational.

Feminist psychologists, including many who would count themselves as conventional researchers in other respects, are generating alternative forms of social practice and changing the science's narrative field. Even the simple claim that the scientist's gender influences scientific conduct challenges basic ideas about science as a set of abstract norms. Thus, despite significant differences among feminist psychologists in their conceptions of science (epistemology), they are collectively engaged in "liminal science," that is, science at the threshold of or betwixt and between fixed conceptions (Morawski 1994). To occupy a liminal zone is not necessarily to be stuck in or by something; rather, it is to be less encumbered or detained. The liminal actor has the potential to subvert, transmute, transform, or reaffirm the reigning world view.

The collective effect of feminist work in psychology notwithstanding, researchers have adopted various epistemological stances. As I describe in subsequent sections, these stances translate into two different methodological styles: (1) what can be called limited revisions or remedial methods, and (2) more inclusive revisions or transformative methods.

Remedial Methods

Many feminist psychologists have opted for interventions that adhere to the conventional canons of inquiry but revise techniques that are visibly gender biased. Their approach is sometimes called feminist empiricism, although this is a misnomer because empirical techniques are employed in scholarship as diverse as feminist materialism and psychoanalysis. Researchers engaging in these remedial projects are unified by their beliefs that science is the search for objective knowledge, that this search has been tainted by sexist attitudes, but that it can be restored to its democratic, good-science ideals by the infusion of feminist awareness. These projects are not new: Feminist psychologists have been detecting bias in sex difference research for more than a century. As early as the 1890s, Mary Whiton Calkins (1896), Cordelia Nevers (1895), and Amy Tanner (1896) contested Joseph Jastrow's study of sex differences in cognition. Strategies of feminist remediation can be found in Helen Thompson's (1903) landmark empirical study of sex differences. They are visible too in Ruth Herschberger's (1948) fictional female chimpanzee who castigates psychologists for their sexist research methods. Similar ideals guided Georgene Seward's (1946) attempt to create sex-fair interpretations of post–World War II sex difference research: She showed how empirical evidence suggested "a democratic reformation of sex roles" in society (249).

Most recently, this remedial tradition has been highlighted through the work of Alice Eagly. Her research demonstrates the power of empiricism—its persuasive force as the "master's" technique, as well as its analytic precision—but it also reveals the limitations of remedial strategies. Eagly's (1987b) studies of sex differences use conventional research techniques to uncover systematic research biases. Her insistence (Eagly 1987a, 1990) that researchers should check for sex differences in all empirical analyses is persuasive, yet it intimates the limitations and ambiguities of the dominant rules of inquiry. For instance, while arguing for such systematic data checking, Eagly found herself up against other researchers who used the same methodological norms to claim that such systematic analysis violated procedures for theory testing (i.e., that such systematic testing was unwarranted unless there were theory grounds to suspect sex difference); that routine sex difference testing could function as self-fulfilling prophecy (an empirically derived construct), thus creating sex differences where none previously existed; and that such testing may not, in fact, yield valid evidence of real sex differences but merely measures of epiphenomena (Baumeister 1988). Eagly's (1995) earnest plea for researchers of sex differences to apprehend their own sex biases, even feminist sex biases, led her to appeal to some abstract vision of "scientific" work as a corrective to these biases. Because she could offer no specific or fail-safe conception of that work, her position depends on an abstract belief in some value-free method.

Remedial feminist projects have had notable successes in altering the narrative field of psychology; among their achievements is the profound one of making gender a legitimate category of analysis. Yet in retaining an unquestioned commitment to abstract conventions of inquiry, these projects can neither certify exact methods nor investigate gender in all scientific places, notably in the very epistemic roots of science.

Psychology's canon of empirical experimentation ultimately, and in its very conception, exonerates the observer and observations from scrutiny, thus blocking any deep interrogation of the scientific actor and the politics of science. Its logic is protective: If methods are held to be without politics or sexism, then only their improper use politicizes them. Further, that world view incorporates a naive view of language, reducing linguistic problems to representations requiring observational confirmation. For instance, feminist reformists are caught within a circle of defining the terms "sex" or "gender," but ultimately are unable to question the meanings of these observation terms. The deeper or more nuanced (and gendered) features of scientific visions, practices, and language cannot be ameliorated through remedial tools alone.

Transformative Strategies

The tendency to distinguish empiricist from postempiricist (interpretive, materialist, constructionist, postmodern, etc.) feminist work not only repeats the above-noted misnomer but also implies fixed boundaries between such epistemological traditions where, in fact, no simple lines of demarcation exist (Keller 1995). The exemplars cited above illustrate the transgressions and fluid quality of even studiously remedial work. Thus, Thompson (1903) prefaced her experimental study of sex differences with the claim that science required a utopia if the aim was a fully "trustworthy investigation of sex alone"; she admitted that "the complete fulfillment of these conditions, even in the most democratized community, is impossible" (2). Similarly, Tanner (1896) became exasperated over the assumptions about the two sexes and about women's natural predispositions; she realized that language and cultural assumptions about sex could not be eliminated from empirical work. And Eagly's (1995) analysis of psychologists' presuppositions, sexist and feminist alike, perhaps ironically demonstrates the necessity of attending to the psychology of the observer as well as that of the observed.

Such remedial work extends beyond mere rule adherence: The studies tell of the limits of a single method, the need to attend to language, the inadequacy of common practices of objectivity and validity, the gender politics of scientific institutions, the significance of the observer to an estimation of the knowledge produced, and a desire to connect science honestly with social change. In the past two decades, substantial feminist research has taken these conclusions as starting points for designing new modes of inquiry. Some of this work adds two presuppositions largely absent from the earlier feminist efforts: (1) an acknowledgment of the diversity, complexity, and historical variability of human experience and actions; and (2) a preference for understanding and interpreting, rather than simply predicting and controlling, experience and behavior.

Here feminist psychologists enter a place between orthodox science and something else, a place affording freedom to explore new methods and theories, generate new language, and reappraise the objects of study. However, theirs is not and has not been an unbridled freedom; in fact, the emergence of a new feminist psychology in the 1960s and 1970s relied on existing psychological knowledge and expertise, particularly concepts of psychological identity, consciousness raising, and psychotherapeutic techniques (Herman 1995). Nevertheless, this space has provided opportunities for experimenting with theory, language, method, and social action—experimentation that also was enabled by the increased numbers of women scientists, the maturation of feminist theories, and a cultural atmosphere more sensitive to matters of gender. And the opportunities have been seized, yielding, in just two decades, a diverse array of methodological innovations. No single literature review could adequately survey these new methods, nor could a reviewer at the present time accurately predict their viability. Collectively, however, these projects venture to transform several key scientific assumptions: objectivity, subjectivity, validity, and the very idea of science.

Objectivity

Objectivity is a signature characteristic of psychology, constituting such a pervasive, almost moral, feature of our science that it is difficult to generate a concise definition. It has become a primary epistemic aspiration of our studies, a technical criterion for what counts as valid knowledge, and an attribute of the investigator.

Several problems have emerged from feminist analyses of objectivity. First, objectivity represents impersonal, value-free, and, hence, universal understandings about the world (the binary of subjectivity, which represents personal, volitional, and, hence, ideographic understandings about the world). Thus, scientific objectivity involves discernment and denigration of subjectivity (Daston and Galison 1992).

Second, although objectivity is based on the premise that one can observe from no specific position—that there is some Archimedean point of observation free from the conditions of perception or the characteristics of the observer—no such position can be located. In fact, numerous studies have revealed how objectivity is gendered, reflecting masculine ideals in its privileging of detachment, control, manipulation of nature, and emotions of disinterestedness (Bordo 1987; Keller 1985; Merchant 1980). Lamb's (1991) analysis of the language used in conventional research on spousal battering and Lopes's (1991) study of the language of rationality in cognitive research demonstrate that objectivity is situated somewhere and conveys a stereotypic voice of authority.

Third, objectivity as conventionally defined produces a tension between truth and social action. Modern science's project of human betterment is inimical to an objectivity defined as devoid of values and morality. Feminist research, grounded in a commitment to women's rights and well-being, reveals the tensions between attaining such a disinterested ethos and realizing justice.

Such problematics have motivated feminist efforts to reconfigure objectivity as a scientific goal and practice that is not dichotomous and gendered (or otherwise imbued with dominance), makes a place for the observer, and admits both the complexity and the greater ambitions of science (Haraway 1988, 1994; Harding 1991; Keller 1985). These theories of objectivity reject Cartesian bifurcations of mind and body, self and other, fact and value. They relinquish the ideal of generic knowers laboring in freedom from historical circumstances. Knowing is situated and worldly: It involves intricate webs of social interactions and transpires in temporal planes. Knowing is relational in multiple senses: the knower's position in a social order, the relations within a community of knowers, and the connections between knowers and the world to be known. In this last sense, knowing is reflexive in that it can be realized only with various gazes back and forth, acts comprising what is commonly known as observing. Conceived in terms of these feminist notions of knowers and knowing, objectivity is an accomplishment of multiple practices, one that has moral and material as well as methodological substance.

The steps from these new conceptions of objectivity to research domains are tenuous; above all, they are complicated by the press of the dominant modes of inquiry. Yet such steps are being taken daily by feminist researchers who strategically revise our conceptions of knowers and the knowing process.

The role and nature of the observer has been reconsidered in three ways: locating the self of the observer, furnishing different identities or situations as integral to objectivity, and relinquishing classic procedures of control and mastery. Lykes (1989) discovered and then integrated into her analysis the disparity between feminist aspirations for collaborative researcher and participant relations and the contractual relations structured into standardized procedures, notably informed-consent techniques. The Guatemalan women participating in her study saw the consent form as shifting the relationship between themselves and the interviewers. Lykes reflected on the subtle message of power contained in the form itself, and she ultimately used the form to initiate fuller clarification of her role and relationship to the participants. Analyzing a dialogue between herself and a client at a rape crisis center, Fine (1989) explored her multiple selves as a researcher, including their contradictions, and offered insights into the transformation of the observer. These studies frame objectivity in terms of the social relations of the investigative context.

Feminist psychologists thus are at the forefront of rethinking their status as knowers in relation to participant "others," especially those differing in race, class, and gender. These formative practices sometimes reveal the enormity of the undertaking. Hurtado and Stewart (1997) examined how "whiteness" is naturalized and made ephemeral in psychological research; its invisible yet hegemonic presence, particularly in researchers, requires multiple methodological innovations and extensive critical analysis. Discovering better, more objective research methods entails finding "ways to retain a critical, counterhegemonic presence in the research" (309–310): addressing the limitations of one's position, seeking different standpoints, and employing complex collaborative methods that better enable representation of multiple perspectives. In a study of gay scientists' approaches to social-scientific study of homosexuality, Terry (1996) has described the perils and seductive traps that attend research centered around one's own identity. Terry identified the different historical conditions that predispose researchers to select and promote one theory over another: In a contemporary climate where genetics supplies a popular world view, "scientists may feel that 'nature' really is more liberating than 'nurture,' if only because the former is more manipulable than before and the latter is imagined as hostile, hopeless, and homophobic" (288).

Another approach to analyzing the practices of knowing is to scrutinize critically the sociohistorical context of research programs. In this spirit, Parlee's (1994) study of the emergence of premenstrual syndrome research informs us how investigative procedures are determined by many interests and agents that extend far beyond laboratory walls to include physicians, pharmaceutical companies, feminist activists, therapists, and ordinary people. Her study shows too how invested agents, including feminist psychologists, may discover that their scientific engagements have inadvertent outcomes that sometimes are contrary to what was originally intended. In a series of studies on laboratory procedures, Bayer (1992, 1997) has reported how seemingly basic experimental designs and mundane technologies reproduce certain social relations. Thus, small-group research rehearses stereotyped family structures, and technical innovations that stand in for the experimenter actually reinforce dominance while they purport to minimize experimenter bias. While Parlee's study suggests that knowers should attend more carefully to the dynamic context of their decisionmaking about methods, Bayer's investigations indicate a need to assess the social meanings conveyed through techniques and apparatus.

Subjectivity

A definition of objectivity as that which controls or eradicates subjectivity (Daston and Galison 1992) yields an impoverished appreciation of subjectivity. Historical analyses have revealed how psychology's notions of subjectivity reflect dominant cultural understandings of the individual while also inadvertently contributing to the emergence of new understandings (Cushman 1990; Hacking 1995; MacIntyre 1985; Pfister and Schnog 1997; Richards 1987; Rose 1985; Sampson 1981).

Acknowledging the historicity of subjectivity does not mean condemning the scientific project. On the contrary, such awareness bequeaths a fresh opportunity to comprehend subjectivity. Feminists have seized the opportunity; they have been especially productive in analyzing that feature of subjectivity known as gender. The introduction of the term "gender" as a central category of inquiry corresponds with the rise of feminist research: It was deployed to distinguish between biological and social theories about male and female differences to weed the empirical garden of unwarranted nativist assumptions (Unger 1979). Yet it has become apparent that "sex," too, is a cultural category that has been forged from shared beliefs about the nature of the world (Bleier 1984; Butler 1990; Kessler and McKenna 1978; Lacqueur 1990). Investigation must proceed cautiously, then, to avoid the fabrication of another unwarranted bifurcation. Feminist psychologists have argued that gender is context-dependent; that gender differences are not polar but multiple; and that studying gender requires analyzing its historical, structural, and performative dimensions (Deaux and Major 1987; Fine and Gordon 1989; Lott 1985; Unger 1989; Wallston 1981). Related work has demanded that matters of agency and power be integrated into models of gender (Kitzinger 1991; Morawski and Bayer 1995; Parlee 1979; Sherif 1982; Unger 1989). Reappraisals of the gendered subject indicate the need to reconsider the "ontogenesis of the subject," including the development of sexuality and bodily experiences (Malone 1997), race, and class (Reid 1993).

Overall, these revisions of our understanding of gender intimate the larger project to develop richer, more accurate theories of subjectivity. These theories will replace the conventions of associating subjectivity with either some abyss of internal mental processes or the stereotypical image of an autonomous, independent, and rational subject. Without falling back on older notions of intentionality, new enterprises will articulate the dynamics of agency while attending to how power relations and social structure contribute to subjectivity. The reflexivity of this work also needs to be addressed, in the form of an ongoing scrutiny of how our scientific projects reappropriate, mirror, or change human behavior and thought (Morawski 1994).

These mandates for understanding subjectivity pose heavy challenges for creating appropriate research methods. Qualitative methods, grounded in extensive contextual analyses, currently comprise the most available techniques for investigating agency and context, as well as the best means for eliminating unwarranted assumptions about individual actors. An example of such work can be found in the study of narratives. Narratives are a "cognitive instrument" (Mink 1978) that organize human experiences and make them meaningful. Narratives serve as mediations between individual actions and material and social-structural conditions; they reflect the dynamics of ongoing negotiations, interpretations, and construals just as they indicate the constraints operating in these dynamics. Narrative inquiry offers a means of tracing the evolution of gendered self-identity

(Personal Narratives Group 1989). In the case of women's experiences, these studies have located the culturally gendered templates for making sense of one's life (Quinn 1987; Wiersma 1988) and the complex influence of social norms (Ginsburg 1989; Helson 1989). Narrative studies offer the opportunity to explore experiences of agency and their relation to psychological well-being (Stewart and Malley 1989).

Other explorations of subjectivity begin at a very different place: They focus on transforming the research relationship into a more "collaborative" or "participatory" one. By establishing such arrangements, researchers are able conduct ongoing appraisals not only of their presuppositions about subjectivity, but also of the multiple power relations undergirding scientific research. Such new arrangements are further justified on methodological grounds: They recognize scientifically that social context, including the investigative context, is an integral feature of cognitions and actions. One concrete means to realize a collaborative arrangement is to engage participants in the collection, analysis, interpretation, and eventual evaluation of research (Doell 1991; Fonow and Cook 1991; Hoff 1988; Imber and Tuana 1988; Mies 1983; Stephenson, Kippax, and Crawford 1996; Taylor, Gilligan, and Sullivan 1996).

Challenges

Once made familiar with the significant if sometimes nuanced attempts to transform objectivity and subjectivity, a reader can find, in the pages of psychology journals, myriad instances of such strategies. Small, diverse methodological innovations are altering the narrative field of psychological science. Their impact, of course, sometimes incites criticism: Some backlashes are in evidence in recent writings that assert the perils of self-report methods (and not their ability to enrich data), and in evolutionary psychology theories that explain rape and heterosexual mating as natural acts (and not as complicated social practices). Critical reaction notwithstanding, feminist investigations have changed the landscape of psychology.

Working at this threshold, the gains are not always easy to perceive, nor are the future challenges. Feminist psychologists have engaged the problems of objectivity—knowers and knowing—and the contours of subjectivity. And although these engagements are realized through an appreciation of science as a culture consisting of complex practices and politics, that culture cannot be altered easily. Some of the more pressing troubles circulate around the evaluation, acceptance, and dissemination of knowledge. It can no longer be assumed that facts are simply that which corresponds to some external reality; nor can feminist scholars hold that valid knowledge contains no value premises. In these understandings, feminist inquiry concurs with Cronbach's (1988) redefinition of validity as a pervasive practice that is situated within a community and must explicitly incorporate assessment of the consequences of research findings. Plural methods require plural modes of assessment; so-called "applied" research need no longer be held suspect; no study, however honorable its politics, should be exempted from critical analysis; and evaluating knowledge must proceed more democratically by encompassing the appraisal of participants and other interested parties.

Proposed techniques for revising how knowledge claims are assessed and utilized include evaluating findings in terms of their effects in the larger culture (Fine 1985; Lather 1991; Striegel-Moore 1993; Worell 1990) and extending accountability to the larger community (Yllö 1988). Above all, the commitment to producing knowledge that leads to positive change in the world means that the procedures for assessing truth claims must include evaluation of how those claims provide enhancement or new awareness (Lather 1991). As Rouse (1996) has noted, these changes are not simply about politics or beliefs, because feminist science scholars value reliable scientific knowledge. Feminist aims assume that "knowledge is neither external to nor merely instrumental for justice, but is itself a valued end for which justice is integral" (208).

A far greater challenge, and one inevitably faced when thinking deeply about the adjudication of knowledge, resides not in furnishing creative research designs, but in modifying the near environment in which researchers conduct their science, learn, teach, and judge the efforts of other scientists. Reid (1993) has cogently enumerated the hazards that are part of the very structure of this environment. In describing barriers to feminist psychologists' knowing women of color, Reid named three notable ones: "personal affiliation," or researchers' personal connection to an area of investigation; "effort maximization," or the economy of getting maximum benefits for work exerted; and "investigator training," or the practice of training new researchers mainly in traditional methods. To this list can be added what can be called "evaluative conservatism," or the tendency to apply canonical standards (sometimes in conjunction with feminist ones) when assessing feminist research projects, students, publications, colleagues, job searches, and candidates for awards.

These barriers, located in the near environment, sometimes unknowingly accepted by us, and often tacitly deployed through routine decisions and judgments, persist as a vestige of our liminality. Such "institutional capture" (Smith 1987) threatens nothing less than the viability, longevity, and future development of feminist methods of inquiry. The challenge to feminist scientists, then, lies just as much in everyday actions as in meticulous and innovative research designs. Whenever these actions are within the scope of our influence or control, as is frequently the case, our greatest contribution to feminist methods is changing the environment in which science is generated.

References

Baumeister, R. 1988. Should we stop studying sex differences altogether? *American Psychologist* 43:1092–1095.

Bayer, B. M. 1992. Histories of inclusion: The importance of gender to small group research, 1940–1990. Paper read at Cheiron Society, Windsor, Ontario.

———. 1997. Between apparatuses and apparitions: Phantoms of the laboratory. In *Reconstructing the psychological subject: Bodies, practices, and technologies*, eds. B. Bayer and J. Shotter. Newbury Park, CA: Sage.

Bernstein, R. J. 1983. *Beyond objectivism and relativism: Science, hermeneutics, and praxis*. Philadelphia: University of Pennsylvania Press.

Bleier, R. 1984. *Science and gender: A critique of biology and its theories on women*. New York: Pergamon.

Bordo, S. 1987. *The flight of objectivity: Essays on Cartesianism and culture*. Albany: State University of New York Press.

Butler, J. 1990. *Gender trouble: Feminism and the subversion of identity*. New York: Routledge.

Calkins, M. W. 1896. Community of ideas of men and women. *Psychological Review* 3:426–531.

Cronbach, L. J. 1988. Five perspectives on the validity argument. In *Test validity*, eds. H. Wainer and H. I. Braun. Hillsdale, NJ: Laurence Erlbaum.

Cushman, P. 1990. Why the self is empty: Toward a historically situated psychology. *American Psychologist* 45:599–611.

Danziger, K. 1990. *Constructing the subject: Historical origins of psychological research*. New York: Cambridge University Press.

Daston, L., and P. Galison. 1992. The image of objectivity. *Representations* 40: 81–128.

Deaux, K., and B. Major. 1987. Putting gender into context: An interactive model of gender-related behavior. *Psychological Review* 94 (3): 369–389.

Doell, R. G. 1991. Whose research is this? Values and biology. In *(En)Gendering knowledge: Feminists in academe*, eds. J. E. Hartman and E. Messer-Davidow. Knoxville: University of Tennessee Press.

Eagly, A. H. 1987a. Reporting sex differences. *American Psychologist* 42:756–757.

———. 1987b. Sex differences in influenceability. *Psychological Bulletin* 85: 86–116.

———. 1990. On the advantages of reporting sex comparisons. *American Psychologist* 45:560–562.

———. 1995. The science and politics of comparing women and men. *American Psychologist* 50 (3): 145–158.

Fine, M. 1985. Reflections on a feminist psychology of women. *Psychology of Women Quarterly* 9:167–183.

———. 1989. Coping with rape: Critical perspectives on consciousness. In *Representations: Social constructions of gender*, ed. R. Unger. Amityville, NY: Baywood.

Fine, M., and S. M. Gordon. 1989. Feminist transformations of/despite psychology. In *Gender and thought*, eds. M. Crawford and M. Gentry. New York: Springer-Verlag.

Fleck, L. [1935] 1979. *Genesis and development of a scientific fact*. Chicago: University of Chicago Press.

Fonow, M. M., and J. A. Cook. 1991. *Beyond methodology: Feminist scholarship as lived research*. Bloomington: Indiana University Press.

Fuller, S. 1988. *Social epistemology*. Bloomington: Indiana University Press.

Gigerenzer, G. 1991. From tools to theories: A heuristic of discovery in cognitive psychology. *Psychological Review* 98:257–267.

Ginsburg, F. 1989. Dissonance and harmony: The symbolic function of abortion in activists' life stories. In *Interpreting women's lives*, ed. P. N. Group. Bloomington: Indiana University Press.

Hacking, I. 1995. *Rewriting the soul: Multiple personality and the sciences of memory*. Princeton, NJ: Princeton University Press.

Haraway, D. 1986. Primatology is politics by other means. In *Feminist approaches to science*. New York: Pergamon.

———. 1988. Situated knowledges: The science question in feminism and the privilege of partial perspective. *Feminist Studies* 14 (3): 575–599.

———. 1989. *Primate visions: Gender, race, and nature in the world of modern science*. New York: Routledge.

———. 1994. A game of cats' cradle: Science studies, feminist theory, cultural studies. *Configurations* 1:59–71.

Harding, S. 1986. *The science question in feminism.* Ithaca, NY: Cornell University Press.

———. 1991. *Whose science? Whose knowledge? Thinking from women's lives.* Ithaca, NY: Cornell University Press.

Harris, B. 1988. Key words: A history of debriefing in social psychology. In *The rise of experimentation in American psychology,* ed. J. Morawski. New Haven, CT: Yale University Press.

Hawes, S. E. 1993. *Reflexivity and collaboration in the supervisory process: A role for feminist poststructural theories in training of professional psychologists.* Paper read at National Council of Schools of Professional Psychology Conference, Las Vegas, Nevada.

Helson, R. 1989. E. Nesbit's forty-first year: Her life, times, and symbolizations of personality growth. In *Representations: Social constructions of gender,* ed. R. Unger. Amityville, NY: Baywood.

Herman, E. 1995. *The romance of American psychology: Political culture in the age of experts.* Berkeley: University of California Press.

Herschberger, R. 1948. *Adam's rib.* New York: Pellegrini and Cudahy.

Hoff, L. A. 1988. Collaborative feminist research and the myth of objectivity. In *Feminist perspectives on wife abuse,* eds. K. Yllö and M. Bogard. Newbury Park, CA: Sage.

Hornstein, G. A. 1988. Quantifying psychological phenomena: Debates, dilemmas, and implications. In *The rise of experimentation in American psychology,* ed. J. Morawski. New Haven, CT: Yale University Press.

Hurtado, A. 1996. Strategic suspensions: Feminists of color theorize the production of knowledge. In *Knowledge, difference, and power,* eds. N. Goldberger, J. Tarule, B. Clinchy, and M. Belenky. New York: Basic Books.

Hurtado, A., and A. Stewart. 1997. Through the looking glass: Implications of studying whiteness for feminist methods. In *Off white: Reading on race, power, and society,* eds. M. Fine, L. Weis, L. C. Powell, and M. Wong. New York: Routledge.

Imber, B., and N. Tuana. 1988. Feminist perspectives on science. *Hypatia* 3 (1): 139–144.

Keller, E. F. 1985. *Reflections on gender and science.* New Haven, CT: Yale University Press.

———. 1995. Gender and science: Origin, history, and politics. *Osiris* 10:27–58.

Kessler, S. J., and M. McKenna. 1978. *Gender: An ethnomethodological approach.* New York: Wiley.

Kitzinger, C. 1991. Feminism, psychology, and the paradox of power. *Feminism and Psychology* 1:111–130.

Kuhn, T. S. 1962. *The structure of scientific revolutions.* Vol. 2 of *International encyclopedia of unified science.* Chicago: University of Chicago Press.

Lacqueur, T. 1990. *Making sex: Body and gender from the Greeks to Freud.* Cambridge, MA: Harvard University Press.

Lamb, S. 1991. Acts without agents: An analysis of linguistic avoidance in journal articles on men who batter women. *American Journal of Orthopsychiatry* 61 (2): 250–257.

Lather, P. 1991. *Getting smart: Feminist research and pedagogy with/in the postmodern.* New York: Routledge.

Latour, B. 1987. *Science in action: How to follow scientists and engineers through society.* Cambridge, MA: Harvard University Press.

Leahey, T. H. 1980. The myth of operationism. *Journal of Mind and Behavior* 1:127–143.

Leary, D. E. 1980. The intentions and heritage of Descartes and Locke: Toward a recognition of the moral basis of modern psychology. *Journal of General Psychology* 102:283–310.

Lopes, L. L. 1991. The rhetoric of irrationality. *Theory and Psychology* 1:65–82.

Lott, B. 1985. The potential enrichment of social/personality psychology through feminist research and vice versa. *American Psychologist* 40 (2): 155–164.

Lykes, M. B. 1989. Dialogue with Guatemalan Indian women: Critical perspectives on constructing collaborative research. In *Representations: Social constructions of gender*, ed. R. Unger. Amityville, NY: Baywood.

MacIntyre, A. 1985. How Psychology makes itself true-or-false. In *A century of psychology as science*, eds. S. Koch and D. Leary. New York: McGraw-Hill.

Malone, K. R. 1997. Feminism and psychoanalysis consider sexuality and the symbolic order: Would social construction join us? In *Reconstructing the psychological subject: Bodies, practices, and technologies*, eds. M. Bayer and J. Shotter. Newbury Park, CA: Sage.

Merchant, C. 1980. *Death of nature: Women, ecology, and the scientific revolution.* New York: Harper and Row.

Mies, M. 1983. Toward a methodology for feminist research. In *Theories of women's studies*, eds. G. Bowles and R. D. Klein. London: Routledge.

Mink, L. O. 1978. Narrative form as cognitive instrument. In *The writing of history: Literary form and historical understanding*, eds. R. H. Canary and H. Kozici. Madison: University of Wisconsin Press.

Morawski, J. G. 1994. *Practicing feminisms, reconstructing psychology: Notes on a liminal science.* Ann Arbor: University of Michigan Press.

———. 1997. White experimenters, white blood, and other white conditions: Locating the psychologist's race. In *Off White: Readings on race, power, and society*, ed. M. Fine, L. Weis, and L. C. Powell. New York: Routledge.

Morawski, J. G., and B. M. Bayer. 1995. Stirring trouble and making theory. In *Bringing cultural diversity to feminist psychology*, ed. H. Landrine. Washington, DC: American Psychological Association.

Nevers, C. 1895. Dr. Jastrow on community of ideas of men and women. *Psychological Review* 2:363–367.

Parlee, M. B. 1979. Psychology and woman. *Signs* 5:121–133.

———. 1994. The social construction of premenstrual syndrome: A case study of scientific discourse. In *The good body: Asceticism in contemporary culture*, eds. M. G. Winkler and L. B. Cole. New Haven, CT: Yale University Press.

Personal Narratives Group, ed. 1989. *Interpreting women's lives: Feminist theory and personal narratives.* Bloomington: Indiana University Press.

Pfister, J., and N. Schnog. 1997. *Inventing the psychological: Toward a cultural history of emotional life in America.* New Haven, CT: Yale University Press.

Porter, T. M. 1995. *The pursuit of objectivity in science and public life.* Princeton, NJ: Princeton University Press.

Quinn, N. 1987. Convergent evidence for a cultural model of American marriage. In *Cultural models in language and thought*, eds. D. Holland and N. Quinn. Cambridge: Cambridge University Press.

Reid, P. T. 1993. Poor women in psychological research: Shut up and shut out. *Psychology of Women Quarterly* 17:113–150.

Reinharz, S. 1992. *Feminist methods in social research.* New York: Oxford University Press.

Richards, G. 1987. Of what is history of psychology a history? *British Journal of the History of Science* 20:201–211.

Riley, D. 1988. *"Am I that name?" Feminism and the category of "women" in history.* Minneapolis: University of Minnesota Press.

Rose, N. 1985. *The psychological complex: Psychology and society in England 1869–1935.* London: Routledge and Kegan Paul.

Rouse, J. 1987. *Knowledge and power: Toward a political philosophy of science.* Ithaca, NY: Cornell University Press.

———. 1996. Feminism and the social construction of scientific knowledge. In *Feminism, science, and the philosophy of science*, eds. L. H. Nelson and J. Nelson. London: Kluwer.

Sampson, E. E. 1981. Cognitive psychology as ideology. *American Psychologist* 36:730–743.

Seward, G. H. 1946. *Sex and the social order.* New York: McGraw-Hill.

Sherif, C. W. 1982. Needed concepts in the study of gender identity. *Psychology of Women Quarterly* 6 (4): 375–398.

Smith, D. E. 1987. *The everyday world as problematic: A feminist sociology.* Boston: Northeastern University Press.

Stephenson, N., S. Kippax, and J. Crawford. 1996. You and I and she: Memory-work and the construction of self. In *Feminist social psychologies*, ed. S. Wilkinson. Buckingham: Open University Press.

Stewart, A. J., and J. E. Malley. 1989. Case studies of agency and communion in women's lives. In *Representations: Social constructions of gender*, ed. R. Unger. Amityville, NY: Baywood.

Striegel-Moore, R. H. 1993. Toward a feminist research agenda in the psychological research of eating disorders. In *Feminist perspectives on eating disorders*, eds. P. Fallon, M. Katzman, and S. Wooley. New York: Guilford.

Suls, J. M., and R. L. Rosnow. 1988. Concerns about artifacts in psychological experiments. In *The rise of experimentation*, ed. J. Morawski. New Haven, CT: Yale University Press.

Tanner, A. 1896. The community of ideas of men and women. *Psychological Review* 3:549–550.

Taylor, J. M., C. Gilligan, and A. Sullivan. 1996. Missing voices, changing meanings: Developing a voice-centered, relational method and creating an interpretive community. In *Feminist social psychologies*, ed. S. Wilkinson. Buckingham, England: Open University Press.

Terry, T. 1996. The seductive power of science in the making of deviant subjectivity. In *Science and homosexualities*, ed. V. A. Rosario. New York: Routledge.

Thompson, H. 1903. *The mental traits of sex: An experimental investigation of the normal mind in men and women*. Chicago: University of Chicago Press.

Unger, R. K. 1979. Toward a redefinition of sex and gender. *American Psychologist* 34 (11): 1085–1094.

———. 1989. Sex, gender, and epistemology. In *Gender and thought*, eds. M. Crawford and M. Gentry. New York: Springer-Verlag.

Wallston, B. S. 1981. What are the questions in psychology of women? A feminist approach to research. *Psychology of Women Quarterly* 5 (4): 597–617.

Wiersma, J. 1988. The press release: Symbolic communication in life history interviewing. In *Psychobiography and life narratives*, eds. D. P. McAdams and R. L. Ochberg. Durham, NC: Duke University Press.

Wooglar, S. 1988. *Science: The very idea*. New York: Tavistock.

Woolf, V. 1938. *Three Guineas*. New York: Harcourt, Brace and World.

Worell, J. 1990. Feminist frameworks: Retrospect and prospect. *Psychology of Women Quarterly* 14:1–5.

Yllö, K. 1988. Political and methodological debates in wife abuse research. In *Feminist perspectives on wife abuse*, eds. K. Yllö and M. Bograd. Newbury Park, CA: Sage.

6

■　　■　　■　　■　　■　　■　　■　　■　　■

Education, Research, and Action

*Theory and Methods of Participatory
Action Research*

Mary Brydon-Miller

"YOU CAN'T MIX YOUR POLITICS and your psychology." This was
the rationale given by a would-be dissertation committee member for his
unwillingness to work with me on a Participatory Action Research (PAR)
project. Nearly twenty years later, it seems that mixing politics and psychology can still present a challenge to those interested in applying their
skills and training to addressing social issues, especially when that means
working outside the bounds of traditional positivist research. The goal of
PAR is transformation. This refers both to the transformative processes of
social change and community empowerment that guide the practice of this
research and to the fundamental transformation of the field that will be
necessary if such practices are to be generally accepted as legitimate forms
of knowledge generation. Participatory Action Research provides a framework within which such transformation can take place, allowing those of
us committed to working with communities to achieve positive social
change to put our psychology to work in support of our political, social,
and economic values.

Participatory Action Research has been defined as a process of research, education, and action (Hall 1981). It is a practice in which the distinction between the researcher and the researched is challenged as participants are afforded the opportunity to take an active role in addressing issues affecting themselves, their families, and their communities (Gaventa 1988). Researchers using this approach explicitly commit to working with members of communities that have traditionally been exploited and oppressed in a united effort to bring about fundamental social change (Maguire 1987).

The current theory and practice of PAR draw on influences from many different disciplines and from researchers and practitioners around the world. According to Budd Hall, the term "participatory research" was first used in the early 1970s by Marja Lissa Swantz to describe work then being conducted in Tanzania that drew on the knowledge and expertise of community members in creating locally controlled development projects. Orlando Fals-Borda used the term "participatory action research" to describe similar efforts in Colombia, emphasizing the social change component of the work (see Lykes, this volume, for a more extensive discussion of the development of PAR in Latin America). At about the same time, Rajesh Tandon in India was developing a similar approach to conducting community-based research (Hall 1997). To a large extent these early efforts focused on the areas of adult education, agricultural development and economic reform.

In the United States and Canada, efforts at developing community-based action research programs were led by researchers at the Highlander Research Center in New Market, Tennessee (Gaventa 1993; Horton 1993), and the International Council for Adult Education in Toronto, Ontario (Hall 1993), as well as by individual researchers such as Donald Comstock and Russell Fox in Washington State (1993) and Ken Reardon and his group of researchers in East St. Louis (1993). A particularly important contribution was made by Patricia Maguire in her book *Doing Participatory Research: A Feminist Approach* (1987). This book, based on her dissertation research with the Battered Family Services in Gallup, New Mexico, added an important voice on the feminist perspective on participatory research processes.

Many of these researchers were influenced by the work of Paulo Freire, the Brazilian educator and writer whose book *Pedagogy of the Oppressed* ([1970] 1993) introduced his readers to the notion of conscientization and the principles of radical educational reform. Freire regards both educator and student—or, by extension, researcher and researched—as equal and active participants in the formation of the educational or research process. "In doing research," he observes, "I am educating and being educated with the people" (1982, 30). Freire's work in literacy training in Brazil and around the world provided a model of how researchers could draw on the knowledge and experience of local people, transforming that knowledge into a critical consciousness of the forces that have shaped their economic and social realities. According to Freire, only with this understanding can individuals and communities take part in processes of social change that will confront economic and political inequalities. "Those promoting participatory action research believe that people have a universal right to participate in the production of knowledge which is a disciplined process of personal and social transformation" (1997, xi).

Practitioners of PAR draw on a variety of theoretical sources, particularly Marxism (Oquist 1978), feminism (Cancian 1992; Joyappa and Martin 1996; Maguire 1987), and critical theory (Antonio 1981; Bernstein 1976; Comstock 1994; Comstock and Fox 1993; Fay 1975; Habermas 1971; Held 1980). (See Crotty 1998 for a fine introduction to a broad range of theoretical perspectives in social research.) My own perspective is based largely on the work of Brian Fay (1975) and the critical theorists cited above, who propose that knowledge generation is not limited to the boundaries established by positivism and suggest that both interpretive and critical approaches to the practice of knowledge generation are also legitimate ways of approaching the research process.

Jürgen Habermas (1971) explored such valid, alternative forms of knowing in his analysis of the forms of human knowledge and their relationship to human interests. Habermas discusses three distinct "categories of processes of inquiry for which a specific connection between logical-methodological rules and knowledge-constitutive interests can be demonstrated" (308). The empirical-analytic knowledge familiar from positivism supports the technical interests that allow us to establish control over our physical environment. As Richard Bernstein points out, Habermas "is not criticizing or denigrating this type of knowledge. On the contrary, insofar as he claims that it is grounded in the dimension of human life that involves human survival, he is stressing its importance and its basic quality for any social life" (1976, 194). But, as Bernstein goes on to explain, "Habermas' primary object of attack is the ideological claim that this is the only type of legitimate knowledge, or the standard by which all knowledge is to be measured" (194).

A second and vital form of human knowledge that cannot be understood through empirical-analytic inquiry, based in human relationships, is what Habermas refers to as the practical interests of humankind, expressed through human communication and language. These interests can only be understood through interpretive or historical-hermeneutic methods in which "access to the facts is provided by the understanding of meaning, not observation" (Habermas 1971, 309; see also Crotty 1998; Tappan, this volume).

Finally, in addition to these two forms of knowledge, Habermas posits critical knowledge, knowledge born of social action that supports the emancipatory interests of humankind. (In a similar vein, Susan Smith's [1997] discussion of these three forms of research contrasts empirical-analytic with interpretive and critical, or what she terms "liberatory," forms of research.) Critically informed inquiry generates a form of knowledge that results in and grows out of the liberation of those generating the knowledge; it is simultaneously knowledge based in action and action based in knowledge. It is only through this dialectical process of action and reflection that the praxis of critical theory—or, to use Freire's term, conscientization—can be achieved (Freire [1970] 1993).

Habermas discusses the necessary relationships between these three categories of knowledge and the interests associated with them. Bernstein states this relationship emphatically: "an adequate social and political theory must be empirical, interpretive, and critical" (1976, 235). He then goes on to suggest that while this emancipatory interest is in some respects "derivative" of the others, it is at the same time "the most basic cognitive interest" (198). The empirical-analytic and historical-hermeneutic methods—or "sciences," as Habermas terms them—do generate valid forms of knowledge, but if we are to act in the interest of humankind, they must be placed in the service of the critical sciences. Comstock (1994) summarizes this goal of critical science succinctly: "A critical social science must directly contribute to the revitalization of moral discourse and revolutionary action by engaging its subjects in a process of active self-understanding and collective self-formation. In this way, science becomes a method for self-conscious action rather than an ideology for the technocratic domination of a passive populace" (626). Participatory Action Research provides a model for integrating these various forms of inquiry within a framework of critical social science and in the interest of human liberation.

In PAR, the role of the researcher in pursuing social justice and human liberation through a process of critical praxis is explicit, as is the political nature of the work, demonstrating the important distinction between PAR and more traditional positivist research. Critically informed approaches to research reject the notion that knowledge generation can or should be apolitical and value-free. As James Farganis states, "all scientific knowledge about social reality carries with it, either implicitly or explicitly, certain ideological, political and evaluative convictions" (1975, 483). Embracing the political nature of any research process allows us to act in a more direct and open manner in addressing social issues and, according to Comstock, "requires the involvement of the researchers in the subjects' political activity" (1994, 637). Our convictions can now become central and mutually acknowledged components of the research process, and the research process itself can be seen and evaluated in terms of its ability to generate broad community participation and on its political, social, and economic impact.

Basic Tenets and Methods of Participatory Action Research

Despite the wide array of theoretical bases that inform Participatory Action Research, we can articulate a basic set of methodological tenets that define its practice. Hall (1981) provides a set of criteria that characterize PAR and can be summarized in three basic guidelines:

- PAR focuses on communities and populations that have traditionally been exploited or oppressed.
- PAR works to address both the specific concerns of the community and the fundamental causes of the oppression with the goal of achieving positive social change.
- PAR is a process of research, education, and action to which all participants contribute their unique skills and knowledge and through which all participants learn and are transformed (see also Fals-Borda and Rahman 1991).

Methodologically, it is more difficult to typify. PAR can and does use what might seem to be fairly traditional methods of social scientific inquiry such as community questionnaires and interviews. But in addition to more standard methods, PAR also utilizes a variety of other approaches, including popular theater, political action, group discussions, community seminars, educational camps, intercultural exchange programs, video productions, and storytelling, to name just a few (see, e.g., Arratia with de la Maza 1997; Brydon-Miller 1993; Debbink and Ornelas 1997; Rahman 1993; Tobias 1982).

Whatever specific techniques are used, the fundamental difference between this approach and traditional research is that in PAR the members of the community themselves, drawing on the expertise of the researcher, determine what questions to ask and which methods to use. Together they develop or adapt the research instruments, carry out the research, and take part in analyzing the results. Finally, and most important, the community members themselves own the results of the research and can determine how the information is to be used in addressing the concerns they have articulated.

Clearly, the researcher has distinct interests in this process and its outcome as well. She must determine what community to work with, and she may specify issues of particular interest to her. In addition, she may feel that the results of a given PAR process have broader implications for our understanding of social issues and processes of social change that should be made available through presentations and publications. Community members themselves may have little interest in participating in these activities, nor do they have the professional and scholarly incentives to do so. Nonetheless, they should be made aware of these intentions from the beginning of the process and encouraged to view their efforts as important contributions to research in the field.

One model of the PAR process, based in large part on the work of Maguire (1987) and Walter Fernandes and Rajesh Tandon (1981), begins with the establishment of relationships between the researcher and members of the community (see Figure 6.1). The success of any PAR project depends on the depth of mutual trust and commitment held by all participants. In cases in which the community is already well-organized and has clearly articulated concerns, they may approach the researcher. When the

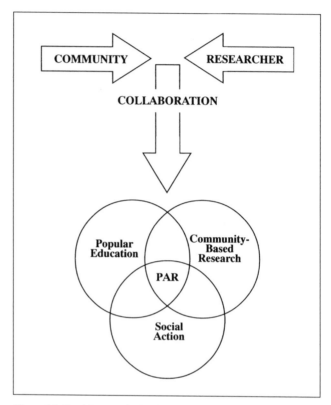

Figure 6.1. Participatory Action Research process.

community is less self-directed or has not yet coalesced around an issue, it may be the researcher who establishes the contact. Randy Stoecker (1999) calls this the "Initiator" role and discusses the challenge in such cases of shifting control from the researcher to the community. The researcher may in some cases be a part of the community group, an "insider." Understanding this insider versus outsider status and its implications is critical to effective PAR, and researchers must consider their roles and actions carefully if the process is to be one of empowerment rather than cooptation (Brydon-Miller 1993; Greenwood and Levin 1998).

The collaboration itself may combine popular education, community-based research, and/or social action, depending on the needs of the community. Ideally, the PAR process should integrate these three elements, with each aspect of the work informing the others through the collaborative efforts of the research team; however, the order and emphasis of these elements must be adapted to fit each individual project. Whatever the process, the final stage is one of shared reflection and consolidation of the learning that has taken place, and a reexamination of the political, social, and economic conditions facing the community. The appropriate role of the researcher is fluid and, to quote my friend, the late poet Joel Oppenheimer, you just have to "Be There When It Happens."

Participatory Action Research and Psychology

The practice of Participatory Action Research is beginning to gain ground in the field of psychology (Chesler 1991; Nastasi et al. 1998; Nelson et al. 1998). Of course, psychologists have a long history of commitment and contribution to their communities; but this has been regarded largely as a form of volunteerism distinct from our work as researchers. We have not attempted to integrate our lives and the knowledge we have gained as community organizers with the "real work" of research. Those who have attempted to bridge this gap have found it difficult to convince others in the field of the legitimacy of their work and the insights gained from it, especially when the work has been based on the principles of collaboration and critical learning described here. However, there are signs that this is changing. As the examples discussed below and the other contributions to this volume suggest, there are researchers in the field who see the potential that such work has for our discipline, and they are beginning to find an audience in professional conferences, journals, and volumes such as this one.

Susan Yeich and Ralph Levine's (1992) work on the relationship between participatory research and the conceptualization of empowerment, in which they describe the establishment of a Homeless Persons Union in East Lansing, Michigan, illustrates the kinds of contributions such efforts can make, theoretically as well as practically. Working with homeless persons in the community, this union engaged in a variety of activities, including "speaking to university classes, presenting workshops at conferences, meeting with politicians, registering homeless and low-income people to vote, testifying at state legislature hearings and city council meetings, organizing public demonstrations, receiving media coverage, networking with other organizations, fundraising, recruiting members, and working with university faculty on a resource book for homeless people" (Yeich and Levine 1992, p. 1901). While they were taking these concrete steps to address issues of homelessness in the community, they were also examining larger questions regarding the nature of empowerment. As the authors point out, "the idea of a researcher designing an intervention to empower other people is somewhat contradictory. Empowerment seems to be a process that one must do for oneself—not something that someone can do for or to another" (p. 1907).

Similarly, S. Darius Tandon and his colleagues have used a PAR process to study grassroots community leadership within the African-American community in Chicago (Tandon et al. 1998; Tandon, Kelly, and Mock, this volume). This collaboration has involved local leaders in all aspects of the research, including "selecting topics and methods, training interviewers, conducting and coding interviews, and utilizing interview findings" (Tandon et al. 1998, 672). Again, the research serves dual goals of generating specific community change while contributing to a greater understanding of the nature of leadership as it pertains to minority communities.

In another example, Fred Piercy and Volker Thomas (1998) discuss the use of participatory evaluation research in family therapy. In addition to reviewing the history of PAR and associated practices, the authors outline a number of specific methods for increasing active client participation and control in the evaluation of family therapy practices.

Another similar approach, defined by Robert Newbrough, is Community Action Research. Newbrough, citing the Liberation Theology movement, among other influences, has suggested the development of research processes "in which persons are empowered, supported and develop a sense of community so that they can take responsibilities for the common good" (1995, 27).

William Foote Whyte uses the term Participatory Action Research to describe his work in the field of organizational behavior (1989, 1991). However, Whyte's work does not, in general, acknowledge the traditions of PAR discussed above, nor does it specifically identify the importance of fundamental social transformation and empowerment that are at the heart of PAR as it is defined here (see, e.g., Pace and Argona 1991 on their work with the Xerox corporation). However, much of the work citing Whyte's influence does reflect these values. For example, E. Sally Rogers and Victoria Palmer-Erbs's (1994) work with participatory approaches to psychiatric rehabilitation, Ira Harkavy's projects with the Philadelphia public school system, and Davydd Greenwood's ongoing research with the Mondragon worker cooperatives (Greenwood, Whyte, and Harkavy 1993) all support liberatory practices in their work.

More recent work by Davydd Greenwood and Morten Levin (1998) uses the term Action Research to describe practices that are quite consistent with the PAR approach discussed here. The authors trace their practice to the early work of the social psychologist Kurt Lewin and to the philosophical roots in pragmatism of William James and John Dewey. In fact, there is an extensive body of Action Research that in both its mission and methods is very consistent with the PAR approach discussed here (Carr and Kemmis 1985; Kemmis and McTaggart 1988; see also the online journal *Action Research International*).

Given the foundations of Participatory Action Research in the developing world, it is fitting that a significant contribution to the current thinking about the theory and practice of PAR in psychology should come from a critique of the research in cross-cultural psychology (Moghaddam and Studer 1997). Disappointingly, much of the work in this area has sought simply to test the replication of existing theory and research in non-Western cultures, but Tod Sloan (1996) discusses the need for psychologists working in the developing world to become actively involved in processes of social change. Drawing on the work of Fals-Borda (1988), Freire ([1970] 1993), and Ignacio Martin-Baro (1994), among others, Sloan suggests that "the researcher must take a stance, choosing between conformist pseudo-neutrality and critical engagement in social transformation" (41). A similar position is reflected in the work of Josephine Jordan (1987) from the University of Harare, Zimbabwe, whose proposal for a developing world psychology reflects the need to establish more indigenous approaches to research embedded in community issues and local knowledge. Jordan's own work with street children in Harare, in which she emphasizes their strategies for survival rather than their victimhood, illustrates this position (personal communication).

I would advocate integrating these various bodies of research within the context of an explicit commitment to political and social change. Without this commitment, participation can become simply another means of supporting the status quo and of coopting community members through a rhetoric of involvement. PAR has the potential to transform our notions of the practice and purposes of psychological research. However, integrating this method into our discipline will require flexibility and reflection. It will require us to reconsider what constitute valid forms of knowledge generation, and to acknowledge the inherent political nature of all the work we do. It will demand greater involvement and commitment on our parts to our own communities and to addressing issues of social justice around the world. At the same time, it will allow us to place our skills and training as psychologists in the service of our personal and political values, giving our work new energy and meaning. For those of us committed to addressing social issues in an open and democratic fashion, it provides a way to integrate our politics and our psychology—to the benefit of both.

References

Antonio, R. 1981. Immanent critique as the core of critical theory: Its origins and development in Hegel, Marx and Contemporary Thought. *British Journal of Sociology* 32 (3): 330–345.

Arratia, M., with I. de la Maza (1997). Grounding a long-term ideal: Working with the Aymara for community development. In *Nurtured by knowledge: Learning to do participatory action-research*, eds. S. E. Smith, D. G. Williams, and N. A. Johnson, 111–137. New York: Apex Press.

Bernstein, R. J. 1976. *The restructuring of social and political theory.* Philadelphia: University of Pennsylvania Press.

Brydon-Miller, M. 1993. Breaking down barriers: Accessibility self-advocacy in the disabled community. In *Voices of change: Participatory research in the United States and Canada*, eds. P. Park, M. Brydon-Miller, B. Hall, and T. Jackson, 125–143. Westport, CT: Bergin and Garvey.

Cancian, F. M. 1992. Feminist science: Methodologies that challenge inequality. *Gender and Society* 6 (4): 623–642.

Carr, W., and S. Kemmis. 1985. *Becoming critical: Education, knowledge, and action research.* London: Falmer Press.

Chesler, M. 1991. Participatory action research with self-help groups: An alternative paradigm for inquiry and action. *American Journal of Community Psychology* 19 (5): 757–768.

Comstock, D. E. 1994. A method of critical research. In *Readings in the philosophy of social science,* eds. M. Martin and L. C. McIntyre, 625–639. Cambridge, MA: MIT Press.

Comstock, D., and R. Fox. 1993. Participatory research as critical theory: The North Bonneville, USA, experience. In *Voices of change: Participatory research in the United States and Canada*, eds. P. Park, M. Brydon-Miller, B. Hall, and T. Jackson, 103–125. Westport, CT: Bergin and Garvey.

Crotty, M. 1998. *The foundations of social research: Meaning and perspective in the research process.* London: Sage.

Debbink, G., and A. Ornelas. 1997. Cows for Campesinos. In *Nurtured by knowledge: Learning to do participatory action-research,* eds. S. E. Smith, D. G. Williams and N. A. Johnson, 13–33. New York: Apex Press.

Fals-Borda, O. 1988. *Knowledge and people's power.* New Delhi: Indian Social Institute.

Fals-Borda, O., and M. A. Rahman. 1991. *Action and knowledge: Breaking the monopoly with participatory action-research.* New York: Apex Press.

Farganis, J. 1975. A preface to critical theory. *Theory and Society* 2:483–508.

Fay, B. 1975. *Social theory and political practice.* London: Unwin Hyman.

Fernandes, W., and R. Tandon, eds. 1981. *Participatory research and evaluation: Experiments in research as a process of liberation.* New Delhi: Indian Social Institute.

Freire, P. [1970] 1993. *Pedagogy of the oppressed.* New York: Continuum.

———. 1982. Creating alternative research methods and learning to do it by doing it. In *Creating knowledge: A monopoly? Participatory research in development,* eds. B. Hall, A. Gillette and R. Tandon, 29-37. Participatory Research Network Series, no. 1. New Delhi: Society for Participatory Research in Asia.

———. 1997. Foreword. In *Nurtured by knowledge: Learning to do participatory action-research,* eds. S. E. Smith, D. G. Williams, and N. A. Johnson, xi–xii. New York: Apex Press.

Gaventa, J. 1988. Participatory research in North America. *Convergence* 24 (2–3): 19–28.

———. 1993. The powerful, the powerless, and the experts: Knowledge struggles in an information age. In *Voices of change: Participatory research in the United States and Canada,* eds. P. Park, M. Brydon-Miller, B. Hall, and T. Jackson, 21–40. Westport, CT: Bergin and Garvey.

Greenwood, D. J., and M. Levin. 1998. *Introduction to action research: Social research for social change.* Thousand Oaks, CA: Sage.

Greenwood, D. J., W. F. Whyte, and I. Harkavy. 1993. Participatory action research as a process and as a goal. *Human Relations* 46 (2): 175–192.

Habermas, J. 1971. *Knowledge and human interests.* Boston: Beacon.

Hall, B. 1981. Participatory research, popular knowledge, and power: A personal reflection. *Convergence* 14 (3): 6–17.

———. 1993. Introduction. In *Voices of change: Participatory research in the United States and Canada,* eds. P. Park, M. Brydon-Miller, B. Hall, and T. Jackson, xiii–xxii. Westport, CT: Bergin and Garvey.

———. 1997. Preface. In *Nurtured by knowledge: Learning to do participatory action-research,* eds. S. E. Smith, D. G. Williams, and N. A. Johnson, xiii–xv. New York: Apex Press.

Held, D. 1980. *Introduction to critical theory: Horkheimer to Habermas.* Berkeley: University of California Press.

Horton, B. D. 1993. The Appalachian land ownership study: Research and citizen action in Appalachia. In *Voices of change: Participatory research in the United States and Canada*, eds. P. Park, M. Brydon-Miller, B. Hall, and T. Jackson, 85–102. Westport, CT: Bergin and Garvey.

Jordan, J. 1987. Developing world psychology: Lessons from cross-cultural psychology. In *Growth and progress in cross-cultural psychology*, ed. C. Kagitcibasi, 60–102. Berwyn, PA: Swets North America.

Joyappa, V., and D. J. Martin. 1996. Exploring alternative research epistemologies for adult education: Participatory research and feminist participatory research. *Adult Education Quarterly* 47 (1): 1–14.

Kemmis, S., and R. McTaggart, eds. 1988. *The action research planner*. Victoria, Australia: Deakin University Press.

Maguire, P. 1987. *Doing participatory research: A feminist approach*. Amherst: The Center for International Education, University of Massachusetts.

———. 1996. Considering more feminist participatory research: What has congruency got to do with it? *Qualitative Inquiry* 2 (1): 106–118.

Martin-Baro, I. 1994. *Writings for a liberation psychology*, eds. A. Aron and S. Corne. Cambridge, MA: Harvard University Press.

McTaggart, R. 1991. Principles for participatory action research. *Adult Education Quarterly* 41 (3): 168–187.

———, ed. 1997. *Participatory action research: International contexts and consequences*. Albany: State University of New York Press.

Moghaddam, F., and C. Studer. 1997. Cross-cultural psychology: The frustrated gadfly's promises, potentialities, and failures. In *Critical psychology: An introduction*, eds. D. Fox and I. Prilleltensky, 183–201. London: Sage.

Nastasi, B., K. Varjas, S. Karkar, and A. Jayasena. 1998. Participatory model of mental health programming: Lessons learned from work in a developing country. *School Psychology Review* 27 (2): 260–276.

Nelson, G., J. Ochocka, K. Griffin, and J. Lord. 1998. "Nothing about me, without me": Participatory action research with self-help/mutual aid organizations for psychiatric consumer/survivors. *American Journal of Community Psychology* 26 (6): 881–912.

Newbrough, J. R. 1995. Toward community: A third position. *American Journal of Community Psychology* 23 (1): 9–37.

Oquist, P. 1978. The epistemology of action research. *Acta Sociologica* 21 (2): 143–163.

Pace, L., and D. Argona. 1991. Participatory action research: A view from Xerox. In *Participatory action research*, ed. W. F. Whyte, 56–69. Newbury Park, CA: Sage.

Piercy, F. P., and V. Thomas. 1998. Participatory evaluation research: An introduction for family therapists. *Journal of Marital and Family Therapy* 24 (2): 165–176.

Rahman, M. A. 1993. *People's self-development: Perspectives in participatory action research, a journey through experience.* London: Zed Books.

Reardon, K., J. Welsh, B. Kreiswirth, and J. Forester. 1993. Participatory action research from the inside: Community development practice in East St. Louis. *American Sociologist* 21 (4): 69–91.

Rogers, E. S., and V. Palmer-Erbs. 1994. Participatory action research: Implications for research and evaluation in psychiatric rehabilitation. *Psychosocial Rehabilitation Journal* 18 (2): 3–12.

Sloan, T. S. 1996. Psychological research methods in developing countries. In *Psychology and the developing world*, eds. S. C. Carr and J. F. Schumaker, 38–45. Westport, CT: Praeger.

Smith, S. 1997. Deepening participatory action-research. In *Nurtured by knowledge: Learning to do participatory action-research*, eds. S. E. Smith, D. G. Williams, and N. A. Johnson, 175–263. New York: Apex Press.

Stoecker, R. 1999. Are academics irrelevant? Roles for scholars in participatory research. *American Behavioral Scientist* 42 (5): 840–854.

Tandon, S. D., L. S. Axelton, J. G. Kelly, and D. A. Strickland. 1998. Constructing a tree for community leaders: Contexts and processes in collaborative inquiry. *American Journal of Community Psychology* 26 (4): 669–696.

Tobias, K. J., ed. 1982. *Participatory research: An introduction.* Participatory Research Network Series, no. 3. New Delhi: Society for Participatory Research in Asia.

Whyte, W. F. 1989. Introduction to action research for the twenty-first century: Participation, reflection, and practice. *American Behavioral Scientist* 32 (5): 502–512.

———, ed. 1991. *Participatory action research.* Newbury Park, CA: Sage.

Yeich, S., and R. Levine. 1992. Participatory research's contribution to a conceptualization of empowerment. *Journal of Applied Social Psychology* 22 (24): 1894–1908.

Alive and Well in Psychology

Exemplars

Part III

A. Interpretive Methods

7

■　　■　　■　　■　　■　　■　　■　　■　　■

White Working-Class Girls, Femininities, and the Paradox of Resistance

Lyn Mikel Brown

"IN RECENT YEARS, while gender and race have become common currency," Valerie Walkerdine (1990) notes, "it has become almost impossible to speak about class" (157). The psychological literature on class in the United States is sparse; on white girls and class, nearly nonexistent. In the introduction to her memoir, *Landscape for a Good Woman*, Carolyn Kay Steedman (1987) notes that what *has* been written about class attributes a superficial, uncomplicated "psychological sameness to the figures in the working-class landscape." This is partly because, she explains, "delineation of emotional and psychological selfhood has been made by and through the testimony of people in a central relationship to the dominant culture, that is to say by and through people who are not working class" (14).

Psychological studies that include class as a variable, with notable exceptions (Fine 1988; Fine and Macpherson 1992; Pastor, McCormick, and Fine 1996; Way 1995), give little sustained attention to the effects of social and material location on girls' emerging subjectivities. Indeed, amid growing attention to the psychological struggles and losses many middle-class white girls sustain as they negotiate dominant cultural notions of femininity (Brown and Gilligan 1992, 1993; Gilligan 1990), very little attention has been given to poor and working-class white girls, and researchers rarely interrogate directly the very notions of culture and femininity on which their work rests.

Given that, as Signithia Fordham (1993) argues, "in a socially, culturally, and racially stratified society like the United States, culturally specific routes to womanhood are inevitable" (8), it becomes important to appreciate the ways in which differences in social location, and the political ramifications of such differences, are taken in and made sense of. How do those of us who stand in different relationship to the dominant (i.e., white, middle-class, and still, with respect to economic and political power, male) culture come to understand ourselves and our relationships with each other? How do we negotiate the connections between the wider society and the values and norms of our local communities? Such questions about and explorations of the impact of social and material location on individual subjectivities and interpersonal relationships are best explored through in-depth qualitative analysis of the language and forms of discourse of different groups of people in different contexts.

In this chapter, I present the Listening Guide, a method that enables such an analysis. I then illustrate this method through my exploration of the ways in which sixth-, seventh, and eight-grade white girls from working-class and working poor families in rural Maine understand, express, and react to dominant cultural constructions of femininity. Interpreting data gathered over the course of a year from videotaped focus groups and individual interviews, I identify and underscore the contradictory nature of what constitutes appropriately feminine discourse and behavior for these girls—discourse and behavior that is radically different from the dominant white middle-class cultural ideal and offers these girls a wide range of physical and verbal expression not usually available under the rubric of conventional femininity. I suggest that while such behavior may signal the girls' ambivalent relationship with middle-class propriety and, in some cases, resistance to the dominant ideologies of femaleness as passive, accommodating and helpless, it may also work to cement the girls' lower caste status.[1]

A Relational Method

In order to understand and interpret the meaning of a person's words, one has to ask (and answer) two interrelated questions: "Who precisely is speaking, and under what concrete circumstances?" (Bakhtin 1981, 340). In addition, one must also ask: Who is listening and what is the nature of her relationship with the speaker, especially with respect to power? Such questions acknowledge the complicated social landscape in which discourse occurs and the various forces, personal and political, that move one to speak and act in certain ways.

The Listening Guide incorporates attention to such questions, because it is responsive to the polyphonic nature of voice, the nonlinear, nontransparent interplay and orchestration of feelings and thoughts, as well as to power and to the fact that "positionality weighs heavily in what knowledge [and in what ways of knowing] comes to count as legitimate in historically specific times and places" (Lather 1991, 116; brackets mine). The method requires that I examine systematically my own positionality and regulatory power with respect to the girls with whom I work. The Listening Guide offers a way to trace the movement in girls' understanding of themselves and others as they take in the voices around them, both appropriating and resisting different perspectives on relationship (Brown et al. 1991; Brown and Gilligan 1991, 1992; Brown et al. 1989).

Over the course of a year I videotaped a focus group of white girls from working-class and working poor families who live in Mansfield, a small rural Maine town. Because I planned to explore the interactions among the girls' understandings of themselves and their relationships with each other, and to examine their local conventions of femininity as well as their appropriation of or resistance to dominant cultural notions of femininity, these girls were chosen, with the help of a local informant, for their outspokenness and strong opinions, and in some cases for their critical perspective on and behavioral resistance to authorities. The thirteen girls who participated in this group ranged in age from eleven to fourteen.

The group met weekly in their public school to discuss their feelings about themselves, their relationships with each other, their families, their teachers, and their reactions to pressures to accommodate to culturally dominant notions of "appropriate" femininity. Because I wanted the girls to feel at ease and to be able to speak comfortably and openly, Diane Starr, a school staff member whom the girls knew well and trusted, facilitated the group conversations. I did, however, get to know the girls as well, and they understood that I would be viewing their tapes. At the end of the year I revisited these issues in individual interviews.

My choice of a small, purposeful sample was deliberate and necessary for a labor-intensive Listening Guide analysis. I wished to bring to the surface the often subtle psychological associations the girls made during their conversations, particularly about femininity, and to use their physical movements and facial expressions to complicate my interpretations. My goal was not only to avoid generalizing to the wider population of white working-class and poor girls, but also to explore the significance and highlight the impact of local understandings and constructions of self and femininity that make overly simplistic generalizations problematic.

The Listening Guide requires one to attend to a person's narrative or dialogue at least four separate times, listening each time in a different way. In this study, I listened to (and viewed, in the case of the videotapes) each interview and group session five times. First I attended to the overall shape of the dialogue and to the research relationship—that is, I considered and documented how my own position as a white middle-class academic with a working-class Maine childhood affected the girls' perceptions of me, our interactions, and my interpretations of their voices. The second time through the videotapes and interviews I attended to the girls' first-person voices, to the ways they spoke for and about themselves. Since, as Anne Campbell (1987) has illustrated, much of our sense of who we are arises from who we believe we are not, I also listened to the girls' gossip and put-downs of their peers and siblings to establish whom they considered "Other" and why. In the third "listening" I attended to the girls' discussions of personal anger and social critique: What people, events, or experiences provoked their anger and criticism? How and to whom did they express their strong feelings? What form did their anger take? Who or what forces constrained their expressions of these strong feelings?

The final two times through the girls' conversations and interviews, most pertinent to the present analysis, I focused on the ways the girls defined and spoke about appropriate feminine behavior and, in particular, the ways they accommodated to and resisted conventional or culturally dominant constructions of femininity. More specifically, in the fourth listening/viewing, I identified ventriloquized voices and performances of conventional femininity. In Mikhail Bakhtin's (1981) terms, "ventriloquation" is the very natural process "whereby one voice speaks *through* another voice or voice type" (Wertsch 1991, 59). My hope was to document the girls' verbal and behavioral expressions of voices, characteristics, and qualities of feminine behavior idealized or denigrated by the dominant culture and to understand the ways in which the girls appropriated and struggled with such voices.

In the fifth listening, I attended to the ways in which the girls resisted dominant cultural constructions of femininity. That is, I documented the girls' voices and gestures of strength, fluidity, irreverence, and creativity, often grounded in local understandings of themselves and acceptable or appropriate feminine behavior, and I explored the ways these voices and gestures interacted to attenuate the pull of convention. Here class and culture, relevant throughout the various listenings/viewings, took center stage as the voices and values of the girls' immediate community came into conflict with those of the dominant culture, particularly as the latter are inculcated in the school classroom. Here also any notion of identity as continuous, unitary, or linear was called into question as the girls struggled with different voices, some clearly more publicly legitimized than others, and as they learned the power of context and audience and the necessity of performing conventional femininity or impersonating the "right" kind of girl. In other words, this analysis documents how context and power relations affect girls' interactions and conversations, such that the selves they present to one another and to the camera are not the only selves available to present.

With each listening or viewing, I used a different colored pencil to trace the girls' voices through typed transcriptions of the videotapes and audiotapes, a standard practice for this method, which allowed me to follow the movement of their group conversations and individual voices and provided a visual orchestration of the five listenings. I documented each listening on worksheets, recording in one column the girls' voices and in another my interpretation of their words. From these worksheets I created interpretive summaries, and from these summaries I generated my findings, examples of which I present below. Since I watched the videos as well as worked with the transcriptions, I was able to document gestures and movements that greatly enhanced my interpretations.

In addition to recording evidence of the five listenings in the group conversations and individual interviews, I constructed a matrix for each girl (Miles and Huberman 1984), noting in brief form her local constructions of femininity and her expressions of—her ventriloquation of and reactions to—dominant constructions of femininity. Thus, this approach not only aided my analysis of the group's conversations, but also allowed me to conceptualize how the girls differed from one another with respect to the five listenings.

The Girls

The thirteen girls in this study live in Mansfield, a small town in rural central Maine. Some of the girls' fathers work in the woods cutting trees; others drive trucks or haul gravel; one is a self-employed mechanic; another is unemployed because of a physical disability. More than half of the girls' mothers work part-time; one as a licensed practical nurse, another at a wood mill, and others in local stores or as waitresses in town. Seven of the girls live with both parents, three live in single parent homes, and one lives with a step-parent.

The range of the Mansfield girls' experiences forbids any simple rendering of their early adolescence. Of the thirteen, six have experienced physical abuse at the hands of a father or other male relative. At least one girl is intimately familiar with the court and child-welfare systems, having testified against an abusive father; two others, sisters, experienced homelessness after fire took their trailer; others know the poverty that lies just on the other side of their parents' unstable jobs and meager benefits. A number of the girls in the group are sexually active, and two are on the pill. These girls speak fondly and with excited anticipation of their sexual and emotional relationships with the migrant workers from Honduras and Mexico who come through the Mansfield area during the summer months.

The Mansfield girls met in an upstairs school classroom after lunch, during their recess period. They usually began their videotaped sessions jockeying for position, some grabbing chairs, others sitting on desks or on the floor in a relaxed, haphazard manner. Videos of their interactions reveal a lively, physical, and often boisterous group of outspoken girls, vying for the attention of the camera, shouting, often pushing each other before settling into more concentrated conversation. Meetings often ended with the girls crowding the camera, laughing and pushing.

Performing Femininities

During a seemingly ordinary gathering one autumn afternoon, four of these white working-class girls illustrate the regulatory fictions of idealized femininity and also the failure of such fictions to define or contain them. After much jockeying for position, some pushing and laughing, the girls excitedly arrange themselves in front of the video-camera. "How would you describe the ideal girl?" Diane begins. The room is animated and the discussion moves at rapid-fire pace. Amber, a small, tough twelve-year-old, is the first to answer. "OK. The ideal girl is very pretty. . . ." Stacey, also twelve, slim and herself conventionally pretty, immediately points to herself and interjects, "Me."

> *Amber:* Talented—
> *Stacey* (smiling, with a look of false modesty): "Me again."
> *Amber:* Smart, everybody likes her, everybody. . . . (Stacey shrugs her shoulders, throws up her hands, as if to say "me, again.") That's about it.
> *Diane Starr* [hereafter DS]: What do you mean by pretty?
> *Amber:* Pretty, beautiful, good-looking. Long hair. I don't know. Pretty eyes. Nice figure. (Donna and Amber look at Stacey accusingly.)
> *Stacey:* My idea of a perfect girl is somebody who's tall and pretty, and they have, like, perfect hair and perfect skin. They get good grades. Not afraid to make mistakes and stuff.
> *DS:* Does anyone know anyone like these perfect people? You guys know anybody like this?

At this question the girls look at one another. "No," they say in low voices. Diane continues, "Have you ever seen anybody like this?" The girls shake their heads no. "Does this person exist?" Amber is certain she does "somewhere in the world"; maybe she is "not perfect, but close to perfect," she determines. The others, however, are not so sure, although they think they might like to become someone like this. "I already am," Stacey interjects, then adds, "Just kidding."

Perhaps in response to this last comment, Amber continues:

Amber: I know someone who's really pretty, but her attitude is blown way out of proportion . . . is right out of it. . . . Yeah, major attitude problem.

Stacey: Snobby.

Patti: Yeah, people who have attitudes. . . . Nosy.

DS: What do you mean, like stuck up?

Stacey: Yeah, two-faced.

Donna: They don't keep secrets. . . .

Amber: She's accusing. . . .

Donna (Says to everyone, but looks at Patti pointedly): You can tell them anything and they give you good advice. You can trust them . . . I don't know.

DS: So now we're getting a different picture of the perfect girl. Not so much looks.

Amber: Personality plays a big part of it.

Donna: You have to be able to trust them. A person that doesn't take over . . . in a group.

Stacey: Oh, yeah. They are trying to be the center of attention.

At this point Patti, at age eleven one of the youngest in the group, interrupts: "No one's actually perfect," she says in a loud voice. "I'd wanna be different than everybody else." But her comment is lost in a hum of debate, not about whether the girls want to be different from others, but about how they wish they could be different from who they are. Stacey begins in earnest: "I wish I was skinnier. A lot! I wish I could lose at least ten pounds." Amber concurs, "At least twelve or fifteen pounds!" To this Donna, tall and very thin, laments, "I only weigh 102." As the conversation turns inward and the girls murmur in low voices to one another about the ideal weight, Patti, the only one of the girls who is not small or thin, looks down. Sitting away from the other girls, she visibly pulls herself out of the conversation.

DS: So what would be the ideal weight?

Donna: Eighty.

Stacey (in a definitive tone): The ideal weight is 110.

Amber: One hundred and ten is *not* the ideal weight! I weigh 110! I should weigh at least eighty-five.

Stacey: I want to weigh between 105 and 110.

Donna: I would like to weigh 122.

Stacey: I think everyone wants to lose weight no matter what. Everybody
   wants to be better and lose weight.
DS: No matter *what* your weight?
Stacey: Yeah. No matter what your weight.
Amber: Well, I'm always trying to be better. Taller. Skinnier.
Stacey: Well, I don't know, I could be. . . . I could be happier.
Amber: If I was taller and skinnier.

As the girls continue to argue about how much they should weigh and
how tall they should be, Donna pulls her right foot up on her seat to tie
her shoe. This ordinary act has the unlikely effect of shifting both the tone
and the substance of the conversation. It is as though Donna's movement
signals something farcical in what has just taken place. What began as sincere and serious suddenly turns into a sort of theater of the absurd: "I want
bigger feet," Amber says emphatically. "I want smaller feet!" Stacey exclaims. The girls laugh; Patti's face lights up as she rejoins the group. Diane
decides to continue the new mood:

DS: I want straight hair.
Stacey: I want curly hair.
Patti: I wish I had smaller feet.
DS: Unfortunately, I gain a shoe size every time I get pregnant.
Stacey: Then I'm never going to get pregnant!

As the conversation turns to who has "big clown feet" and "shoes that
look like hot dogs," the girls break from their orderly row of chairs. Amber
jumps up and moves toward the camera. "I want to get closer. I want to
get closer!" she exclaims, perhaps symbolizing her desire to shatter the distance between her and the image she has projected. At this the entire
group jumps in front of the camera, first putting their faces up close, then
hopping on one foot, holding onto one another in order to keep their balance as they raise their feet toward the camera lens in a kind of clumsy cho-
rus line.

Stacey: See my feet? They're all my feet!
DS: Are they clown feet?
Stacey: Yes, these are my clown feet. Smell!

The girls shout to the camera, "These are mine! These are mine!" In the background Donna and Amber hug. The girls then compare their heights in an exaggerated manner. Standing back-to-back, they laugh and shout, "Who's taller?" "Am I taller? I hope not!" Amber pushes in front of everyone and says directly to the camera: "Ain't I short!? I'm only four-eleven." The girls, laughing, compare themselves to one another and then with Diane, who has joined them in front of the camera. "What about me! What about me?" they shout, laughing uncontrollably. As the drama ends, Patti, who has taken Diane's place behind the camera, announces, "You are watching Channel Five News!"

In the meeting just described, four different girls' voices converge initially to re-create an image of the "perfect girl" recognizable to anyone who opens the pages of a teen fashion magazine: beautiful, tall, long hair, perfect skin, pretty eyes, nice figure; she must be talented and get good grades; she is liked by everybody, with a personality to match her looks. That these girls do not know or have not actually seen anyone like this does not dissuade them from expressing their desire to be like her. She is the standard against which others are measured, or so it would first appear—accusatory looks say that either you have come too close or you have swayed too far from her likeness. That dissonant voices are lost in the group construction of this image—Patti's wish to be different from the ideal, for example, and Donna's desire to weigh more rather than less—speaks to its potential to control their collective imagination.

And yet even as they speak, the limits and even the absurdity of this ideal are communicated among the girls through their body movements and facial expressions. As they talk with great seriousness about trust and loyalty, about always being nice, about having a good attitude and not demanding attention, signs of envy, competition, irritability, mistrust, and betrayal seep into the spaces between them. Their bodies convey what is not directly addressed or acknowledged: the "psychic excess" that falls outside the narrow confines of such an ideal (Butler 1991, 24).

Thus, while the dialogue among Donna, Patti, Stacey, and Amber is ostensibly about their desire and struggle to imitate narrow conventions of white middle-class femininity, they simultaneously signify their inevitable failure and persistent refusal to do so. What falls outside the ideal, what can never be fully expressed inside its boundaries, erupts within the intervals of the girls' gestures and interactions (Butler 1991, 24). At the height of intense debate, an unremarkable, barely discernible act threatens to reveal as an illusion—indeed, an absurdity—what had seemed so true and possible and intensely important.

The girls' consistent failure to approximate the ideal thus provides an opening that threatens to reveal the perfect girl for who she is, a "phantasmic ideal" of feminine identity (Butler 1991, 21). The potential of this threat to be disruptive or subversive depends on the girls' relationships. Indeed, the association between Donna's tying her shoe and the girls' heightened mood ignites a dramatic shift in relationship. As the girls' concerns about beauty elevate to the level of parody, their collective voices gather momentum and their expressions toward one another change. Gone are the accusatory looks and the argumentative voices. Their wariness and defensive postures vanish as they jump from their seats, wrap their arms around each other, and move together. They are at once raucous, active, funny, loud, and loving—they are not a "pretty" sight. Now the camera, rather than other girls, becomes the audience and witness to their performance; they are, in a sense, in this together, undivided, and from this group display comes their power to re-direct and re-define the terms of the situation.

The significance of this collective, relational act cannot be overstated, since by definition the ideal girl is isolated in her perfection. By comparison, all other girls are deficient, and so the ideal girl elicits the envy, competition, and disloyalty commonly associated with girls' and women's relationships. In their initial construction of this ideal, the girls too are separate: they are bodies in a row facing the camera, each concerned with comparing herself with the image. The fiction of the feminine ideal, in this sense, serves to divide girls psychically and socially, to disconnect them from themselves and one another. Only when this fiction is disrupted and made ridiculous do the girls move together.

In another session, Corrine responds to Diane's request that she settle down by dramatically crossing her legs, folding her hands in her lap, pursing her lips, and cocking her head. In the perfect parody of a proper lady, at once sincere and ridiculous, she looks wide-eyed into the camera, feigning rapt attention. In another session, when a boy pokes his head into the classroom, Susan, her face red with anger, yells "Tommy, get out!" and then turns to the camera, smiles, and says sweetly, "Thank you." Through such shifts in identity the Mansfield girls reveal to the camera—to Diane and to me—the embodiment of the ideal girl: physically controlled and emotionally contained, compliant, innocent, cooperative, attentive; always nice and sweet and polite, positive, up-beat, and sincere.

These girls clearly choose when and for whom to perform this particular character. Stacey, for example, shifts from her usual self-assured voice to a tentative, uncertain waver as she reenacts a scene with her school counselor; Rachel reveals a sudden look of wide-eyed innocence when Diane confronts her about her swearing. During one session an animated conversation about anger and physical abuse hangs in the air when a teacher unexpectedly enters the classroom and asks to know what the girls are talking about. Almost simultaneously, the girls' facial expressions lighten, their voices rise, the cadence of their speech quickens, and without missing a collective beat, the conversation shifts, in well-rehearsed form, to a review of their earlier discussion of the "ideal girl": "I think the ideal girl is someone who gets all straight A's," Tracy begins. And the others follow suit: "And is a popular kid in school," and "gets a lot of boyfriends," and "never does anything wrong."

In this last instance, the ideal girl makes her appearance as character and subject matter; the girls soon signal their animosity toward her. Since this particular teacher is one of their favorites, she is invited to join them in their resistance. In a few moments the girls, Diane, and their teacher are laughing, as together they make a farce of this ideal: They wonder aloud if the ideal girl has "nose hairs," if she looks "like a Barbie doll," if she has "big boobs," revealing their psychic and social distance from the regulatory fictions of white middle-class femininity. Here, too, they reveal their desire to share this critical distance with women they trust.

These parodies of and transformations into sweet, nice girls reveal not only the Mansfield girls' distance from the expected white middle-class feminine ideal, but also their collective awareness of this identity and their understanding of the power it holds for certain audiences—very often their teachers and other school authorities, as well as the camera, since they know I will be watching. Their sarcasm and animosity seem to reflect their anxiety around this ideal and what their failure to meet it might suggest to these authorities.

At the same time, they reject the authority of the ideal by poking fun at those who most resemble her. Speaking in syrupy, sing-song falsetto voices, moving their bodies to imitate stiff, controlled postures, for example, they ventriloquate and perform their middle-class women teachers and administrators. "Be nice," Rachel sarcastically warns the other girls; "Respect the talker," Susan says in a "proper" tone, hands neatly folded in her lap. "Thank you for your honesty," Amber mimics in a high, sweet voice.

Perhaps in defense of the feelings of intense anger, sadness, and disappointment such middle-class adult voices arouse, these working-class girls also perform feminine identities dramatically different from this conventional ideal. Resistant, defiant voices of toughness and invulnerability, of danger and daring, disrupt the categories and fictions of white middle-class propriety promoted in their school. As they do with their teachers, the girls take great pleasure in shocking Diane and me with these voices and personas, with their language, gestures, and behavior. In one session, Rachel looks into the camera and gives the finger, stopping only when, laughing, she registers the surprise on Diane's face.

But perhaps more than anything else, the girls' heated arguments and debates among themselves reveal the parameters of the feminine ideal—not only what it requires of them and their relationships, but also their anxiety and rage at the ways it justifies unfairness and exclusion. Shifting in and out of their desire and disdain for perfection and idealized relationships, challenging one another at the level of experience, they bring into bold relief what such fictions promise and also what they demand: the level of not knowing or denial needed to operate as though the ideal were real and therefore possible.

Conclusion

Throughout the year, in their group conversations and individual interviews, these girls demonstrate their acute awareness of the expectations to perform idealized notions of white middle-class femininity even as they experience the complexity of their lives—a complexity that assures them and others that they are, as it were, a bad fit within such a narrow context. The contradictions they live during early adolescence bring to the surface a multitude of voices and visions that vie for their allegiance. The range of their feelings and behaviors puts them at odds with the expectations of middle-class teachers and other adults invested in the conventional feminine ideal, and thus underscores their displacement in school and in white middle-class society. Cast against idealized notions of femininity, their strong voices sound off-key, become unrecognizable, difficult to hear; their bold, self-protective actions, necessary for their survival, become signs of failure or distress. Ironically, therefore, the very behavior that frees them from stereotypical gender conventions may also label them, according to white middle-class notions of femininity, psychologically troubled, socially inferior, or marginal.

The Listening Guide provides a way to elucidate the struggles these working-class girls experience as they negotiate and contest the contradictory voices and visions of appropriately feminine behavior and constructions of self competing for their attention. The girls' shifts away from idealized understandings of femininity, while garnering approval from authorities, negate the knowledge and relational strengths they have developed and thus attenuate their power. However, their resistance—the knowing looks, rolling eyes, irreverent gestures and movements, the group arguments and open disagreements as well as the polyphonic nature of their speech and their subtly subversive shifts in voice—cement their closeness and give power to their collective refusal to be deluded into believing that the performance is real. The Listening Guide method, responsive to different voices, brings such contradictions to the surface for interpretation. By attending to power relations, particularly the ways participants accommodate to or resist dominant cultural norms and expectations, and including the power of the researcher to affect her participants' responses, the method requires the researcher to consider the context in which people speak and the constraints and possibilities they perceive. Such consideration offers a complex rendering of individual selves who have access to multiple voices and intentions, who are aware of legitimized norms and practices, but who are never in simple relationship to them.

Throughout the year, in session after session, their anxieties, struggles, and insights, born of a keen awareness and persistent experience of their difference from the ideal, reveal the limits of socialization. Their shifts in identity and changing performances, their struggles to integrate fragments of experience and conflicting experiences, disrupt any illusion of smooth continuity in identity formation and exemplify over and over again their power to authorize themselves in ways that disrupt the "proper."

As these analyses show, these girls are not passive, unconscious characters, manipulated or duped by the larger social context, nor are they always active, always fully conscious, or totally outside of relationship with the people and voices that populate their social context. Their pain and struggle, however, is accompanied by possibility. Among and between the girls, resistant voices, gestures, and interactions disrupt the regulatory fictions of idealized femininity, revisioning both who they are and who they might become.

Note

1. Paul Willis (1977) makes a similar point in his study of British working-class lads in *Learning to Labor*. While there are a great many differences between these girls and his "lads," I find most helpful Willis's emphasis on the cultural tension between school ideology and the boys' lives and his exploration of the processes by which the boys' active opposition to school authorities serves to reproduce their working-class standing.

References

Bakhtin, M. 1981. *The dialogic imagination.* Austin: University of Texas Press.

Brown, L., E. Debold, M. Tappan, and C. Gilligan. 1991. Reading narratives of conflict and choice for self and moral voice. In *Handbook of moral behavior and development: Theory, research, and application*, eds. W. Kurtines and J. Gewirtz. Hillsdale, NJ: Lawrence Erlbaum.

Brown, L., and C. Gilligan. 1991. Listening for voice in narratives of relationship. In *Narrative and storytelling: Implications for understanding moral development*, eds. M. Tappan and M. Packer. New Directions for Child Development, no. 54. San Francisco: Jossey-Bass.

———. 1992. *Meeting at the crossroads: Women's psychology and girls' development.* Cambridge, MA: Harvard University Press.

———. 1993. Meeting at the crossroads: Women's psychology and girls' development. *Feminism and Psychology* 3 (1): 11–35.

Brown, L., M. Tappan, C. Gilligan, B. Miller, and D. Argyris. 1989. Reading for self and moral voice: A method for interpreting narratives of real-life moral conflict and choice. In *Entering the circle: Hermeneutic investigation in psychology*, eds. M. Packer and R. Addison. Albany: State University of New York Press.

Butler, J. 1991. Imitation and gender insubordination. In *Inside/out: Lesbian theories, gay theories*, ed. D. Fuss. New York: Routledge.

Campbell, A. 1987. Self-definition by rejection: The case of gang girls. *Social Problems* 34:451–466.

Fine, M. 1988. Sexuality, schooling, and adolescent females: The missing discourse of desire. *Havard Educational Review* 58:29–53.

Fine, M., and P. Macpherson. 1992. Over dinner: Feminism and adolescent female bodies. In *Disruptive voices*, ed. M. Fine. Albany: State University of New York Press.

Fordham, S. 1993. "Those loud black girls": (Black) women, silence and gender "passing" in the academy. *Anthropology and Education Quarterly* 24:3–32.

Gilligan, C. 1990. Teaching Shakespeare's sister. In *Making connections: The relational worlds of adolescent girls at Emma Willard School*, eds. C. Gilligan, N. Lyons, and T. Hanmer. Cambridge, MA: Harvard University Press.

Lather, P. 1991. *Getting smart: Feminist research and pedagogy with/in the postmodern*. New York: Routledge.

Miles, M., and A. Huberman. 1984. *Qualitative data analysis*. London: Sage.

Pastor, J., J. McCormick, and M. Fine. 1996. Makin' homes: An urban girl thing. In *Urban girls*, eds. B. Leadbeater and N. Way. New York: New York University Press.

Steedman, C. K. 1987. *Landscape for a good woman*. New Brunswick, NJ: Rutgers University Press.

Walkerdine, V. 1990. *Schoolgirl fictions*. London: Verso.

Way, N. 1995. "Can't you see the courage, the strength that I have?" Listening to urban adolescent girls speak about their relationships. *Psychology of Women Quarterly* 19:107–128.

Wertsch, J. 1991. *Voices of the mind*. Cambridge, MA: Harvard University Press.

Willis, P. 1977. *Learning to labor*. New York: Columbia University Press.

■   ■   ■   ■   ■   ■   ■   ■   ■

8

Using Feminist Research Methods to Explore Boys' Relationships

Niobe Way

MORE THAN THIRTY YEARS AGO, psychologists and psychiatrists studied adolescent boys and created theories of human development that were more accurately theories of development for white, middle- and upper-class boys. Among the many claims they made, one that still lives with us today in our academic journals, books, and popular magazines, is that a central conflict in human development takes place during adolescence and involves the struggle for individuation and autonomy. Adolescents, according to these developmental theories, seek an individuated selfhood or an autonomous sense of self. Such claims have been and still are represented as claims about human development inclusive of all people rather than claims about a certain gender, culture, time, and place.

Responding to the absence of girls and women in these studies and developmental theories, psychologists such as Carol Gilligan and Jean Baker Miller began exploring the experiences of working- and middle-class adolescent girls and women. Their aim was, and still is, to bring the experiences and voices of girls and women into our psychological theories. This body of feminist research inspired numerous studies of culturally diverse adolescent girls and women (Belenky et al. 1986; Brown and Gilligan 1992). Most of these studies have used relational and voice-centered research methods—methods grounded in feminist theory—that reveal the richness and complexity of girls' and women's experiences.

One of the central findings from this relatively new body of work is that the struggles for adolescent girls and women are not about individuation and autonomy but about staying in relationship with others and with themselves (Brown and Gilligan 1992; Gilligan 1982). Feminist researchers and clinicians argue that adolescent girls' and women's identities are embedded in relationships rather than constituted by differentiation and separation from others (Chodorow 1978; Miller 1976). Since such representations of girls' and women's development have entered the dialogue, it is now common to hear researchers, clinicians, and the general public claim that whereas adolescent boys and men are concerned with individuation and autonomy, adolescent girls and women are concerned with establishing, maintaining, and being in relationship (Miller 1991; Thomas 1996).

These beliefs about adolescent boys' and men's interest in autonomy and individuation, however, are based on theories of male development created during an earlier historical period than the more recent theories of female development, and with predominantly white, middle- and upper-class populations. Not only that, they are based on studies of boys and men that used fundamentally different research methods from those used by contemporary feminist researchers studying girls and women. Psychologists using voice-centered, relational research methods have focused almost exclusively on the development of girls and women, whereas psychologists studying the development of adolescent boys and men have typically used surveys, questionnaires, observations, or structured interviews to understand development. Because the methods we use determine the kinds of "findings" we get in our research, problems clearly arise when research findings are compared that are based on entirely different methodological approaches to the study of human development.

Although we have acquired, over the past fifteen years, a deeper and more complex understanding of the relational experiences of a socioeconomically and culturally diverse group of girls and women, we currently have little understanding of the relational experiences of an ethnically, socioeconomically, and culturally diverse group of adolescent boys and men[1]—particularly from a developmental perspective.[2] What do adolescent boys and men from diverse cultural and socioeconomic backgrounds want in their relationships? How do they experience their relationships over time? The model of male development often cited as the counterpoint to girls' and women's development may no longer be an accurate representation of male development, even among white, middle- and upper-class boys and men. When we begin to examine boys' and men's relational experiences using a feminist approach, and when we begin to include African Americans, Latinos, and Asian Americans as well as those from poor and working class families, we may end up with an understanding of male development quite different from what is currently found in the developmental literature.[3]

The central aim of this chapter is to describe a project I conducted to address this problematic interplay of theory and method by longitudinally examining the experiences of close friendships among an ethnically diverse group of urban adolescent boys from low-income families. Relying on a relational, voice-centered, and explicitly feminist approach to research, my colleagues and I interviewed adolescents boys from an urban high school over a three-year period to understand the ways in which urban, poor, and working-class African-American, Latino, and white adolescent boys experienced their close friendships and how these experiences changed over time.

A Feminist Approach

Grounded in women's experiences, a voice-centered, relational approach to research aims to listen closely to the subtleties of human voices and stories. This feminist method of investigating lives underscores the complexity of development, the "nonlinear, nontransparent orchestration of feelings and thoughts" (Brown and Gilligan 1992, 3). I consider this approach to be explicitly feminist because it grows out of listening to girls and women (Gilligan 1982; Fine 1991; Ladner 1971), and much of the theoretical groundwork that supports it is based in feminist theory (see Bordo 1990; Harding 1986; hooks 1989; Nicholson 1990).

Feminist methods typically emphasize the relational nature of research.

The patterns that are "found" by researchers are products of what occurred between two or more people—the researcher(s) and the researched. The narrative in an interview or the responses in a survey are never a pure or "innocent" representation of the "Other" (see Fine 1991), but are jointly constructed. In my research, this relational assumption led me to allow for both stability and spontaneity. Although a specific set of interview questions was being posed to each participant in my study, room was given during the interview for the participant and the interviewer to follow new and unexpected pathways. This semi-structured approach to interviewing explicitly acknowledges both the interviewer's agenda (e.g., to understand a particular topic from the participant's perspective) and the participant's agency or power (e.g., to introduce important new knowledge that the interviewer had not anticipated).

Understanding and attuning oneself to the power dynamics within the research relationship is also a common goal in feminist, voice-centered research. What is said and not said by both the interviewer and interviewee is determined, in part, by the power dynamics within the research relationship, and it may be either empowering or disempowering for the interviewee and interviewer depending upon the specifics of the interview protocol, context, and goal. Although I, as an interviewer and principal investigator, have the power to choose the questions and to interpret the adolescents' responses in the present study, the adolescents have the power of knowing their own experiences and deciding what to tell me and what not to tell me. Attuning myself to who is speaking and from what vantage point strengthens the rigor of my research because it encourages me to see and hear the unexpected.

Feminist research also assumes that an individual's words cannot be separated from the cultural context in which they are embedded. To discuss how a person speaks about her or his world means to understand that these experiences are intimately connected to her or his specific location in the world. Holding such assumptions, the interviewers in my study are consistently pushing and probing during the interviews toward understanding what types of cultural expectations, hopes, desires, and stereotypes are influencing the stories of the participants as well as the interviewers' own questions, thoughts, interpretations, and comments during and after the interviews. Such understandings are then incorporated into the "findings" of the research.

A Study of Boys' Relationships

Using a feminist approach to research, I sought to understand the close friendships of urban adolescent boys. The sample for this longitudinal, qualitative study comprised nineteen boys who attended a public high school in a large northeastern city during the first year of the study. At the time of the first interview the adolescents were fifteen or sixteen years old. They were randomly drawn from a larger pool of students who were interviewed as part of a school-wide study of high-risk behavior.[4] Those who were freshman or sophomores at the time of the first interview were interviewed each year for three years (N = 11), whereas those who were juniors at the time of the first interview were only interviewed for two years (N = 8). They identified themselves as African-American (12), Puerto Rican (4), El Salvadoran (1), Bolivian (1), or Irish American (1). They all came from poor or working-class families and were all raised in the United States. Social class was inferred from the parents' educational background and current occupations.

The participants were interviewed in English by me or one of four ethnically and socioeconomically diverse colleagues.[5] Three of the interviewers, including myself, had been working for several years as counselors at the high school where the students were recruited. We were, therefore, quite familiar with the school and many of the students.[6] Working within a relational approach, I made concerted efforts to have the adolescents interviewed by the same interviewer each year. This, however, was not always possible due to scheduling conflicts. The interviews, which were one-to-one, in-depth, and semi-structured, typically lasted between one and a half and two hours. The interview protocol focused on questions about current close friendships and about the changes in these friendships over time (e.g., "Describe your close or best friend(s)." "How do you think this friendship has changed over time?"). Although each interview included a standard set of questions, follow-up questions were open-ended in order to capture the adolescents' own ways of describing their relationships. All interviews were audiotaped and transcribed.

The data analysis of the interview transcripts included two techniques: narrative summaries (Miller 1988) and a variation of a data analytic technique called the Listening Guide (Brown et al. 1988). The intent of narrative summaries is to condense the stories told by each participant while quoting the participant extensively in order to maintain the flavor of the discussion (Miller 1988). In the present analysis, I created brief summaries of each discussion of friendships in each interview. Following this step, I identified themes across and within these narrative summaries. The interviews were then read for each theme. Reading for themes entails highlighting each passage, sentence, or word in the transcription that suggests the particular theme for which one is reading. This process of highlighting helps to create a trail of evidence for the themes one is following. My technique of listening for themes is based on the Listening Guide (Brown et al. 1988). Unlike Narrative Summaries, the Listening Guide encourages the listener to pay close attention to the form (i.e., how the story was told) as well as the content of the interview, and to follow one's own process of interpretation. Both of these data analytic techniques encourage the listener to attend closely to the voices of the adolescents and to attune oneself to the relational elements of the research process.

Stories of Friendships

Guillermo, a Bolivian-American adolescent with jet black hair pushed behind his ears, watches me closely as I prepare to interview him for the first time during his junior year. Once we begin the interview, he immediately reveals what will be a key theme for him over the two years he is interviewed (italics represent the interviewers' questions):

> *Do you have a close or best friend this year?* Not really I think myself. The friend I had, I lost it [he moved away]. . . . That was the only person that I could trust and we talked about everything. When I was down, he used to help me feel better. The same I did to him you know so. I feel pretty lonely and sometimes depressed . . . because I don't have no one to go out with, no one to speak on the phone, no one to tell my secrets, no one for me to solve my problems. *Why don't you think you have someone?* Because I think that it will never be the same, you know, I think that when you have a real friend and you lose it, I don't think you find another one like him. . . . I tried to look for a person but it's not that easy.

A "real friend" for Guillermo is someone with whom he can "go out" and to whom he can talk about "everything" and entrust his "secrets." Unable to find another such friend, Guillermo speaks about his loneliness and depression. Intimate and emotionally supportive male friendships—"chumships," according to Harry Stack Sullivan (1953)—are what Guillermo appears to have "lost." Guillermo's discussions of having no close or best friends and his yearning for the type of friendship he had at a younger age were echoed by many of the adolescent boys in the study. They told us that while they *wanted* to have close or best male friends, they did not have such friends *any longer*.

The following year, I ask Guillermo again about his close friendships. He says to me that he has a close friend, but he sounds ambivalent:

> *Do you have a close or best friend?* If you could call it that. Because I don't tell him my secrets, right, you know. I told you that I had a very good friend in Miami and with him it was very different. I used to tell him a lot of things. But this guy, I don't trust him that much. Even though I hang around with him all day and we talk about things. Maybe he considers me his best friend and tells me things. I tell some things, but not all of them.

Lacking trust in his current friend, Guillermo limits the extent to which he will reveal his intimate life to this friend. Yet Guillermo tells me that he will confide in his girlfriend. While Guillermo has not found a close male friend, he has found a close female friend.

Along with Guillermo, almost all of the adolescent boys in the study spoke about their difficulties trusting their male peers. By their junior or senior year, 79 percent of the boys claimed *not* to trust other boys, 58 percent reported not having close or best friends because they did not trust their male peers, and 50 percent spoke about yearning for intimate same-sex friendships and of having had such friendships at an earlier age.[7] As they grew older, the boys' earlier "chumships" seemed to disappear. Several threads wove together these boys' narratives of friendship: distrusting their male friends; not having close or best male friends because of a lack of trust; yearning for close, intimate male friendships; and articulating a relational language filled with vulnerability and passion. In order to present evidence for these themes, I will focus on the narratives of two boys—Malcolm and Albert. By listening to these two boys, one can hear the themes detected in the data and also hear the ways in which their stories offer different perspectives on a particular theme.

Malcolm

Like Guillermo, Malcolm tells a story of not trusting his male peers, not being close to other boys, and feeling that the person he trusts the most is his girlfriend. Wearing baggy pants, a brightly colored shirt, and untied sneakers, Malcolm, a tall, slim African-American adolescent, says in his freshman year that he used to have a best friend in junior high school but that no such friend currently exists:

> *Do you have a best or close friend?* Oh no, nobody. Not even around my way. It's like everybody else is just associating. No it's just like things like friendship take time. . . . You have to just take it slow and be able to know for true who's your friend, who's not.

Malcolm is cautious about whom to call a friend, calling those he knows "associates" until he is more certain. Although he does not directly state that he is wary of trusting his peers, Malcolm implies such a belief in his phrase "you have to take it slow." His "associates," Malcolm explains "are not the people that you really get into deep depth conversation with." He keeps these relationships superficial both in conversation and in his daily contact. The boys in the study often referred to having "associates" who were not considered trustworthy enough to be called "friends."

In his sophomore year, Malcolm says in response to Mike's questions concerning whether or not he has a close or best friend:

> No, right now, I don't know, I don't like to be crowded too much. No . . . just my girlfriend really. I be chilling with her, but besides that I'm getting tired of being crowded really. . . . *What does that mean?* Well it could just be one person. But sometimes that one person just get aggravating—not what he says and stuff, it's just that he's being that he's there. 'Cause it's just most of the time I like to be alone, . . . I don't like to have people always around me.

With little affect in his voice, Malcolm expresses little interest in having a close or best male friend and, in fact, claims to feel uncomfortable ("crowded") with his male peers. When he discusses his girlfriend with Mike, however, his desires concerning male friendships become more complicated than this dismissive attitude initially suggests:

With my girlfriend, I could relax . . . we could do certain things that you can't—don't do with other guys. Well, you can do it, but it's just not the same feeling. Like when you're walking with a girl because with a girl you can express certain feelings and stuff you know. . . . You can talk about certain things and with boys it's just harder to like . . . some of the things you may want make you seem like you're gay or something. . . . It's more relaxing when you're with a girl so you can just chill. Seems like you have more to talk about.

Although Malcolm may desire close, intimate, male friendships, he seems to find it too risky ("make you seem like you're gay") so he chooses, instead, to spend intimate time with his girlfriend, with whom he need not fear breaking social norms.

Although he freely expresses himself with his girlfriend, Malcolm points out, with a vulnerability apparent in his hushed tones, that he does not think of his girlfriend as his best friend: "'Cause if you have a best friend you know, you express yourself more and you like—you like feel lost without them. So, you know, with her it's really just we have a close relationship where we can express things." Distinguishing between close friendships and those that one "feel[s] lost without," Malcolm describes the nuances of friendships. According to Malcolm, being close with another person "where [you] can express things" does not necessarily indicate a strong and deep attachment to that person.

Such distinctions between close and best friends are heard throughout the boys' interviews. The boys were consistently attuned to the layers and subtleties of friendships and their understandings revolved around the concepts of trust, betrayal, and loss. Adolescent boys, who have been described repeatedly as activity oriented rather than relationship oriented (see Belle 1989), carefully describe why certain peers were only "associates" and not friends, and why other peers were only close friends and not best friends. Best friends were those whom one could trust and without whom one would "feel lost"; "associates" were those with whom one spends time, but whom one does not "really" trust.

In his junior year, Malcolm—whose colorful hip-hop fashions contrast with his slightly more depressed tone—tells me, his interviewer this year, why he finds it difficult to have close or best male friends:

> I might talk with people but it won't get real deep. . . . There is nobody there
> to talk to. . . . *Do you think you have a close or best friend in your life right now?*
> Right now, no. . . . I had a couple like once when I was real young, around
> ten. . . . But right now, nobody really 'cause it seems that as I've grown, you
> know, everybody just talks behind your back and stuff. You know, so I just
> let it go because it seems like no people that I've been meeting can hold up
> to their actions. . . . Something might've happened like between me and a
> person where other people felt that we shouldn't even be friends no more.
> So they sit there and talk about me to that person while I'm not around or
> something and that person will just talk about me too, you know. . . . I al-
> ways hear "He talks about you, he says this or he says that." . . . So I just
> don't really bother with it, trying to make, you know, best friends. Say what-
> ever you want behind my back, I don't care. Whatever you do behind my
> back, I don't care.

Although there are suggestions in earlier interviews that Malcolm struggles with trusting his peers, it is not until his junior- year interview that he
makes these difficulties explicit. Malcolm has seemingly given up hope of
having the kind of close friend he had when he was younger, because people in his world do not "hold up to their actions." Following this direct
and angry statement, however, Malcolm distances himself by claiming not
to "care" about his friends betraying him. Malcolm may not *want* to care,
but he seems to have isolated himself from his friends in response to *caring* precisely about how his friends are treating him.

The apparent consequence of distrust for Malcolm is that he chooses
not to have close or best male friends. When I ask him if he wishes that he
had a close or best friend, he says:

> Somewhat, because then they [his "associates"] wonder why like I don't call
> them and stuff or you know. Because it's you know I really don't wanna be
> with them. . . . It's not somebody I could trust. Because like there's even
> times when I found stuff missing. Like I try to like hang out in my room and
> I find that things are gone, you know they're gone. Certain things like my
> tapes are missing and stuff.

Having friends for Malcolm involves not only verbal betrayal but also acts
of stealing. In his interview, Malcolm wonders aloud why his friends do
these things to him and speculates that they may be jealous of his success
in school, where he receives a lot of attention from the teachers. This type

of official recognition of boys as they struggle to be considered important may be particularly resented by peers.

Like Malcolm, the other boys in the study repeatedly used a language of vulnerability and intimacy when describing close or best male friends (e.g., "you feel lost without them"). Such "feminized" language from boys speaking about other boys surprised me and prompted me to question my assumptions about adolescent boys. Even though these boys came into the interview office *looking* "hip-hop," cool, laid back, and macho (pants riding low on their hips, Walkmen around their necks, sneakers untied), they did not *speak* in such ways. Rather, they spoke about pain, frustration, fear, and loss. Boys who have been portrayed in the research literature as more interested in doing things with other boys than with sharing their thoughts and feelings (Belle 1989) spoke to us about male friendships that "break you apart" and that "you feel lost without," about "deep depth" friendships, and about wanting friends with whom you "share your secrets," "tell everything," and "get inside."[8]

Albert

Albert, an athletic-looking Puerto Rican adolescent who speaks softly and seems hesitant about being interviewed each year of the study, suggests to Stacy, his male interviewer, that he also shares many of the same beliefs as Malcolm and Guillermo. During his sophomore year, Albert says matter-of-factly: "I don't have friends because I don't like walking around here, like I be hanging with people getting killed and I try to play it safe and stay home now." Boys commonly drew a connection between violence and having friends. Many types of fear seemed to discourage male friendships: fear of betrayal, theft, and violence.

When Albert is asked by Stacy if there is anybody in his life he would call a close or best friend, he explains in a hushed voice barely audible on the audiotape:

Now, no . . . I'm lonely here, but I have to deal with it. . . . I was trying to find one . . . I was going to find a good friend you know like my first one that I had back in New York. . . . I've met a friend but I don't know if they do things like that because I don't talk to them that much. You know, so I go to class and that's it . . . I never be talking to nobody.

Albert, who recently moved to the city in which the study took place, mentions an earlier close friendship. He hopes to find a similar type of friend in his new life in high school.

In his junior year, Albert, whose voice sounds a bit more self-assured, explains to Stacy that he still does not have a close friend:

> I got friends and everything but I don't consider them as close friends not now. *Why?* No, 'cause it's like I haven't known them that good. I know them this year and a part of last year you know so I don't know them good. . . . I would like a friend that if I got anything to say to him or like any problems or anything I'll tell him and he'll tell me his problems, you know? . . . Some friends be your friend when you're not in trouble, when you have money or something. Once you don't have a lot of money or something they'll be like back off. But a real friend will stick right there with you. He won't back off.

Albert speaks about his lack of close friends, but also about his desires to have such friends. He does not claim to want friends with whom to "do things," but with whom to share each other's problems. Victor, an African-American student, suggests a similar theme in his junior-year interview:

> *Do you have a close or best friend this year?* . . . I don't say I do. 'Cause . . . I feel that a friend is going to be there for you and they'll support you. Whether they're good and bad times . . . you could share your feelings with them, your true feelings, . . . that's why I don't think I have any real close friends. I mean things can travel around in a school, and the story would change from person to person. Yeah basically, I hate it, I hate it, 'cause you know I wouldn't mind talking to somebody my age that I can relate to 'em on a different basis.

Albert and Victor, along with most of their male peers, discussed their frustration and anger at their peers' unreliable behavior and their longing for friends "that would be there" and with whom they could share their "true feelings."

When I interview Albert in his senior year, he looks tired and worn out. He tells me with exasperation that he still does not have a best friend:

> A best friend? No, just friends. . . . *Why?* You know I can't trust—I don't trust 'em too much, you know. . . . I had a friend . . . and he [tried to steal my girlfriend] and, you know, [I] can't trust nobody else. [I have] kind of

friends, you know, but to have another best friend, that would be pretty hard, now . . . can't trust nobody else no more.

Although there had already been indications in his earlier interviews that he was struggling to trust his peers, Albert's current experience of betrayal seems to have deepened his sense of distrust. Albert suggests an inflexibility that was common among the boys. Once their male peers had betrayed their trust (on one or more occasions), they often stated that they refused not only to continue to be close with those particular peers, but to trust *any* of their peers. The boys' sensitivity to betrayal by their same-sex peers seemed acute and dramatic.

Albert continues on this theme of distrust in his senior- year interview:

Can't trust people no more, you know. Before you could, but now, when you got a girl, and they think that she's cute, you know, they still might go try to rap to her and everything you know. You can't trust 'em like before that they will be serious. Like that friend I had in New York, my best friend [the friend he referred to in his sophomore year], you know . . . I could trust him with my girl, you know, and he could trust me with his girl, you know. . . . People ain't like that no more, you know . . . back then you could trust.

Like Guillermo and Malcolm, Albert believes that when he was younger, trusting others was easier. He remembers his best friend from junior high school (whom he mentions each year) as someone he could trust and with whom, he says later in his interview, he could "talk to and he would talk to me, too." Growing up appears to involve a great loss for these boys.

Discussion

Core themes regarding trust, betrayal, and loss were evident in the boys' interviews. As the boys grew older, they increasingly spoke of not trusting other boys, fearing that other boys would betray their trust, and yearning for the types of friendships they had when they were younger. Because many researchers have noted that trust is one of the most important ingredients in adolescents' friendships, and that betrayal is a commonly perceived threat to such friendships (see Savin-Williams and Berndt 1990; Youniss and Smollar 1985), it was not surprising that betrayal and distrust were pervasive concerns among these adolescents. It was surprising, however, that the boys spoke so frequently about not trusting any or very few of their peers. Previous studies of adolescent boys' have rarely reported such high levels of distrust among boys.[9] Almost all of the adolescent boys, by their junior or senior years, stated that they could not trust their same-sex peers, and many stated that they did not trust *any* of their peers.

Reasons for this high level of distrust may lie indirectly or directly with the experiences of racism and harassment that these adolescents regularly experience. All the boys in the study spoke of daily harassment from the police, of being watched carefully in every store, street, subway station, school building, and neighborhood they entered. They are watched by adults both outside and inside their own communities. When an entire auditorium of students from the high school in which the study took place was asked if they had ever been stopped by the police, approximately 90 percent of the boys raised their hands. These predominantly ethnic minority boys repeatedly told us stories of being strip-searched, asked for their identification, and questioned by police. They receive clear messages about not being trusted by many of the adults in their lives. This lack of trust experienced on a daily basis is likely to have an effect on these boys' abilities to trust each other (Epstein and Karweit 1983).

The fear of "seem[ing] like you're gay" (from Malcolm's interview) may also deter adolescent boys from trusting other boys and from pursuing relationships with them. As Diane Raymond notes, "Indeed, homophobia is so pervasive and so powerfully internalized that individuals may voluntarily abandon close friendships rather than risk charges of homosexuality" (1994, 120). The shift from having close, intimate male friendships during junior high school (or early high school) to not having such relationships during high school suggests that boys are falling out of relationship with other boys right at the point in their lives when messages about the presumed link between manhood and heterosexuality are entering their minds. Raymond (1994) also notes that "[i]ntense same-sex friendships that continue after adolescence [and after childhood]—particularly those between men—are often discouraged, judged immature, and occasionally severely punished" (120). Not trusting other boys may allow adolescent boys to distance themselves from their own culturally unacceptable and therefore potentially risky desires for close, intimate relationships with other boys.

The type of school where this study was undertaken may further explain the pervasiveness of distrust among these adolescents. All of the participants attended a particularly large, underfunded, and chaotic inner-city school that lacked any real means to create a community within the school. The rates of suspension and dropout were among the highest in the city. Each student is met with a metal detector when he or she enters the building, the school is staffed by security guards who patrol the hallways, and the school doors are locked shortly after the school day begins to prevent stragglers and criminals from entering. Nancy Karweit and S. Hansell (1983) state: "Negative features in a school environment—ridicule, discrimination, low expectations, stereotypes, repressions, punishment, isolation—may increase the dissociative quality of the setting and affect the thought processes and social behaviors of the students" (60). Although none of the students in the present study specifically discussed conditions in their school, the social relations and behaviors of the adolescents who participated in this study may be deeply influenced by their school. The school in which they spend a substantial part of their day conveys to them that they are not trustworthy, and these messages of distrust are mostly likely seeping into their interpersonal relationships.

Finally, the prevalence of distrust found in this study may be traced to the quality of the adolescents' relationships with their parents. Those who do not have trusting, close relationships with their parents may not have such relationships with their peers (see Gold and Yanof 1985). However, students in the study who reported distrusting their peers were just as likely to state positive feelings toward their parents (or the person with whom they resided) as negative ones. Some spoke about lacking trust in their peers but having trusting and close relationships with their parents, whereas others spoke about not trusting their peers and not having close or trusting relationships with their parents.

It is important to note that some of the parents in this study specifically warned their children not to trust their peers who were not family members. These types of messages may reflect a belief system, common within many close-knit, oppressed communities, that those who are not part of one's immediate or extended family should not be trusted (Stack 1974). Such messages may make it particularly difficult for adolescents to have close, trusting nonfamilial friendships.

These stories of trust, betrayal, and desire among adolescent boys raise critical questions. What are the implications for developmental theory if these boys are not speaking about wanting autonomy and independence in their relationships (although they may be autonomous and independent in these relationships) but about wanting intimate, self-disclosing, same-sex relationships? Research has shown repeatedly that adolescent girls are more likely than adolescent boys to have intimate, self-disclosing same-sex friendships (Furman and Buhrmester 1985; Savin-Williams and Berndt 1990; Way and Chen forthcoming). The present study suggests, however, that adolescent boys, at least from urban low-income environments, may desire intimate same-sex relationships as much as their female peers; girls may simply be more encouraged, successful, or skillful in fulfilling such desires.

Clearly, the findings presented in this paper may reveal patterns specific to the population studied. Researchers have, in fact, found significant ethnic/racial and social class differences in the quality and characteristics of adolescent and adult friendships (DuBois and Hirsch 1990; Gallagher and Busch-Rossnagel 1991; Jones, Costin, and Ricard 1994; Walker 1994; Way and Chen forthcoming). The findings, however, may also reveal patterns that exist among many different populations of adolescent boys, including white, middle-class boys. Because our methods with white, middle-class adolescent boys have not included voice-centered, relational approaches, we do not know whether the patterns detected in the present study would also be found among these boys if we used such methods with them. Perhaps they, too, would speak about not having but desiring intimate male friendships[10] or about not trusting their male peers. The methods used by feminist researchers studying girls and women should be used in research studies of culturally, ethnically, and socioeconomically diverse boys and men, so that we may begin to expand our knowledge of the relational worlds of boys and men. Like adolescent girls, adolescent boys appear to be struggling in their same-sex relationships. It is critical not only to determine the pervasiveness of this struggle among different groups of boys, but also to assess ways to help boys have the relationships they seek.

Notes

Acknowledgments: Parts of this chapter have been published previously in "Between Experiences of Desire and Betrayal: Friendships among Urban Adolescents," in B. Leadbeater and N. Way, eds., *Urban Girls: Resisting Stereotypes, Creating Identities* (New York: New York University Press, 1996).

1. Investigators are beginning to examine the relational experiences of ethnically and socioeconomically diverse adult men (see Franklin 1992; Hansen 1992; Walker 1994).

2. Although there have certainly been many interview studies conducted with adolescent boys, these studies have rarely focused on listening closely—in an open-ended and exploratory way—to the nuances and subtleties of the boys' stories.

3. Karen Walker's (1994) and Clyde Franklin's (1992) research indicates that, in fact, our models of friendships are radically transformed when we listen to the stories of ethnically and socioeconomically diverse adult men.

4. This project was a part of a larger cross-sectional project, funded by the National Institute of Drug Abuse (Principal Investigator: Perry London), examining the psychosocial correlates of high-risk behavior. It was also a part of a longitudinal study examining the ways in which urban adolescents speak about their worlds, which was funded, in part, by The Henry Murray Research Center, Radcliffe College (see Way 1998).

5. Besides me, the interviewers were Helena Stauber, Michael Nakkula, Jamie Aronson, and Stacy Scott.

6. The students who were being counseled by us, however, did not participate in the study.

7. The reason I indicate proportions of participants who suggested each theme and quote precisely the words of the adolescents is to allow my readers to have an accurate representation of the interview data.

8. Karen Walker (1994) found that white, working-class men in her qualitative study of adult men often spoke about having intimate, same-sex friendships.

9. Kneia DaCosta (1996) also noted that the theme of distrust of one's peers and classmates permeated the narratives of the urban adolescents she interviewed.

10. John Reisman (1990) found in his study of male college undergraduates at a midwestern university that many males wished for "greater opportunities for personal disclosure" in their same-sex friendships.

References

Belenky, M. F., B. M. Clinchy, N. R. Goldberger, and J. M. Tarule. 1986. *Women's ways of knowing.* New York: Basic Books.

Belle, D. 1989. Studying children's social networks and social supports. In *Children's social networks and social supports.* New York: John Wiley and Sons.

Bordo, S. 1990. Feminism, postmodernism, and gender-scepticism. In *Feminism/Postmodernism*, ed. L. Nicholson. New York: Routledge.

Brown, L. M., D. Argyris, J. Attanucci, B. Bardige, C. Gilligan, K. Johnston, B. Miller, R. Osbourne, J. Ward, G. Wiggins, and D. Wilcox. 1988. *A guide to reading narratives of moral conflict and choice for self and moral voice.* Cambridge, MA: Center for the Study of Gender, Education, and Human Development, Harvard University, Monograph #2.

Brown, L. M., and C. Gilligan. 1992. *Meeting at the crossroads: Women's psychology and girls' development.* Cambridge, MA: Harvard University Press.

Chodorow, N. 1978. *The reproduction of mothering: Psychoanalysis and sociology of gender.* Berkeley: University of California Press.

DaCosta, K. (1996). *Urban black adolescents' appraisals of social and academic concerns.* Poster presented at the Sixth Biennial Meeting of the Society for Research on Adolescence, Boston, March.

DuBois, D. L., and B. J. Hirsch. 1990. School and neighborhood friendship patterns of blacks and whites in early adolescence. *Child Development* 61: 524–536.

Epstein, J. L., and N. Karweit. 1983. *Friends in school: Patterns of selection and influence in secondary schools.* New York: Academic Press.

Fine, M. 1991. *Framing dropouts: Notes on the politics of an urban high school.* Albany: State University of New York Press.

Franklin, C. W., II. 1992. Friendship among black men. In *Men's friendships*, ed. P. Nardi. Newbury Park, CA: Sage.

Furman, W., and D. Buhrmester. 1985. Children's perceptions of the personal relationships in their social networks. *Developmental Psychology* 21:1016–1024.

Gallagher, P., and N. Busch-Rossnagel. 1991. *Self-disclosure and social support in the relationships of black and white female adolescents.* Poster presented at the Society for Research on Child Development, Seattle, March 25–29.

Gilligan, C. 1982. *In a different voice: Psychological theory and women's development.* Cambridge, MA: Harvard University Press.

Gold, M., and D. S. Yanof. 1985. Mothers, daughters, and girlfriends. *Journal of Personality and Social Psychology* 49 (3): 654–659.

Hansen, K. V. 1992. Our eyes behold each other: Masculinity and intimate friendship in antebellum New England. In *Men's friendships*, ed. P. Nardi. Newbury Park, CA: Sage.

Harding, S. 1986. *The science question in feminism.* Ithaca, NY: Cornell University Press.

hooks, b. 1989. *Talking back: Thinking feminist, thinking black.* Boston: South End Press.

Jones, D. C., S. E. Costin, and R. J. Ricard. 1994. *Ethnic and sex differences in best friendship characteristics among African-American, Mexican-American, and European-American adolescents.* Poster presented at Society for Research on Adolescence, San Diego, February 10.

Karweit, N., and S. Hansell. 1983. Sex differences in adolescent relationships: Friendship and status. In *Friends in school: Patterns of selection and influence in secondary schools*, eds. J. Epstein and N. Karweit. New York: Academic Press.

Ladner, J. 1971. *Tomorrow's tomorrow.* New York: Anchor Books.

Miller, B. 1988. *Adolescent friendships: A pilot study*. Unpublished qualifying paper. Cambridge, MA: Harvard Graduate School of Education.

———. 1991. *Adolescents' relationships with their friends*. Ph.D. dissertation. Cambridge, MA: Harvard Graduate School of Education.

Miller, J. B. 1976. *Toward a new psychology of women*. Boston: Beacon Press.

Nicholson, L. 1990. *Feminism/postmodernism*. New York: Routledge.

Raymond, D. 1994. Homophobia, identity, and the meanings of desire: Reflections on the cultural constructions of gay and lesbian adolescent sexuality. In *Sexual cultures and the construction of adolescent identities*, ed. J. Irvine. Philadelphia: Temple University Press.

Reisman, J. M. 1990. Intimacy in same-sex friendships. *Sex Roles* 23:65–82.

Savin-Williams, R. C., and T. J. Berndt. 1990. Friendship and peer relations. In *At the threshold: The developing adolescent*, eds. S. Feldman and G. R. Elliot. Cambridge, MA: Harvard University Press.

Stack, C. 1974. *All our kin: Strategies for survival in a black community*. New York: Harper and Row.

Sullivan, H. S. 1953. *The interpersonal theory of psychiatry*. New York: Norton.

Thomas, M. 1996. *Diversity in women's friendships*. Paper presented at Association for Women in Psychology, Portland, Oregon, March 14–17.

Walker, K. 1994. Men, women, and friendship. *Gender and Society* 8 (2): 246–265.

Way, N. 1995. "Can't you hear the strength, the courage I have?" Listening to urban adolescent girls speak about their relationships. *Psychology of Women Quarterly* 19 (1): 107–128.

———. 1996. Between experiences of desire and betrayal: Close friendships among urban adolescents. In *Urban girls: Resisting stereotypes, creating identities*, eds. B. Leadbeater and N. Way. New York: New York University Press.

———. 1998. *Everyday courage: The lives and stories of urban teenagers*. New York: New York University Press.

Way, N., and L. Chen. Forthcoming. Friendship patterns among African American, Latino, and Asian American adolescents from low-income families. *Journal of Adolescent Research*.

Youniss, J., and J. Smollar. 1985. *Adolescent relations with mothers, fathers, and friends*, Chicago: University of Chicago Press.

9

■　　■　　■　　■　　■　　■　　■　　■　　■

Echoes of Sexual Objectification

Listening for One Girl's Erotic Voice

Deborah L. Tolman

GOOD GIRLS DON'T WANT SEX; what they really want is love. Even
in an era of teen magazines offering girls tips on how to hone their sexual
skills, there remains an assumption that the "sexual" part of adolescent sexuality is the domain and desire of boys. The familiar story that organizes
"normal" female adolescent sexuality is a romance narrative (Kirkman,
Rosenthal, and Smith 1998) in which a (good) girl, who is on a quest for
love (Thompson 1984), does not feel sexual desire—strong, embodied,
passionate feelings of sexual wanting. In this story, sexual desire is male; it
is intractable, uncontrollable, and victimizing. There continues to be no
readily available image or story of a "normal" girl who has and responds
to her own sexual desire (Tolman 1994b). The romance narrative positions girls as more and less willing sexual objects, rendering their sexual
subjectivity difficult at best (Carpenter 1998). Michelle Fine observed
that, "[t]rained through and into positions of passivity and victimization,
young women are currently educated away from positions of sexual self-
interest" (1988, 42).

The problem is, however, that sexual desire is part of the human condition. Sexual desire is an embodied compass, providing us with potent in-

formation about ourselves and our relationships. To construct female sexual desire in adolescence as normative challenges psychology's covert but persistent collusion with a culture that denies and denigrates girls' sexual feelings (Fine 1988; Tolman 1994b). Anchored in an expectation that adolescent girls can and should experience sexual desire—not that they should or will necessarily act on these feelings, but that they should be able to recognize and acknowledge what is a part of the self—I have gathered descriptions of and narratives about experiences of sexual desire from more than fifty mid-adolescent (ages 15–18) girls, from urban and suburban areas, who are diverse in race, ethnicity, and religion. Understandably, I have found that feeling and responding to their own sexual desire—knowing, listening to, and taking into account their own bodily sexual feelings—poses a dilemma for these girls (Tolman 1994a, 1994b, 1994c, 1996a, 1996b; Tolman and Higgins 1996). Feeling desire meant for these girls that either (1) they were at odds with cultural context(s) that discourage them from living full-bodied lives, or (2) at odds with or dissociated from their own feelings.

The ways in which we do and do not "story" sexuality into being define how we make meaning out of our bodies and our relationships (Plummer 1995), as does access to critiques and alternatives to sanctioned stories. In this chapter, I will present a case from my current exploration of how girls' knowledge and experiences of their bodies and of their desire are shaped, enabled, and undermined by stories available in the culture about intimate relationships and sexuality. In this case, I listen to a white, middle-class, seventeen-year-old girl, Isabel, who has described this part of her life in a two-hour clinical interview with me. The fact that she is white and middle class matters, because cultural stories about girls' sexuality are profoundly raced and classed: White middle-class girls are positioned as aspiring "good" sexual objects, whereas poor girls and girls of color are constructed in opposition to create such goodness by serving as the placeholders for "bad" (Tolman 1996a).

Listening under the Cultural Stories of Female Adolescent Sexuality

Central to my investigation is a method of narrative analysis called the Listening Guide (Brown et al. 1989), which I have utilized to develop an understanding of adolescent girls' sexuality in terms of their own desire. The Listening Guide is a feminist approach to narrative analysis that makes explicit and central the relationship between the researcher listening and the research participant speaking, and which involves multiple readings of the same narrative from specific perspectives (Brown et al. 1989; Gilligan, Brown, and Rogers 1990). It is distinctly different from traditional methods of coding, in that one listens to, rather than categorizes or quantifies, the text of the interview.

The Listening Guide is particularly appropriate for understanding girls' narratives about their sexual desire because it enables the reader to "bring to the surface the 'undercurrent' of female voices and visions as it filters through an androcentric culture" (Brown and Gilligan 1992, 4). This method is oriented towards identifying such "contrapuntal" voices of human experience (Gilligan 1982, 1); in this case, voices at odds with the accepted cultural voices that speak to and about female adolescent sexuality.

This method of listening has been key in helping me to learn something new about female adolescent sexuality. It has enabled me to take in the voices of girls trying to speak about an unspeakable topic—their own desire. In addition to listening to the narrative for the story and for the narrator's representation of her self (see Brown, this volume; Way, this volume), the "I" or self voice, I listen for two voices specific to my expectation that girls' sexual desire is normative: what I call an "erotic voice" (Lorde 1984), that is, a girl's knowledge and narration of her own sexual feelings; and a "voice of the body," that is, a girl's indication and description of her bodily feelings and responses (Tolman 1994b).

The Listening Guide provided me with a means of reentering relationships I have formed with adolescent girls through interviewing them. Like a therapist, as a listener I bring myself knowingly into the process of listening, learning from my own thoughts and feelings in response to what a girl is saying in her story, and using clinical methods of empathy and associative logic to follow or make sense of her story. This attention to myself increases my ability to stay clear about what my own ideas and feelings are and how they do and do not line up with a girl's words, thus avoiding "bias" or imposing my own story over the girl's. Lyn Brown and Carol Gilligan have described the relationship of the listener to the speaker in the text of the narrative as both responsive and resistant (Brown and Gilligan

1992). In other words, listening for an aspect of experience that has been rendered invisible by an oppressive ideology, such as learning about girls' desire within the context of patriarchy, involves an interpretive process that weaves together the speaker's words and other aspects of her storytelling that the Listening Guide forefronts.

This case study illuminates two distinct uses of the Listening Guide. The first is to develop detailed case studies, which this one exemplifies, in which a specific theme or theoretically interlocking themes are explored in depth. Such case studies are most often grouped together to identify common and divergent patterns (e.g., Brown and Gilligan 1992; Tolman 1994b), yielding robust, empirically driven theory grounded in intensive examination of a group of participants who share some set of characteristics (Fine 1996). The second way in which the Listening Guide can be used is in a case study of an individual who in some ways departs from the "norm," thus uncovering a pattern or common experience within a group that might not otherwise be audible in their narratives and/or experiences (e.g., Steiner-Adair 1991; Zemsky 1991).

Object Lessons of the Romance Narrative

After my interview with sixteen-year-old Isabel, I feel like I need to come up for air. The interview is not what I had expected. Isabel has regaled me with an unexpected barrage of cultural conventions. I know that Isabel, as a white, middle-class girl, has had to deal with an image of herself as not having or acting on any of her own sexual feelings, if she is to be considered good. As a smart girl like I was, I know that she is probably thought of as a "brain"—that is, someone without a body and thus without the ability or desire to be sexual. I know Isabel to be a self-declared feminist. I hear these contradictory constructions of self in her interview, as she voices what amounts to a struggle and wish to feel desire and to be sexual in her body, something she thinks about and writes about in her journal a lot, but something that she is speaking about for the first time in this interview and has in fact experienced very little.

When I analyze the narratives in this interview, I notice two things. An erotic voice surfaces very rarely during this two-hour inquiry about her subjective experiences of her sexuality. In contrast, a voice of the body is prevalent. This pattern makes me wonder what Isabel is saying about her body. Why does her voice of the body not occur alongside an erotic voice—a more common pattern in other interviews? What can I learn about girls' experience of sexuality by the absence of an erotic voice in how Isabel speaks about her body, her experiences, her knowledge, and her fantasies?

The first clue is that Isabel interrupts my opening questions to tell me about an association she is having to my general questions about girls' sexuality. In one of the few times in this interview that an erotic voice appears, Isabel tells me that she is associating my saying "sexuality" with the character Celie in *The Color Purple*. She recalls that "she was totally sealed off from her whole body and um, because people kept telling her you know, not to look down there." She reminds me that Celie was raped by her father and forced to give "her life and her body and everything" to her husband. Isabel describes how Celie "broke um, this whole uh fear that she had of herself, just by looking . . . she was looking at her vagina. . . . And, and she was all, all of a sudden like a new person, with a really deep and um, and understanding of herself." Isabel notes the link between Celie becoming "so much more connected and at one with herself, but also so much more of a sexual person, just because she knew who she was." In Isabel's reading of the story, Celie is then able to enter an authentic romantic relationship because this experience had made her "so sure of herself."

As a set piece for our interview, Isabel introduces a story about the transformation that brings together an erotic voice and a voice of the body for a woman who had been "totally sealed off from her whole body," who had learned not to know her own body, and who had experienced sexual violation. I interpret Isabel's insertion of this story into our interview as indicating that she knows the possibility of an erotic connection, to self, through one's own body, and to others—knowledge and experience that makes a woman "so sure of herself." In so doing, Isabel is tipping me off in several ways to help me hear her. She wants me to know about and, I think, join her in shaping and pursuing her own query about herself, her body, and her thoughts, hopes, and fantasies about relationships. In fact, Isabel has had very little direct experience in exploring her sexuality with others. She prepares me to hear that she, too, feels "sealed off from her whole body" in the land of relationships. I also hear her telling me that she knows about how women's oppression is accomplished in part through suppression, or maybe possession, of women's sexuality, as well as the empowering effect of a woman gaining "a really deep . . . understanding of herself" through knowing and owning her own body. Celie's sense of self seems to Isabel to stand in contrast to how she and, she says, adolescent girls feel about themselves: "It's so hard to be at one with yourself when you don't know who you are . . . you have these biological hormones going and so it's, it, it doesn't always get together, like the sexuality part."

Isabel frames this interview with her knowledge of an erotic voice, but this voice then quickly disappears as she tells me about her sexuality; she voices her sexuality as a wish rather than an experience as she divulges to me the contours of her fantasies and experiences. What sets Isabel apart from other girls is that the question of her own desire matters to Isabel. Isabel notices, talks about, questions, and worries about the absence of sexual feelings in her life. I attribute this insight to her feminist perspective. However, when Isabel speaks explicitly about sexual desire, contradictions abound. On the one hand, she tells me she is worried that she is "asexual" because she has not felt a "sexual urge":

> maybe I'd go to a college campus just to hunt out the guys, and they're just not there. And maybe it's because I don't know them, but nothing's like striking a chord. Um, and then I, I guess in the past like month, or I mean it's been going on for awhile, but I just start to get really scared, like, "Oh my God, I'm asexual," (laughs) you know, I'm like nothing's happening. I'm not finding anybody and when I fantasize, I don't fantasize about having sex. And, and I don't think that I'm a lesbian, which would be fine with me if I were, but I just don't think I am. And I don't think um, I mean I'm pretty sure that I'm like heterosexual, but there's no sexual urge there. And I keep like checking, like, you know, like, um, tracing my birthday back, and like, I'm only sixteen. So maybe it's coming next year. Like, it better hurry, 'cause you know, there's just like no impetus there for like, losing virginity.

As she tells me about her search for a boyfriend, I hear an echo of my inquiry in her own questions about herself. For her, the act of searching for a boyfriend also seems to be a search for herself, for a sign that will tell her something about who she is. In part, I hear Isabel wondering what, in fact, desire is. Is it something associated with age, so that being "only sixteen" might explain her silent body, the absence of a "sexual urge"? Perhaps she is confused about the object of her desire, her sexual identity—but she considers and rejects this possibility. Isabel says that the absence of desire is making her "scared"; knowing about her own desire is, in part, a way of knowing herself that Isabel actually misses. Notable also is Isabel's conception of her own desire as the "impetus" for having sex; this sense of entitlement to her own feelings, this refusal to engage with a romance narrative in which she has the privilege of trading sex for love, sets Isabel's statements apart from other girls in their curiosity, fear of losing a boyfriend, having a certain amount of time elapse in a relationship, or desire to fit in as the "impetus" for having sex (Billy, Brewster, and Grady 1994; Thompson 1990; Tolman 1994a).

In contrast, Isabel speaks frequently in this interview about her body. Her reflections give me some clues about the absence of an erotic voice in her life. She does not have very much "real-life" experience with her body in sexual relationships; she narrates a few experiences colored by disappointment and violation. I wonder whether Isabel simply has not had any opportunity to explore such relationships—she says that she hasn't found anyone in her high school whom she wants to date—or whether she keeps herself from having such experiences. But she chooses to respond often and at great length to my questions about her relationship with her body and her struggle and desire to know her body better and to feel her embodied feelings. Her interest in this topic is noticeably more intense than other girls with whom I've spoken. Her access to alternative stories of female sexuality through feminism has provoked her own inquiry.

I notice that while speaking about her body, Isabel speaks as if she is looking at it rather than feeling it—even in response to my direct questions about what her body feels like. In such descriptions, there is no evidence of an erotic voice. Her body is an object that she examines, evaluates, judges, and breaks into parts. She fantasizes her body into other shapes and sizes. Evidence of having been socialized into objectifying her own body (Bartky 1990; Bordo 1993) abounds. A striking example is when I ask her to talk about what her body feels like in a fantasy that is ephemeral and spiritual but distinctly disembodied. This question is meant to be interruptive on my part, to invite her to speak the unspeakable—that is, voice her body—as well as to encourage her to explore the question of a sealed-off body that she herself has raised:

Deb: What does your body feel like?
Isabel: Like when I was walking down like, and James' brother was um, star-

ing at me and I was like, "Wow, I'm so gorgeous" and when I looked back
at that later I was like crazy, 'cause I knew I wasn't, but it's that same kind
of feeling, where all over you, you know like your leg is just absolutely perfect, and your feet are not too big, and, and your shoulders are just like,
you're actually standing up straight for once, um, and you're just gorgeous, and your bones, like are sticking out at the right places (laughs),
you know 'cause you're, like you're, you're so, like you're um, your throat
bones, are just like pushing out a little bit because . . . your cheekbones are
like all high up and, and your hair is like radiating.

Deb: You are giving me this amazing image of what you look like. But I want
to get a sense of what it feels like, how does this feel in your body?

Isabel: I don't, I guess I don't understand. I mean, I feel wonderful, and I feel
absolutely like I love myself and like everybody that I'm walking past is
staring at me, and that this guy that I'm with is like, "Wow, I have the best
of everything, 'cause she's really smart and she's really beautiful." Which
are two (clears throat) things that I'm constantly trying to connect. Um,
like think about the connection between myself, but um, is that what you
mean, like those kinds of things?

When I ask her to tell me about feeling sexy, she describes the experience
of looking sexy; she equates "knowing that I look beautiful" with "Yeah,
I'm so sexy." When I persist in asking her about the feeling, she persists in
describing looking sexy. In fact, this may make her feel sexy, but she voices
her thoughts about her looks, the image she projects as a desirable object:

Deb: What's it feel like, feeling sexy?

Isabel: Oh, it's so wonderful. And sometimes, like once in awhile, on a really
good day, when I'm in a very good mood, it happens in real life, where I
just feel sexy, and, and I know that everybody must be just looking at me
like, "Oh wow, she's like so beautiful." Or like, "Oh my gosh, she must
have thirty boyfriends outside of school." (laughs) Um, or, or just like,
"Wow she looks just so um, amazing. I really wish I looked like her." . . .
Um, but yeah, I mean, the whole like notion of feeling sexy is an integral
part of my life (laughs).

In Isabel's world, sexy is neither about how her body feels nor about her
desire—it is about appearing rather than feeling. Isabel is so accustomed

to experiencing her body as something that she watches and manipulates, that she has difficulty knowing whether she is really experiencing an embodied feeling, whether her body's voice is authentic or just something she is imagining:

> Sometimes when somebody um touches me, just like putting a hand on a shoulder, or stands really close, that also can happen, um, yeah like um, yeah. But it's, I'm more aware of it because when somebody, I mean I'm, it's just a little confusing because when somebody like really gorgeous comes close um, and I'm thinking, I think to my—and, and that same kind of like really inner peace, like warmness happens, I think, "Oh, that's just because your, you want this to happen right now . . . because they're standing close and they're really cute so you start to do this, um, so I don't know if that's me telling my body to do it or if it is just happening. Oh my gosh, I wish it would just happen because I mean, like I'm progressing somewhere (laughs).

In listening for an erotic voice and a voice of the body in her sexuality narratives, I can document how well Isabel has learned to objectify her body. An object has no feelings of its own, no sense of agency, has an absence of subjectivity (Tolman and Debold 1993). Isabel goes on to describe experiences of feeling vulnerable when being objectified by men. In addition, her interview is peppered with narratives in which she describes several experiences of "everyday" or "normalized" violation that most women have encountered (Phillips, 2000; Tolman, 2000). Isabel is fully conscious of the anger she feels as she finds herself joining them in their appraisal of her body, worrying that

> I should look more beautiful right now, so you know I try to stand a little bit straighter, even though I'm so angry, at, in one sense at this guy um, and like if my hair's parted down the middle maybe I'll like part it down the side and stuff so I don't look like a geek or anything like that, but just all these things that um, that are going on. And they're very conflicting, and it's very frustrating. I feel very vulnerable then, um, because I'm not in control.

Isabel tells of the power of having been socialized into knowing and relating to her own body as an object. She gives voice to an experience that many feminist women have and keep to themselves: despite our conscious sense of outrage and anger at this violation, we have been well trained to be the best objects we can be, even at the very moment of violation—which is a moment not only someone else's but of our own consumption as well. Isabel has the strength to be able to know and voice the contradictory nature of her response and her discomfort at feeling "not in control."

Isabel's descriptions of experiencing her own body as an object are explicitly associated with situations she calls "romantic" or potentially sexual. In the romance narrative, the normative path of development demands that girls dissociate from their own agency and embodied feelings, that they become good (hetero)sexual objects for the sexual gaze and conquest of men (Ramazanoglu and Holland 1993). Feminist analyses of the romance narrative delineate how it disempowers women by positing them as objects rather than subjects in their relationships and in their own lives, keeping them out of touch with the knowledge they gain through their own embodied experience (see, e.g., Debold, Wilson, and Malave 1993). It is not inconsequential, then, that the primary theme in Isabel's descriptions of her sexual fantasies is romance. Isabel invokes the romance narrative over and over again in describing girls' sexuality. That her thoughts and few experiences are organized by the romance narrative offers an explanation for how rarely an erotic voice appears in her stories, as well as the extent to which the voice of her body is relentlessly characterized by objectification:

> I have this little fantasy world where um, where everything's just totally romantic and I like wanted to meet this guy who's in college, who's just absolutely gorgeous, and he's just going to be incredible, and he's like, he knows, like he's memorized a hundred selected poems by e. e. cummings, you know, and he just, but he knows like all these other poets, too. He plays the guitar, which is a must, and, and he would like make picnics for me, and we'd just go out and um, and have this wonderful time, and, and we'd just lie close together, but we wouldn't do anything. We would just like lie close together and um, and it would just be so romantic, and I'd feel like I was deeply connected to him. But it never goes beyond that. It never goes like, and then we'd strip off our clothes or something. I mean, maybe we would, but it wouldn't be like, as in any kind of sexual, any like, a deeply sexual connotation, like we were going to have intercourse.

The contradiction between Isabel's knowledge, relayed through Celie's experiences, that she can and should have an erotic voice, and her narration of her own objectification may contribute to or be an artifact of her tendency to speak within the confines of the romance narrative. Interestingly, Isabel shies away from the part of the romance narrative where she is swept off her feet and "taken" by her handsome beau. Perhaps because Isabel has access to an alternative story about herself, her body, and her sexuality, because she knows to have questions and wishes about her own sexual desire, even in her fantasies, she cannot yet write that part of the story.

Listening to (Some)Body: Isabel's Erotic Voice

Despite Isabel's inculcation into the romance narrative, she does in fact have access to her body as a source of powerful feeling and information about relationships. On the heels of telling me about a disappointing experience of being kissed by a boy, which she found "disgusting" but associated with "society's definition of sexual pleasure," she offers a description in which an erotic voice interplays with the voice of her body. I am taken aback when she suddenly shifts into describing a potent experience of embodied pleasure, revealing a close knowledge of the voice of her body *and* of an erotic voice. In fact, the two voices seem to blend into one as she speaks about a feeling that she associates with sexual pleasure:

> *Isabel:* If sexual pleasure is what gives you like this really inner sense of like peace and relaxation and just like thinking that's everything's OK and like, and um, and like when you really can start to feel like your um like your juices or like your blood flowing throughout you, and like everything just becomes relaxed and light, and this is the weirdest thing in the world, but when somebody I really respect, and it either can be male or female, um, but I really think it's beautiful, and, and to be beautiful in my little world of beauty you don't have to be like um gorgeous in a physical sense, you can be just like really mature, and self-assured and powerful, that's what makes um, somebody beautiful. If they start to talk, and, and if they're talking they have to be talking for like more than a minute, obviously, but if they start to talk, and I'm just totally absorbed in what they're saying and their voice, and like the flux of their voice, and they can just be read-

ing poetry, or, or just talking about like biology, or you know, like chemistry, or something, I mean, my chemistry teacher doesn't do that for me, but, but they can just be talking about the most blasé or mundane subject and um, and I just get totally immersed in what they're saying . . . and I have no idea, this is like the one thing that gives me the most pleasure, so I'm just associating sexual pleasure, 'cause I guess that's, I mean sexual pleasure is supposed to give you a lot of pleasure too, so, but—

Deb: Is there something about your body that gets involved with that?

Isabel: Yeah, it's um, it's everything gets really loose . . . and um, and sort of like very warm, and I just, and like I have just this great sense of being one, like being connected when that happens, um, just hearing this person speak, like the words flow right through me, but I can like totally, I mean just crystal clear in my mind like what they're saying, and but, but everything gets involved in what they're saying, and I'm just sitting there like, "Oh, you know, just speak forever, it's just wonderful."

With the exception of the poetry reading, this story has no elements of the romantic narrative. Isabel reveals a deep knowledge of profound pleasure and intense bodily feeling in connection with another person—"just hearing this person speak, like the words flow right through me"—that is not socially constructed as either romantic or sexual, but that she experiences as profoundly embodied and pleasurable. I am struck that Isabel experiences a powerful connection to herself and to other people only in situations that she does not construe as sexual.

Conclusions

Listening for Isabel's erotic voice and the voice of her body, and then relating the absence and presence of these voices to the "I," or self voice, in her narratives, illuminates how she experiences her body explicitly as an object in situations that are socially labeled sexual. In a sense, when asked about her own sexual feelings, Isabel has narrated her own sexual objectification, both as she has internalized it and as she experiences it in her daily living. What sets Isabel apart from many other adolescent girls who have learned to know their bodies as objects rather than as sexual subjects is that she also knows that desire, empowerment, and self-actualization are accessible to her through her own body. Because she has access to alternative narratives through the experiences of Celie and through feminism, I can hear Isabel wondering about the absence of her own erotic voice, initiating a process of resisting her internalized objectification and coming into her body. A key piece of information that resonates with what other girls have told me is that Isabel has not had an opportunity to speak to other girls or to adult women about her experiences, her fantasies, or her questions. This silence, which shrouds active, passionate female adolescent sexuality, is both cause for concern and opportunity for change (Thompson 1990; Tolman and Szalacha 1999). When educating girls into sexual health, we are obliged to teach them not only about the physical and emotional risks of sexuality, but also about the ways in which our sexuality can make us more resilient and more alive and about our entitlement to an erotic voice. By cultivating an erotic voice, we are not going to turn girls into sex fiends. However, we will challenge a system that depends on the erotic silence (Heyn 1997) of girls, which is the lynchpin of our current construction of adolescent sexuality (Tolman in press). By speaking to girls *and* boys about girls' entitlement to their sexual desire, we demand a rewrite of the romance narrative in which girls are sexual subjects rather than sexual objects.

References

Bartky, S. L. 1990. *Femininity and domination: Studies in the phenomenology of oppression*. New York: Routledge.

Billy, J. O. G., K. L. Brewster, and W. R. Grady. 1994. Contextual effects on the sexual behavior of adolescent women. *Journal of Marriage and the Family* 56:387–404.

Bordo, S. 1993. *Unbearable weight: Feminism, western culture, and the body*. Berkeley: University of California Press.

Brown, L. M., and C. Gilligan. 1992. *Meeting at the crossroads: Women's psychology and girls' development*. Cambridge, MA: Harvard University Press.

Brown, L. M., M. B. Tappan, C. Gilligan, B. A. Miller, and D. E. Argyris. 1989. Reading for self and moral voice: A method for interpreting narratives of real-life moral conflict and choice. In *Entering the circle: Hermeneutic investigation in psychology*, eds. M. J. Packer and R. B. Addison, 141–164. Albany: State University of New York Press.

Carpenter, L. 1998. From girls into women: Scripts for sexuality and romance in *Seventeen Magazine*, 1974–1994. *Journal of Sex Research* 35 (2): 158–168.

Christian-Smith, L. K. 1990. *Becoming a woman through romance*. New York: Routledge.

Debold, E. W., M. Wilson, and I. Malave. 1993. *Mother daughter revolution: From betrayal to power*. Reading, MA: Addison-Wesley.

Fine, M. 1988. Sexuality, schooling, and adolescent females: The missing discourse of desire. *Harvard Educational Review* 58 (1): 29–53.

———. 1996. *Disruptive voices*. Ann Arbor: University of Michigan Press.

Gergen, K. J. 1985. The social constructionist movement in modern psychology. *American Psychologist* 40 (3): 266–275.

Gilligan, C. 1982. *In a different voice: Psychological theory and women's development*. Cambridge, MA: Harvard University Press.

Gilligan, C., L. M. Brown, and A. G. Rogers. 1990. Psyche embedded: A place for body, relationships, and culture in personality theory. In *Studying persons and lives*, eds. A. I. Rabin, R. A. Zucker, R. A. Emmons, and S. Frank. New York: Springer Publishing Co.

Heyn, D. 1997. The erotic silence of the American wife. New York: Plume.

Kirkman, M., D. Rosenthal, and A. M. A. Smith. 1998. Adolescent sex and the romantic narrative: Why some young heterosexuals use condoms to prevent pregnancy, but not disease. *Psychology, Health, and Medicine* 3 (4): 355–370.

Lorde, A. 1984. *Sister outsider: Essays and speeches*. Trumansburg, NY: Crossing Press.

Moore, S., and D. Rosenthal. 1992. The social context of adolescent sexuality: Safe sex implications. *Journal of Adolescence* 15 (4): 415–435.

Petersen, A. C., N. Leffert, and B. L. Graham. 1995. Adolescent development and the emergence of sexuality. *Suicide and Life-Threatening Behavior* 25 (Supplement): 4–17.

Phillips, L. 2000. Flirting with danger. New York: New York University Press.

Plummer, K. 1995. *Telling sexual stories*. London: Routledge.

Ramazanoglu, C., and J. Holland. 1993. Women's sexuality and men's appropriation of desire. In *Up against Foucault*, ed. C. Ramazanoglu, 239–264. New York: Routledge.

Steiner-Adair, C. 1991. When the body speaks: Girls, eating disorders, and psychotherapy. In *Women, girls, and psychotherapy: Reframing resistance*, eds. C. Gilligan, A. Rogers, and D. Tolman. Binghamton, NY: Harrington Park Press.

Thompson, S. 1984. Search for tomorrow: On feminism and the reconstruction of teen romance. In *Pleasure and danger: Exploring female sexuality*, ed. C. Vance. New York: Routledge and Kegan Paul.

———. 1990. Putting a big thing into a little hole: Teenage girls' accounts of sexual initiation. *Journal of Sex Research* 27 (3): 341–361.

Tolman, D. L. 1994a. Daring to desire: Culture and the bodies of adolescent girls. In *Sexual cultures: Adolescents, communities, and the construction of identity*, ed. J. Irvine. Philadelphia: Temple University Press.

Tolman, D. L. 1994b. Doing desire: Adolescent girls' struggles for/with sexuality. *Gender and Society* 8 (3): 324–342.

———. 1994c. Dimensions of desire: Final report to the Spencer Foundation. Wellesley, MA.

———. 1996a. Adolescent girls' sexuality: Debunking the myth of the urban girl. In *Urban girls: Resisting stereotypes, creating identities*, eds. B. J. R. Leadbeater and N. Way, 255–271. New York: New York University Press.

———. 1996b. Dimensions of desire: Phase 2. Final report to the Spencer Foundation. Wellesley, MA.

———. 2000. Object lessons: Romance, violation, and female adolescent sexual desire. *Journal of Sex Education and Therapy* 25 (1).

———. In press. Dilemma of desire: Adolescent girls' struggle with/for sexuality. Cambridge, MA: Harvard University Press.

Tolman, D. L., and E. Debold. 1993. Conflicts of body and image: Female adolescents, desire, and the no-body body. In *Feminist perspectives on eating disorders*, eds. P. Fallon, M. Katzman, and S. Wooley, 301–317. New York: Guilford Press.

Tolman, D. L., and T. Higgins. 1996. How being a good girl can be bad for girls. In *Good girls/bad girls: Women, sex, violence, and power in the 1990s*, eds. N. B. Maglin and D. Perry. New Brunswick, NJ: Rutgers University Press.

Tolman, D. L., and L. A. Szalacha. 1999. Dimensions of desire: Bridging qualitative and quantitative methods in a study of female adolescent sexuality. *Psychology of Women Quarterly* 23 (2): 7–39.

Walker, A. 1982. *The color purple.* New York: Washington Square Press.

Zemsky, B. 1991. Coming out against all odds: Resistance in the life of a young lesbian. In *Women, girls, and psychotherapy: Reframing resistance*, eds. C. Gilligan, A. Rogers, and D. Tolman. Binghamton, NY: Harrington Park Press.

■　■　■　■　■　■　■　■　■

10

Embodying Working-Class Subjectivity and Narrating Self

"We Were the Hired Help"

Sandra J. Jones

FEMINISTS HAVE PERSISTENTLY ARGUED that gender, race, and class are interlocking systems of oppression that are experienced and resisted on individual, cultural, and institutional levels (e.g., Collins 1990; Spelman 1988). Despite its inclusion in the list, class is often the least addressed of these systems (Reay 1999).[1] Although psychologists have developed theories of racial and gender identities (e.g., Helms 1993; Miller 1986), there are no comparable theories of how we develop personal class identities and a sense of our place in a class-stratified society. A variety of factors may contribute to a neglect of class in psychological research, such as the myth that the United States is a classless society, the undercutting of class identity by competing identities, and the fact that class, like sexuality, is not always apparent (Aronowitz 1992).

A growing body of autobiographical writing by academics from the working class suggests that the experience of growing up working class informs adult subjectivities (e.g., Dews and Law 1995; Ryan and Sackrey 1996; Tokarczyk and Fay 1993). In addition, the research and writing of a small number of feminist psychologists from the working class identifies a need for a feminist understanding of class (Walkerdine 1996a). A psychological study of class would need to examine class consciousness as a psychological versus a political construct, explore the lived experience of class, and develop an understanding of the ways in which class is learned in childhood (Steedman 1994).

In this chapter, I draw upon my research with female academics from the working class as a way to engage consciousness of class and the ways in which class informs self or subjectivity (Jones 1998a, 1998b). I use the term *self* to refer to one's grasp of oneself, including moods, attitudes, and opinions. Self is constructed intersubjectively at the crossroads of subjectivity, the unconscious, and the social realm through a process of reflexive appropriation (Elliott 1992). Fundamental conflicts centered around class, gender, and race are experienced through social interactions and are deeply inscribed in the unconscious or imaginary dimension of subjectivity. Through analysis of narratives told by one participant, I engage the idea that class is deeply experienced—it gets in your bones—and informs self, whether or not you have the language to articulate class relations.

The Study

I engaged in interpretive research with ten female academics from the working class[2] in order to explore the ways in which class informs self and is interwoven with gender, race, and ethnicity. My use of an interpretive approach draws on feminism (e.g., Reinharz 1992; Stewart 1994) and other critical perspectives in order to expand a focus on individual experience and situate individual behavior within sociohistorical contexts and social relations of power (Charmaz 1983). I conducted two phenomenological interviews[3] with each participant in her home or office that lasted approximately two hours each. The interviews focused on the lived experience of growing up working class and becoming an academic. As secondary sources of information, I observed participants in classrooms and collected documents, specifically, curricula vitae, syllabi, articles written and recommended by participants, and a genogram that recorded the education and occupation of family members across three generations.

Although the participants shared working-class backgrounds, there were differences among them in terms of race, ethnicity, regionality, sexual orientation, family status, religion, age, discipline, and institutional af-filiation and status. Six of the ten participants were white; four were women of color (two African Americans, two Latinas). Region of origin included the northeast, east, midwest, west, southwest, and south. Four of the participants had at least one parent who migrated to the United States (Portuguese, Polish, Eastern European Jewish, Salvadoran), and two had grandparents who had migrated (Italian, Mexican).

In interpretive research, the researcher is the research instrument (Hammersley and Atkinson 1983). Given this, the researcher's positionality and the relationship between researcher and participant are critical. In addition to understanding the particular circumstances of participants in an interview, it is equally important to ask who is listening and what is the nature of the listener's relationship with the speaker, "especially with respect to power" (Brown 1997, 686). Power relations between participants and myself were complicated. Similarities in our experience helped establish rapport and informed my analysis (Maxwell 1996; Seidman 1991). Like my participants, I am a first-generation college graduate from the working class and am acutely aware that our working-class backgrounds situate us differently than colleagues with middle- or upper-middle-class backgrounds. In a variety of ways, we incorporate class issues into our teaching and research, and we tend to feel a special affinity with working-class students.

However, as researcher I was situated in a position of power in regard to the research process and interpretation of results. On the other hand, the participants were tenured or tenure-track professors and situated in a position of higher social status than I was as a doctoral candidate. Although I was older than some participants, they had more experience negotiating class issues in the academy, and I looked to them as potential role models. Therefore, rather than being static, the relations of power between us were continually being negotiated.

Although there were similarities in our experience and orientation, there were important differences as well. For example, all of the participants entered college following high school graduation with the exception of one participant who entered college within two years of graduating. In contrast, I identified myself to participants as a nontraditional college student from the working class who attended college while working full time to support a family. There were also racial, ethnic, religious, regional, sexual orientation, and personality differences that affected the interviewing relationship. My experience as a heterosexual WASP (English-Irish-Scottish) who grew up in a predominantly white, industrialized, small town in New England both informed and constrained my ability to understand participants' life experiences. Differences in social identities and our respective roles of interviewer and interviewee situated us in complicated relations of power and interpersonal connections. As a researcher, I was conscious of power relations and strove for equity, not only as an ethical imperative, but as a means of developing the trust necessary for participants to share their experiences with me (Seidman 1991).

Feminist research that explores lived experience "approaches the researched not as objects to do research on, but as participants in dialogue" (Langellier and Hall 1989, 201). As a way to engage participants in the construction of meaning and check my interpretation of their texts, I employed a reflexive[4] dialogical process. I gave participants a copy of their transcripts with a request that they note clarifications, corrections, and any material that they wanted removed. Some participants made corrections and clarified sections. No one asked me to remove material. After completing the analysis, I sent a draft of my analysis to participants and requested their feedback on my interpretation of their texts.[5] Five of the participants requested minor changes, which I made. If we had encountered differences that we were unable to resolve, I would have included our different points of view in the analysis. I subsequently sent participants a copy of the completed dissertation. In the final analysis, the work is mine, and I take responsibility for the interpretation (Riessman 1993).

Integrating Grounded Theory and Narrative Analysis

I used a combination of grounded theory and narrative analysis to analyze the data. Grounded theory is an inductive approach to analyzing text and developing theory (Glaser and Strauss 1967; Strauss and Corbin 1990). Grounded theory analysts systematically read and code transcripts using descriptive terms that are drawn or "emerge" from the text. Coding is guided by the researcher's focus of inquiry. The entering focus is usually stated in the research question and is informed by the researcher's knowledge, hunches, and assumptions. In inductive research, the focus of inquiry evolves during data collection and coding. As coding proceeds, analysts identify categories and relationships (similarities and distinctions) between categories within and across interview texts. Lower level categories are then grouped into higher level categories or abstract concepts. By grouping categories into a hierarchical structure and identifying the properties of higher level categories, analysts explicate theoretical concepts.

An advantage of grounded theory is that it enables analysts to develop theoretical concepts that can be generalized. However, a drawback of categorizing strategies is that they fracture the text in order to rearrange it into categories. As a result, the original context is lost. In contrast, narrative analysis is a contextualizing process for analyzing contiguous sections of text that comprise a coherent story with a beginning, middle, and end (Gee 1991; Mishler 1986, 1992; Riessman 1993). An advantage of narrative analysis is that it enables analysts to examine text within its original context. A drawback of contextualizing strategies is that they tend to produce highly individualized accounts from which it is difficult to develop theory. However, Joseph Maxwell and Barbara Miller (1996; see also Maxwell 1996) argue that categorization and contextualization are complementary processes for interpreting data and that both are necessary in order to provide a well-rounded account. Taking my lead from Maxwell and Miller, I integrated grounded theory and narrative analysis as a way to negotiate the benefits and limitations of both approaches.

Narrative theorists argue that narrative is the fundamental way in which we make ourselves intelligible to others and to ourselves (e.g., Bruner 1990; Mishler 1986). Thus, narrative analysis is particularly suited to research that employs autobiographical text as a way to examine self. My use of narrative analysis draws on the sociolinguistic work of James Gee (1991), as well as the work of Elliot Mishler (1986, 1992) and Catherine Riessman (1993). Analysis of narratives involves attending to how a story is *said* as a way to interpret the meaning of the story. Narrative analysts attend to relationships between statements within a narrative and the way in which the speaker constructs coherence.

There was a dynamic interaction between my use of grounded theory analysis and narrative analysis. In addition to systematically coding texts, I identified and analyzed particular narratives that I found compelling and that exemplified key dimensions of subjectivity and consciousness of class.

In turn, narrative analysis informed my evolving focus of interpretation. My criteria for a compelling narrative were intuitive: The narratives I selected informed my inquiry focus, moved my understanding forward, and evoked emotions (the participants' and my own). The display of emotions (e.g., tears, laughter, change of pitch) indicates deeply held positions (Harré 1995). The strong cognitive-affective dimension in the narratives that I selected signaled that these stories were important in the process of negotiating self (Riessman 1993).

Once I identified a narrative in a transcript, I listened to the tape to hear how it was spoken, attending to pitch, pauses, intonation, and rate of speech. Drawing on these cues, I structured the narrative into numbered lines. As exemplified in the narrative excerpts that follow, I underlined words that were emphasized (which appear here in italics), noted false starts with a hyphen, and indicated a raised pitch at the end of a line with a carat symbol (^). I indicated short pauses by three periods and longer pauses by a "p" in brackets followed by the length of the pause in seconds. I included my verbal responses in the text, marking them as spoken by the interviewer, as a way to show my involvement in the co-construction of the narrative. Gee (1991) argues that the structure of narratives mirrors that of poetry: poetic "stanzas are a universal part of the human language production system for extended pieces of language" (25). By attending to linguistic cues and topic switches, I grouped lines into stanzas and stanzas into strophes to analyze the structure of narratives. The poetic structure of a narrative, the way in which a story is said, sets up inferences about its meaning.

After structuring the text, I inquired into the meaning of the structure by asking several questions: Why does the speaker organize the narrative in this way, for this listener? What particular words or metaphors are used? What is the plot? How is the narrative linked to other narratives in the interview? Attending to these questions is an interpretive task that requires careful attention to the content and structure of the text in order to construct meaning.

Parsing stories into narrative structures conveys dimensions of meaning that are lost in representations of spoken text as sentences or quotes. By conveying a sense of how the text was spoken, narrative structures help the reader notice patterns. In this chapter, I present excerpts from narratives told by Anne (a pseudonym) to illustrate my analysis. Taken together, these narrative excerpts illuminate consciousness of class in childhood and the ways in which working-class consciousness is embodied and informs self.

Embodying Working-Class Subjectivity

Anne is white, a second-generation Portuguese and a third-generation Italian. At the time of the interviews she was forty-nine. The events described in this narrative took place when she was between the ages of five and eight. The first narrative, which I call "Being Hired Help," is a story about going to work with her father, who had a second job as a weekend gardener for affluent families. I generally began the first interview with each participant by discussing the family genogram. In this context, participants told stories about childhood experiences of being working class—stories that evoked sadness, anger, pride, and joy. Anne told this story in the context of describing her father's work, which she recorded on her genogram.

Narrative: *Being Hired Help (Abridged)*

048   and I would spend the day *gardening* with my father
049   and he would mow the lawns
051   and I would do all the trimming

053   and he would *pay me*
055   which always kind of astounded me do you know
057   he would always pay me really quite *well*

058   and but I have very distinct *memories* of those experiences
059   they're probably some of the most influential *memories* um *in my life* [crying, p:10]

062   Interviewer: We can always stop this if you want to take a- a break [Anne shakes her head side to side, p:18]
063   Anne: Well I think that they were important um—
064   they were important experiences in terms of- of social class [Interviewer: oh]

067   this was like first second third grade
068   and I *knew* what social class was about then

070　of course I couldn't articulate it in the way
071　that I can *semi*-articulate it now . . . you know
072　but it was . . . um it was very clear to me

073　the differences in the *lives* um of these people
074　whose lawns my father was mowing
075　and our *life*

078　I can remember going with my father to these houses and
079　they would not let my father and I use the toilets
080　go into the house and use the *bathrooms*

082　I could remember my mother saying you know
083　"go to the *bathroom* Anne before you leave the house okay"
084　because my father could just- there were lots of bushes around
085　so my father could easily kind of go into the bush [laughs]
086　but I couldn't as *easily*- could not as easily *manage* that . . . alright

087　so I could remember not um you know-
088　*going* to the bathroom beforehand and
089　not *drinking* much while I was there
090　because then I would have to use a *bathroom*
091　and there was no bathroom to be *used*

093　I remember one of them *Mrs. Smith* an older woman
094　and she would occasionally just kind of peek-*peek* out the window alright
095　to I *suppose* make sure- at least in my mind- in my head as a kid
096　to make sure that we were still working
097　you know not taking a little *break* or something

098　I mean I just and- and never appeared
099　I mean never came to the lawn and greeted me
100　and engaged me in any kind of a conversation

101　it was very clear that we were- that we were the hired help you know
103　there was absolutely no question about that

104　and that *bus* ride was not a very long bus ride—
108　so *literally* they you know they could have brought us home

109   and it would have taken them all of about *seven minutes* alright to bring us home

110   and so I always thought as a kid you know
111   like *why wouldn't you do that*
112   here you have this- these *two cars* kind of in this garage you know
113   and so why- and Mrs. Smith even had a *driver*

114   so like why *couldn't they* just bring us home
115   why did we have to kind of get on the bus
116   you know, walk to that *stop* and get on the *bus* and then walk at the other end

The beginning of this narrative and the way in which it was told did not suggest that these were painful experiences. I did not know why Anne began crying after saying these were "influential *memories*" in her life. By listening to Anne's telling of this story, I realized that gardening with her father was one of the locations where she learned her class position. Class was about "differences in . . . lives." She learned what it felt like to be "hired help" and how to conduct herself in that situation. There is a strong visceral dimension in this narrative, a focus on the body and allusions to physical discomfort. As a little girl, she did "all the trimming," and had to "walk" to and from the bus after a long day of labor. Anne's mother taught her strategies for coping with the material conditions. These "practices of survival" (Walkerdine 1997, 40) included ignoring her thirst ("not *drinking* much") and going to the bathroom before leaving, since "there was no bathroom to be *used*." Because she was a girl, Anne did not have the same outlet as her father. Her experience of class relations was interwoven with the experience of being female. In addition to the corporeal dimension of being hired help, Anne described the social relations of class. She was covertly watched—"peek[ed]" at–and not engaged in conversation. Through active participation in the garden, Anne experienced and coped with a set of social practices and physical conditions that informed her working-class subjectivity.

Suffering the humiliations of being treated like hired help raised ethical questions for Anne. The Smiths could have provided some relief by having their driver bring them home. That they did not offer to do so was incongruous to Anne as a child. Research indicates that young children expect the rich to care for the poor by sharing their resources (Leahy 1983). Her question—"why wouldn't you do that?"—reflects the confusion she felt as a child.

I asked Anne if she talked with her father about their experience in the garden. She said they did not: "that would be, I think, too personal for him to talk about when I was that age." In the absence of language, Anne appropriated a way to resist the injuries of class and deal with the pain associated with being working class by "saving face":

> In some ways, I think even as a child, I was able to save *face*. I mean I saw my father saving face, you see, and in turn I could walk away with my father, okay, thinking that, oh you know, these people are *weird*, these people are maybe not very nice, I don't *understand* these people, okay, but my father loves what he is doing. I mean he may be tired. He may be exhausted. He may be *underpaid* for it, but enormous pride.

Twice in this quote, Anne juxtaposes three negative statements with an optimistic concluding statement. This repetition suggests that the weight of oppression (indicated by the repetition of three statements) was counteracted by her father's "pride" and love of gardening. As part of her identification with her father, Anne appropriated a sense of self as working class that included a sense of pride in manual labor. By interpreting her father's behavior as "saving face" and adopting that behavior for herself, she was able to resist some of the negative consequences of being treated like hired help. In so doing, she developed a "defense against oppression" (Walkerdine 1996b, 153). Anne externalized the problem: the Smiths were "weird" and "not very nice."

It is striking to me that Anne's ability to "save face" occurred without any discussion. In the absence of words, she looked to her father ("I saw my father saving face"). There was an interchange between them, something that she experienced and appropriated from his bearing and the way that he conducted himself in this situation—a language of the body that was not verbally articulated (Zandy 1995). Perhaps there was something in the way he stood, walked about the garden, and got on the bus at the end of the day that evidenced the pride he felt in his work. She saw that he walked away from the Smith's garden with his dignity intact, and she in turn was able to do the same.

In his concept of class habitus, Pierre Bourdieu (1985) argues that children are particularly attentive to "gestures and postures . . . always associated with a tone of voice, a style of speech, and . . . a certain subjective experience" (87). Anne's text about saving face and Bourdieu's concept of class habitus resonate with my working-class experience and provide insight into how social relations become material (see also Brennan 1993; Harré 1995; Sampson 1996). Both texts evoke my own sense or tacit knowledge of embodying a way of moving, speaking, feeling, and making meaning in response to class oppression.

Although Anne is no longer working class, the marginality that she experienced as a child continues to inform her subjectivity and work. In the following narrative, "This Is the Best Job in Town," she connects the humiliations her father experienced with her ongoing working-class identity as an academic. I focus on the concluding section of the narrative in order to present stanza and strophe structure.

Narrative: This Is the Best Job in Town (Abridged)

Strophe 5: Identifying as Working Class

STANZA 11: I'M UPPER MIDDLE CLASS AND WORKING CLASS

38 you know what I said about even though I'm kind of upper middle class
39 what is that kind of identification do you know
40 and I still- I really still do have kind of a working-class I think a working-class identification

STANZA 12: PART OF IDENTIFYING AS WORKING CLASS IS MY
CONNECTION WITH MY PARENTS

41 part- part of it is because of my continuing connection with my parents
42 and they're living in my house you know
43 so that's- there's the reality of that right [Interviewer: right]

STANZA 13: PART OF IDENTIFYING AS WORKING CLASS IS HAVING
BEEN MARGINALIZED AS A CHILD

44 part of it I think is my realization that being working class meant growing up that I had been marginalized

45 that I- that I was marginalized

46 and marginalization has given me enormous insight as a sociologist [Interviewer: hmm]

Strophe 6: Positive Marginality

STANZA 14: BEING ON THE MARGINS GIVES YOU A DISTINCTIVE PERSPECTIVE

47 being someone who's on the margins . . . does afford alright

48 the opportunity to look at the world in ways in which you probably would not look at the world [Interviewer: mm hm] alright

49 if you were not on the margins you know [Interviewer: uh huh, right]

STANZA 15: I HAVE VERY GOOD SOCIOLOGICAL INSIGHT

50 and so I think I have very good *sociological insight* [Interviewer: yes] you know

51 and it's something I think that- it doesn't- it doesn't only come with training

52 it doesn't only

STANZA 16: THE INSIGHT THAT I HAVE COMES FROM THOSE LIFE EXPERIENCES

53 I mean particularly if you're interested in *social class* okay [Interviewer: right] alright

54 I think the insight that I have could not have only been the result of the graduate school courses or having a terrific mentor okay [Interviewer: right]

55 that it really does come from those life *experiences* you know [Interviewer: mm hm]

Strophe 7: Finding Value in Being Working Class

STANZA 17: I'M QUITE PROUD OF MY WORKING-CLASS IDENTITY

56 and so for *me* you know that has made such a wonderful difference in my life [Interviewer: uh huh]

57 that- that the working class- that the working class identity

58 even kind of psychologically is something actually that I'm quite *proud of* [Interviewer: mm hm, mm hm] you know

STANZA 18: MY PAINFUL MEMORIES ATTRACT ME TO
WORKING-CLASS STUDENTS

59 so you know because those *painful memories* you know
60 about how I sometimes saw my father treated
61 and being in situations in which he had no control over
62 was feeling so *vulnerable* okay um because of our class position
63 that I find that that's what makes me attracted to the working-class
     students [Interviewer: yes] okay

In this narrative, Anne hits upon a central concept in my grounded theory analysis of interview texts, specifically, an ongoing working-class identity. The titles of strophes represent analytic concepts, namely, working-class identity, positive marginality, and valuing working-class lives. The titles of stanzas are conceptually similar to descriptive codes (lower-level categories) in grounded theory analysis in that they are developed inductively from the words of participants, and they identify a key idea in the text.

In strophe 5, Anne asserts her working-class identity and grounds it in her "continuing connection" and daily interactions with her parents and in her experience of class "marginalization." She downplays her identification as upper middle class, which is based on objective characteristics, such as education, occupation, and income. In terms of these dimensions of social status, she is not working class. Her claim to a working-class identity is based on history, current interpersonal connections, and experiences of oppression: "being working class meant growing up that I had been marginalized."

In strophe 6, Anne constructed a connection between working-class marginality and her work as a sociologist. From her present context, Anne identified a positive outcome of class oppression: "I have very good sociological insight" that "could not have only been the result of . . . graduate work . . . or having a terrific mentor." Having a personal knowledge of marginality helps Anne understand the lives of people who are located on the fringes of society.

The final strophe builds on the preceding strophes and concludes the narrative by linking it to the gardening narrative. Anne is "proud" of being working class. In multiple ways, she values her working-class identity, which "has made such a wonderful difference in my life." In the last stanza, she situated her affective connection to working-class students with "painful memories" of class marginality and her father's "vulnerable" experiences. She intuitively picks out working-class students "as soon as they walk in the room . . . I just *know* it . . . it's like this kindred spirit" (stanza 8). Experiences of working-class marginality profoundly inform Anne's adult subjectivity, class consciousness, affective ties, and academic practice.

Conclusion

Anne's ability to find value in being working class and to feel proud of her working-class identity, in a society that views the working class as something to escape, is quite an accomplishment, particularly within an academic cultural milieu. Anne has transformed painful experiences of marginality into sociological insights. In doing so, she has engaged in what Janet Zandy (1995) calls "a process of self-creation that resists denial of working-class identity and consciousness, indeed, and uses working-class knowledge to produce culture and claim a place as a public intellectual" (7).

The embodiment of working-class subjectivities positions Anne and other academics from the working class differently than colleagues from upper-class backgrounds (Reay 1996). For this group, class issues remain deeply affective, at times evoking visceral reactions. Of elitism in the academy, Anne says: "sometimes it takes my breath away, you know it really does take my breath away, and I have to put, sometimes, a lid on my anger."

In my analysis of the last narrative, I suggested a relationship between narrative analysis and grounded theory. The concepts embedded in Anne's narratives (e.g., being hired help, saving face, valuing working-class lives) generalized across these interviews. For example, I identified excerpts related to the concept of valuing working-class lives in other participants' texts. Participants talked about the importance of valuing working-class lives and their efforts to do so through academic work. One participant argued that identifying what she valued from her working-class background as well as how she had been hurt and limited by it were important in her adult development (Jones 1998a). Examining concepts across participants using grounded theory expanded my understanding of concepts that were situated in narratives and articulated through narrative analysis. At the same time, the rich context in which concepts were embedded in particular stories informed my understanding of concepts across participants.

These narratives provide a glimpse of the ways in which working-class positionality is experienced and embodied by female academics from the working class. Analyses of these texts indicate that children are conscious of class relations, although limited in their ability to understand and articulate them, and that childhood experiences of class marginality continue to inform adult subjectivities (see also Dews and Law 1995; Tokarczyk and Fay 1993). Identifying as working class after achieving upward mobility is related to deeply affective, embodied experiences of class marginality as well as ongoing identifications with working-class families, friends, and students.

Notes

1. Notable exceptions to the neglect of class in psychology include the work of British psychologists Valerie Walkerdine (1996a, 1996b, 1997) and Diane Reay (1996, 1999) and U.S. psychologists Lyn Mikel Brown (1997) and Lois Weis and Michelle Fine (1993).

2. All of the participants identified as growing up working class. They were first-generation college graduates whose parents had been employed in blue-collar occupations (for a categorization of occupations see Gilbert and Kahl 1993).

3. See Hammersley and Atkinson (1983) and Seidman (1991) for a description of interviewing that draws on phenomenology and ethnography.

4. As a way to mitigate the inequality of power between researchers and participants, feminists argue for a reflexive practice that involves self-disclosure and participant involvement in a collaborative process of interpretation (see, e.g., Allen and Baber 1992; Fine 1994; Langellier and Hall 1989; Morawski 1990; Reay 1996).

5. The practice of systematically soliciting feedback from participants about texts and the interpretation of texts is referred to as member checks (Lincoln and Guba 1985; Seidman 1991).

References

Allen, K. R., and K. M. Baber. 1992. Ethical and epistemological tensions in applying a postmodern perspective to feminist research. *Psychology of Women Quarterly* 16:1–15.

Aronowitz, S. 1992. *The politics of identity: Class, culture, and social movements.* New York: Routledge.

Bourdieu, P. 1985. *Outline of a theory of practice.* New York: Cambridge University Press.

Brennan, T. 1993. *History after Lacan.* New York: Routledge.

Brown, L. M. 1997. Performing femininities: Listening to white working-class girls in rural Maine. *Journal of Social Issues* 53 (4): 683–701.

Bruner, J. S. 1990. *Acts of meaning.* Cambridge, MA: Harvard University Press.

Charmaz, K. 1983. The grounded theory method: An explication and interpretation. In *Contemporary field research: A collection of readings,* ed. R. M. Emerson, 109–126. Prospect Heights, IL: Waveland Press.

Collins, P. H. 1990. *Black feminist thought: Knowledge, consciousness, and the politics of empowerment.* New York: Routledge.

Dews, C. L. B., and C. L. Law, eds. 1995. *This fine place so far from home: Voices of academics from the working class.* Philadelphia: Temple University Press.

Elliott, A. 1992. *Social theory and psychoanalysis in transition: Self and society from Freud to Kristeva.* Cambridge, MA: Blackwell.

Fine, M. 1994. Working the hyphens: Reinventing self and other in qualitative research. In *Handbook of qualitative research,* eds. N. K. Denzin and Y. S. Lincoln, 70–82. Thousand Oaks, CA: Sage.

Gee, J. P. 1991. A linguistic approach to narrative. *Journal of Narrative and Life History* 1:15–39.

Gilbert, D., and J. A. Kahl. 1993. *The American class structure: A new synthesis.* Belmont, CA: Wadsworth.

Glaser, B., and A. Strauss. 1967. *The discovery of grounded theory: Strategies for qualitative research.* Chicago: Aldine.

Hammersley, M., and P. Atkinson. 1983. *Ethnography: Principles in practice.* London: Routledge.

Harré, R. 1995. The necessity of personhood as embodied being. *Theory and Psychology* 5 (3): 369–373.

Helms, J. E. 1993. *Black and white racial identity: Theory, research, and practice.* Westport, CT: Praeger Publishers.

Jones, S. J. 1998a. Subjectivity and class consciousness: The development of class identity. *Journal of Adult Development* 5 (3): 145–162.

———. 1998b. *Narrating multiple selves and embodying subjectivity: Female academics from the working class.* Ann Arbor, MI: UMI Dissertation Services.

Langellier, K. M., and D. L. Hall. 1989. Interviewing women: A phenomenological approach to feminist communication research. In *Doing research on women's communication: Perspectives on theory and method,* eds. K. Carter and C. Spitzack, 193–220. Norwood, NJ: Ablex.

Leahy, R. L. 1983. The development of the conception of social class. In *The child's construction of social inequality,* ed. R. L. Leahy, 79–107. New York: Academic Press.

Lincoln, Y. S., and E. G. Guba. 1985. *Naturalistic inquiry.* Beverly Hills, CA: Sage.

Maxwell, J. A. 1996. *Qualitative research design: An interactive approach.* Thousand Oaks, CA: Sage.

Maxwell, J. A., and B. A. Miller. 1996. *Categorization and contextualization in qualitative data analysis.* Unpublished manuscript.

Miller, J. B. 1986. *Toward a new psychology of women.* 2d ed. Boston: Beacon Press.

Mishler, E. G. 1986. *Research interviewing: Context and narrative.* Cambridge, MA: Harvard University Press.

———. 1992. Work, identity, and narrative: An artist-craftsman's story. In *Storied lives: The cultural politics of self-understanding,* eds. G. C. Rosenwald and R. L. Ochberg, 21–40. New Haven, CT: Yale University Press.

Morawski, J. G. 1990. Toward the unimagined: Feminism and epistemology in psychology. In *Making a difference: Psychology and the construction of gender,* eds. R. T. Hare-Mustin and J. Maracek, 150–183. New Haven, CT: Yale University Press.

Reay, D. 1996. Dealing with difficult differences: Reflexivity and social class in feminist research. *Feminism and Psychology* 6 (3): 443–456.

———. 1999. "Class Acts": Educational involvement and psycho-sociological class processes. *Feminism and Psychology* 9 (1): 89–106.

Reinharz, S. 1992. *Feminist methods in social research.* New York: Oxford University Press.

Riessman, C. K. 1993. *Narrative Analysis.* Newbury Park, CA: Sage.

Ryan, J., and C. Sackrey. 1996. *Strangers in paradise: Academics from the working class.* 2d ed. Boston: South End Press.

Sampson, E. E. 1996. Establishing embodiment in psychology. *Theory and Psychology* 6 (4): 601–624.

Seidman, I. E. 1991. *Interviewing as qualitative research: A guide for researchers in education and the social sciences.* New York: Teachers College Press.

Spelman, E. V. 1988. *Inessential woman: Problems of exclusion in feminist thought.* Boston: Beacon Press.

Steedman, C. 1994. *Landscape for a good woman: A story of two lives.* New Brunswick, NJ: Rutgers University Press.

Stewart, A. J. 1994. Toward a feminist strategy for studying women's lives. In *Women creating lives: Identities, resilience, and resistance,* eds. C. E. Franz and A. J. Stewart, 11–35. Boulder, CO: Westview Press.

Strauss, A., and J. Corbin. (1990). *Basics of qualitative research: Grounded theory procedures and techniques.* Newbury Park, CA: Sage.

Tokarczyk, M. M., and E. A. Fay, eds. 1993. *Working-class women in the academy: Laborers in the knowledge factory.* Amherst: University of Massachusetts Press.

Walkerdine, V. 1996a. Subjectivity and social class: New directions for feminist psychology. *Feminism and Psychology: Special Issue on Class* 6 (3): 355–360.

———. 1996b. Working-class women: Psychological and social aspects of survival. In *Feminist social psychologies: International perspectives,* ed. S. Wilkinson, 145–162. Buckingham, England: Open University Press.

Walkerdine, V. 1997. *Daddy's girl: Young girls and popular culture*. Cambridge, MA: Harvard University Press.

Weis, L., and M. Fine, eds. 1993. *Beyond silenced voices: Class, race, and gender in United States schools*. Albany: State University of New York Press.

Zandy, J., ed. 1995. *Liberating memory: Our work and our working-class consciousness*. New Brunswick, NJ: Rutgers University Press.

Zwerling, L. S., and H. B. London, eds. 1992. *First generation students: Confronting the cultural issues*. San Francisco: Jossey-Bass Publishers.

11

▪   ▪   ▪   ▪   ▪   ▪   ▪   ▪   ▪

Phenomenological and Participatory Research on Schizophrenia

Recovering the Person in Theory and Practice

Larry Davidson, David A. Stayner,
Stacey Lambert, Peter Smith,
and William H. Sledge

LOSS OF THE SELF has long been considered a core component of schizophrenia (Auerbach and Blatt 1996; Davidson and Strauss 1992). Most theories of the disorder conceptualize this loss of self as an intrinsic element of the disease process. Recently, however, a growing body of first-person accounts has suggested that for the person with schizophrenia there may be external sources of the loss of self embedded within the mental health system and the broader community (Davidson in press; Deegan 1992). These sources include the stigma that continues to accrue to mental illness in popular culture; patronizing attitudes and practices that have been transferred from long-term state hospitals into community settings; and models of treatment that focus on pathology and dysfunction to the exclusion of processes of improvement, leaving little room for the person to assume an active role in coping with the disorder (Davidson and Strauss

1992, 1995; Estroff 1989, 1995). Taken together, these influences converge to promote a stereotype of the person with schizophrenia as a passive, inept "empty shell" of the person she or he used to be. This stereotype both discourages clinicians from seeking out the person "behind" the illness and conveys to people with schizophrenia that there is little they can do on their own behalf but entrust their plight to the ameliorative efforts of others (e.g., North 1987).

In contrast to this traditional view of mental illness as a pervasive and irremediably incapacitating condition, both rigorous, large-sample, long-term follow-up studies (e.g., Davidson and McGlashan in press; Lin and Kleinman 1988; McGlashan 1988) and smaller sample, intensive studies (e.g., Davidson and Strauss 1992) have demonstrated that a significant proportion of people with schizophrenia improve over time (Harding, Strauss, and Zubin 1992). These studies identify a range of factors that facilitate improvement that are related directly to the person's efforts in coping with the disorder (Strauss et al. 1987) Our research has suggested that the organizing principle that brings these various factors together into a coherent whole is the reconstruction of a sense of self as a social agent (Davidson and Strauss 1992; Davidson in press). In this view, recovery involves reclaiming an effective sense of social agency out of the fragments of disorder, despite the other, external threats to self.

In this chapter, we argue that conventional approaches to research on mental illness provide yet one more source of the loss of self, unwittingly undermining rather than promoting recovery by treating the person with the disorder as a passive object to be investigated and acted upon by others. We present a research approach that promotes, rather than undermines, recovery by eliciting and fostering a functional sense of self utilizing phenomenological and participatory research methods that focus on the agency of the person with the disorder, and involving him or her as an active collaborator in the research enterprise. We provide an example of the application of these methods in addressing the vexing problem of recidivism in the treatment of schizophrenia. In conclusion, we suggest that the application of these methods for and with people with mental illness not only will contribute important knowledge to our understanding of these disorders, but also can contribute significantly to the recovery of the person with the disorder.

The Problem of the "Revolving Door"

Despite progress in treating mental illness, rehospitalization continues to occur at a problematic rate, with current estimates ranging from 30 to 50 percent during the first year following discharge (Klinkenberg and Calsyn 1996; Wasylenki 1994; Weiden and Olfson 1995). Families, clinicians, administrators, and public policy makers alike have become more concerned with the phenomenon of the "revolving door" patient; that is, the person who experiences recurrent inpatient admissions and appears unable to maintain tenure in the community (Coterill and Thomas 1993; Pfieffer, O'Malley, and Shott 1996).

Although empirical literature suggests that rehospitalization may be due as much to social and environmental factors as to clinical ones (e.g., Green 1988; Kent and Yellowlees 1995), conventional approaches to preventing rehospitalization have focused on preventing relapse, assuming that people end up back in the hospital due to exacerbations of their disorder. Based largely on the deficit and dysfunction model of treatment, these approaches have focused almost exclusively on the signs and symptoms of the disorder within a narrow medical model. They have been primarily clinical and psychoeducational in nature, and have involved educating both patients and their families about the nature of serious mental illness, the need for medication, the ongoing vulnerability to stress, and the use of problem-solving strategies to decrease stress and the level of "expressed emotion" in the family environment (Anderson, Hogarty, and Reiss 1980; Falloon 1985; Goldstein 1994; Leff and Vaughn 1981). The most recent advance in this line of investigation has been to develop strategies for educating patients and their families about the early warning signs of relapse and involving them in a close monitoring of symptoms in order to intervene early in the process of decompensation to avert full-blown episodes of the disorder. This approach of "prodromal recognition" and early intervention has shown some promise in reducing relapse rates (Birchwood 1995; Herz and Lamberti 1995).

A Failed Attempt

Situated within an academic medical center, our first attempt to address the "revolving door" problem at our own urban community mental health center was based on this conventional, clinical approach. We instituted a system that closely monitored early detection of signs and symptoms and early intervention to prevent relapse for people with histories of two or more hospitalizations within the previous year. During their inpatient stay, we educated these individuals about their disorders, assisted them in identifying their unique "relapse signature," the unique pattern of early warning signs and symptoms that characteristically precede an episode for a given individual, and we got them involved with their outpatient clinician in developing an "action plan" that stipulated what they should do in the case of the appearance of their relapse signature in order to avert a full-blown episode. While some of this work was done one-to-one between a patient and his or her clinician, we also started twice-weekly "relapse prevention" groups as the primary locus for disseminating this approach. In addition to these groups, which were conducted in the inpatient units, we instituted twice-weekly "relapse prevention" groups in the outpatient clinic in order to provide for close monitoring of symptoms following discharge. Our intent was to engage people in these groups while they were still in the hospital, in the hope that they would continue to attend following discharge.

For the first three months of this initiative, participants completed the relapse signature checklists and participated in both inpatient and outpatient groups *while* in the hospital. Not a single person (out of the first thirty-six who were eligible), however, returned to the outpatient relapse prevention groups following discharge. And as a group, their rate of readmission continued as before. As the ineffectiveness of this program became increasingly evident, we evaluated our initial approach to recidivism and discovered that it had a number of serious limitations.

We have come to understand that these limitations primarily derived from the way we had defined the problem of recidivism. Although the problem of people recycling through acute inpatient stays and appearing unable to adapt to community living was of significant concern to a number of different stake-holders—including policy makers, clinical administrators, clinicians, family members, and patients themselves—our initial conceptualization of the problem was derived from only one of these perspectives: the clinical one. This conceptualization focused solely on the disorder per se, assuming that it was primarily because of their disorder that people were readmitted. Such a view not only did not address the social and material environment to which people returned following discharge from the hospital, but it also did not take into account the person's own perspective. There was little room within such a view, for example, for the possibility that people might choose to return to the hospital as an alternative to life on the streets. By implying that the best people could hope for was to minimize and contain the impact of their disorder by monitoring for and preventing relapses, this view also provided little basis for encouraging people to pursue their own recovery. The problem was seen not so much as the fact that people were getting stuck recycling through recurrent, brief inpatient care and not getting on with their lives, but that their recurrent use of high-cost inpatient care was taking up a disproportionate amount of scarce resources. Redirecting some of these resources to outpatient care (in the form of prodromal recognition and early intervention) might produce a net cost savings, but it did little to promote recovery or community adaptation.

Had the problem been defined primarily from the perspective of the families or the patients themselves, different interventions might have followed. We became interested in learning how people with mental illness might view the problem of recidivism differently, and how they might be involved in a fuller and more constructive way in addressing it. We also were interested in learning what possible functions acute hospitalizations might play in their lives, and if we might be of more assistance to them in their efforts to establish a life in the community. To achieve these aims, we adopted a phenomenological-participatory action research strategy to involve the patients in helping us to understand better what precipitated their readmissions and to develop a new approach to preventing rehospitalization and enhancing community adaptation.

Phenomenological-Participatory Action Research Approach

Our research strategy followed the principles of phenomenological and participatory approaches (Davidson 1987; Davidson 1992; Husserl [1954] 1970; Rogers and Palmer-Erbs 1994; Whyte 1989, 1991) and involved several elements. First, we tracked down twelve recidivist patients to elicit descriptions of their experiences of rehospitalization, the circumstances of this event, and the functions it served in their lives. Recidivism was defined as having had two or more hospitalizations within the last year. We elicited these descriptions by conducting open-ended, phenomeno-logical interviews. The interviews were narrative to allow the participants to describe their experiences leading up to, during, and following this most recent hospitalization, rather than having them address specific questions or issues that we assumed to be relevant (Davidson and Cosgrove 1991). Next, we asked people to focus on their experiences of the new relapse pre-vention interventions in which they participated during their hospitaliza-tion, the factors that led to their not participating after discharge, and what they would find more useful in the future.

Second, we attempted to understand the participants' experiences in their own terms and from their own perspective. That is, our analysis of these data focused on the meaningfulness of the experiences *for the par-ticipants* as opposed to *for us* (i.e., in terms of how their experiences did or did not fit our own theoretical preconceptions regarding the phenome-non). We chose two means to accomplishing this task: (1) utilizing estab-lished qualitative-phenomenological data analytic procedures designed to ground our interpretations in the participants' own life contexts, and (2) involving the participants themselves in understanding their responses.

The established qualitative-phenomenological approach used in this study involved several steps. All of the open-ended, narrative interviews that were conducted were audiotaped and then transcribed. The interview transcripts were then distributed to three of the investigators, two of whom were experienced qualitative researchers and one of whom was a postdoctoral fellow learning to conduct qualitative research. Each of the investigators analyzed the transcripts independently; all three then came together to discuss their findings and reach a consensus.

Phenomenological analysis of the transcripts involved two levels of re-view: within each individual and then across individuals. First, each inves-tigator reviewed each transcript to identify and code the interview data for recurrent themes that characterized each individual's experience, then brought the themes together through a "cut and paste" method into an edited synthesis for that participant. The edited synthesis followed a nar-rative structure, placing the recurrent and salient themes identified in the interview in the temporal context of the participant's ongoing life, thereby retelling the participant's story in a thematic way. The investigators then met to review each of their edited syntheses for each participant, comparing and contrasting the themes they had each identified and coming to a general agreement on the operative and important themes in each story. Areas of disagreement between investigators typically involved explicating implicit meanings identified by some but not all of the investigators, rather than what was already explicitly stated in the interview. In cases such as these, the discussion and consensus that developed focused on how much of what was implicit in the interview data could be explicated with confidence, and how much remained speculative and required further inquiry.

Once the investigators had reached a consensus on an edited synthesis for each of the interview transcripts, they reviewed the twelve edited syntheses as a whole, first independently and then as a group. This review entailed identifying themes that were common across the participants, as well as areas in which the participants might differ. Each investigator composed a general synthesis of these themes, which once again retained the narrative structure of the edited synthesis. The investigators then compared and contrasted these syntheses to produce a general structural synthesis of the findings that held across investigators (Davidson 1994; Giorgi 1970; Wertz 1983). This synthesis consisted of four major themes that are described below.

Once we had completed an initial draft of the major themes we had identified and their interrelationships in the form of a general structural synthesis, we reconvened a group of the original participants and asked for their feedback on our tentative understanding of their responses. We asked them to identify areas of importance that we had missed, and to comment on whether or not we had captured their experiences and concerns in the way we had framed the themes that we had identified. The descriptions we provide below incorporate their feedback.

Following this participatory model, the final stage of our research strategy involved working collaboratively with the participants to translate the implications of these findings into designing a new intervention. We return to describing this final step following our presentation of the findings from the interviews.

Attractions of the Hospital

The first and most striking feature of these interviews was the fact that our agenda, as clinicians, of preventing rehospitalization was not shared by the patients. The open-ended, narrative structure of the interviews allowed participants to describe several attractions of the hospital that made it a place they appreciated being able to return to when needed. These attractions included safety, respite, food, and privacy; several people described hospitalization as a "vacation." Even one person who was hospitalized against his will described it as a "forced vacation." Stated another: "It's like a vacation, you take some time out, and you know, in a place where there is privacy and there is care and there are lots of people to listen to you." This latter element—having people listen to you—seemed most important to participants. They valued the care and concern they experienced while in the hospital. For instance, one person stated: "You see at home you don't have to listen to nobody but yourself. When you come into a hospital it's different. You're around a whole bunch of people that care about you." This same person went on to explain that his sense of being cared about had grown steadily during each of three hospitalizations: "The first time I was scared, the second time I had been here before and I knew what to expect, the third time it was like coming home again. Everyone was like greeting me at the door. . . . The third time was the best I think."

Impoverished Community Life

The appeal of the hospital became apparent when we noted the contrast between participants' descriptions of their stays there and the descriptions they offered of their lives outside of the hospital. For example, recognizing that some of these individuals had been living in homeless shelters where the beds were twelve inches apart shed useful light for us on why they would describe living in a hospital room with three strangers as offering them "privacy." In continuing the "vacation" theme, another person described rehospitalization as providing respite from his life in the community: it's "like hiding away. Where I live it's inner city, so I felt that I had a better chance living here than living in society." Described another participant: "My living situation? I was homeless, broke, unemployed, the same harsh feeling everyday."

The starkest contrast drawn between life in the hospital and life in the community, however, was again in the area of caring and social isolation.

Participants' descriptions of life in the community were striking in their *absence* of any mention of supportive friends or family. Only one person mentioned the support of a parent with whom he lived. A few people told poignant stories of their longing for reunification with their own children, and the problems and obstacles they experienced in this regard. Clearly, this need to have someone to talk to led participants to appreciate having a doctor show up at their bedroom door each morning to ask how they had slept the night before while in the hospital. Another participant said he felt "popular" because so many people on the unit wanted to know how he was feeling. This sense of being "popular" in the hospital provided a welcome relief from feelings of being alone and abandoned on the outside, where there may have been no one who even knew or cared that they existed, much less how they had slept the night before.

Powerlessness, Fatalism, and Apathy

In addition to feeling alone and abandoned, many participants expressed a profound sense of powerlessness and fatalism in the face of their symptoms and other problems in living. Asked if there was anything that she could do to cope with her illness or make things better, for instance, one person could only state: "Just take my medicine and pray." Far from feeling that they could act early to prevent relapse, participants drew a blank when asked what they could do to prevent future readmissions. Said another: "I can't answer that one. Nobody knows the future, you know. I could be talking to you today and end up back in the hospital tomorrow."

This lack of control extended beyond their symptoms to their lives in general, as summed up by one participant whose mental illness was simply the last item in a list of things in his life that he could not change: "[it's] like living in poverty all your life, being oppressed, no income, unemployment, no good jobs, you know what I'm saying: guns, drugs, and all of that." For a few, even the suffering associated with their symptoms and the conditions in which they lived was giving way to numbness and apathy. Said one participant: "My reaction to my suffering is less, less fierce, now I'm becoming cold about it . . . colder and colder. I don't mean I don't care no more, but you know I'm living in this situation for a long time and my reaction to it is like numbed."

Disconnection from Mental Health Services

The last major theme we identified was that participants saw mental health treatment as being of little use to them in dealing with the situations described above. While most spoke of taking their medications as perhaps the only thing they could do, few expressed even a rudimentary understanding of their illness or how their pharmacologic or other treatments might be helpful. For example, one person could only state: "they say I'm a schizophrenic"; another denied any knowledge of her illness and only saw one thing she could do when she felt that she was getting worse: "I just know when I get too sick . . . it's time to come" to the hospital. As we described above, however, coming to the hospital was described primarily in terms of the respite and care it provided rather than the treatment that would be received there. What clinicians conceptualize as providing treatment appeared to be experienced by the patients themselves more like classroom exercises for which they would be graded, having no more relevance to, or impact on, their symptoms and lives than a history lesson. One participant, when asked about the treatments he received in the hospital, said: "Well, it was something like this where they ask you questions. It was like going to school [and] I passed . . . I passed with flying colors. Everybody loved me after I left that place." Like good students, some individuals were quite willing to follow the instructions of their treaters while in the hospital. Said another person of her treatment: "I loved it, because they knew what was wrong with me, and they were trying their best to help me; so I agreed with everything they said. . . . There were a lot of meetings, a lot of doctors, you know, doctors come around every morning to talk to you to see how you're doing. You get your levels, your levels are one to five, one, two, three, four, five; when you come in you're a one. To go, the goal is to leave as a five."

This kind of compliance with unit routines did not translate into meaningful connections for people between treatment and coping with their disorders. When speaking of symptoms, medication, or coping, participants unanimously described their treaters as the only ones who carried responsibility for understanding their illness and treatment. Even a person who described how treaters had varied in their diagnoses, and hence in their conversations about her symptoms and their treatment, felt no investment in this disagreement, appearing to be a passive spectator of a relatively uninteresting dispute between distant, well-meaning experts. Most people described either resisting treatment regimens—citing, for instance, unwanted side effects of medications or their unwillingness to accept a diagnostic label—or spoke of their efforts simply to comply with whatever was said or ordered by treaters in order to follow the path of least resistance. In no case did the participants appear to think that any of these decisions would have any real bearing on their life or suffering.

In keeping with this general tone of disconnection from treatment per se, participants saw no connection between their outpatient treatment and their risk for rehospitalization. Only one person could suggest how his outpatient treater might help him stay out of the hospital, and this was to state emphatically: "he can stay the hell away from me; that's what he can do." With this attitude toward outpatient treatment, it is not surprising that participants said that they did not see it worth the effort and inconvenience required to obtain transportation to the mental health center to make it to their outpatient appointments.

A Community Integration Approach

The participants' stories generated several implications for revising our initial intervention. It was evident from these interviews that efforts to educate people about their disorders and involve them in the process of identifying early warning signs would be extremely difficult to the degree that they felt hopeless about their possibilities for improvement and helpless to do anything on their own behalf. These efforts would be further undermined to the degree that people felt disconnected from treatment and saw no direct benefit from remaining in treatment once discharged. Lastly, prevention of rehospitalization would remain the agenda solely of clinicians and administrators until patients were able to find the appealing features of the hospital—such as respite, privacy, safety, and, above all, care—in the community.

We began our efforts to define and develop an alternative approach by focusing on this last implication and what the participants themselves identified as useful in this regard. Rather than emphasizing our need to prevent readmission, we followed the lead of the participants in assuming that restoring a decent quality of life for themselves in the community would make the hospital less appealing. Our further discussions with the patients and other mental health consumers who had been hospitalized previously but were now leading productive lives suggested several directions for program development to address the restoration of community life.

First, we needed to find a way to address the social isolation and loneliness people experienced in order to provide a sense of belonging in the community that paralleled the feeling of camaraderie and care they experienced inside the hospital. Second, to address their feelings of powerlessnes, fatalism, and apathy in relation to their disorders and lives, we had to find a way to instill hope and provide concrete evidence of the possibilities of recovery and of people achieving some level of mastery over their condition and problems. And lastly, to address the disconnection from treatment, it was crucial for us to find ways to demonstrate that treatment could be of direct benefit—that it could be used in an active, constructive way that enabled people to reclaim their lives.

To achieve these aims, we made several substantive changes in the "relapse prevention" program based on what the participants identified in their interviews as being useful to them. To address their concerns about transportation and their desire to look beyond their disorders, we moved the twice-weekly outpatient groups outside of the mental health center to a community location and shifted the focus from preventing relapse to helping people establish a life for themselves in the community. To address their loneliness and desire for companionship, we placed a core emphasis on the mutual support participants could provide for each other. We fostered the development of a sense of belonging and cohesiveness, both within and outside of the group, as we encouraged people to spend time with each other doing things together in the community. As a result of these changes, the common task of the group members quickly shifted from preventing hospital readmissions to helping each other stay in the community in order to remain a member of the group.

We further strengthened this mutual support component, as well as overcame barriers posed by lack of transportation, by deploying mental health consumers as staff to pick people up and bring them to the group. Based on the participants' desires to be more connected to community activities and resources as well as to each other, these consumer-providers also began to organize and host a weekly social and recreational outing in the community (without clinical staff). These outings had as their only functions allowing participants to experience the positive features of community living, to have fun, and to become friends. In addition to fostering mutual support and community integration, the consumer-providers helped clinical staff to lead the twice-weekly groups, and in this role instilled hope and acted as role models for the possibility of recovery.

Lastly, to address participants' basic needs and feelings of powerlessness, we provided lunch once a week, with plans for what to have for lunch and where to go on outings decided by the participants themselves, offering them tangible experiences of their own agency. In this context, and with the consumer staff as role models, we were able to help people reframe their symptoms as barriers to having a fulfilling life in the community and to offer them coping strategies and other treatments, such as medications, as useful tools for their recovery.

Initially, we conceptualized this revised intervention as an outreach and engagement program to help people establish roots in a network of supportive relationships and enjoyable activities in the community. We expected people to participate for an average of three months following discharge, by which time we expected them to have consolidated their connections to ongoing treatment and supports. Due to this short-term, engagement function, we placed strong emphasis during these first three months on increasing the connection between participants and their outpatient clinicians; for example, staff members would drop participants off at their clinician's office after groups or outings.

As the three-month period came to a close for the first group to participate in the new intervention, however, participants began to express concerns that they would lose the gains they had made if they were deprived of each others' company and assistance and could no longer attend the weekly groups and outings. In the collaborative spirit we had tried to foster to this point, we again asked the members of the group what they would find useful as a next step in their process of community integration. We explained that there was a steady flow of people coming out of the hospital who needed to be invited into the group, and that we had a limited capacity due to staffing constraints. Around this same time, we also began to experience budgetary problems in the program and informed the group members that we were running out of funds for the community outings. We asked them to join us in problem-solving in relation to these two issues.

Rather than feeling disappointed or demoralized, as we might have expected, the participants rallied and made a number of concrete suggestions. They offered to reduce expenditures on the outings to make the money last longer, hold outings more infrequently, and/or participate in free activities as long as they could continue to spend time together. In addition, they participated in a presentation of the program to the administrative and clinical staff of the mental health center, describing how useful the program had been to them in making friends, beginning to reclaim their lives, and—as a by-product—staying out of the hospital. They spoke eloquently about the importance of the community outings and their wish to continue to have access to funds in order to preserve this valued activity. As a result of this presentation, in combination with the preliminary data that suggested the effectiveness of the program, new funds were allocated to the program to cover the additional expenses of future outings so that they could continue for the remainder of the fiscal year.

In lieu of discontinuing their involvement in the group program at the end of the first three months following their discharge, the participants also suggested that they continue to meet as a group but reduce the frequency of meetings to once per week. They would no longer be provided with a free lunch and would have to manage their own transportation to and from the group, but could continue to meet with each other to provide mutual support and assistance in adapting to community living. Additional staff resources of a psychology trainee and a consumer peer counselor were provided to facilitate this new group in response to the participants' request. The participants entitled this group "Friends and Recovery," and initiated a group ritual of holding "graduation" parties, replete with balloons and a cake, for each participant to complete the first three-month intervention without a readmission.

Preliminary outcome data from the first six months of this program are encouraging regarding our initial goal of preventing rehospitalization among recidivist patients, even though it had at this point become an ancillary goal of the program. Compared to a similar group of recidivist patients who did not participate in the intervention, but who had a roughly equivalent number of readmissions and days in the hospital prior to the index admission, readmissions during the first three months after discharge among the first fifteen people to participate were reduced by almost 70 percent, and days spent in the hospital during this same period were reduced by more than 90 percent (Davidson et al. 1997).

Discussion

The "revolving door" phenomenon of recurrent, acute inpatient admissions has provided a good test case for the feasibility and utility of involving people with serious mental illness as collaborators in the research enterprise. This project has demonstrated the importance of treating people with schizophrenia as social agents pursuing their own agendas in trying to carve out a life for themselves. The conventional, clinical view of rehospitalization missed the mark by assuming that readmissions were primarily caused by the deficits associated with the disorder and may also have exacerbated people's preexisting feelings of powerlessness and helplessness over their condition. Eliciting their perspective on this problem and involving them in finding solutions to it appear to have initiated a reversal of this process, offering compelling evidence of their ability to make decisions and act constructively on their own behalf, as well as to benefit their peers.

Adopting this perspective on schizophrenia research does not preclude the complementary usefulness of conventional, objective methods. What it does suggest, however, is that for any method to be useful in identifying factors in recovery it first needs to be grounded in an understanding of the experience and role of the person with the disorder. Recovering the role of the person with the disorder in both our theory and our method may provide a basis for developing research that eventually promotes the recovery of the person in our practice as well.

References

Anderson, C. M., G. Hogarty, and D. J. Reiss. 1980. Family treatment of adult schizophrenic patients: A psychoeducational approach. *Schizophrenia Bulletin* 6:490–505.

Andreasen, N. C. 1984. *The broken brain: The biological revolution in psychiatry.* New York: Harper and Row.

Auerbach, J. S., and S. J. Blatt. 1996. Self-representation in severe psychopathology: The role of reflexive self-awareness. *Psychoanalytic Psychology* 13:297–341.

Birchwood, M. 1995. Early intervention in psychotic relapse: Cognitive approaches to detection and management. *Behavior Change* 12:2–19.

Cotterill, L., and R. Thomas. 1993. A typology of care episodes experienced by people with schizophrenia in an English town. *Social Science and Medicine* 36:1587–1595.

Davidson, L. 1987. What is the appropriate source for psychological explanation? *Humanistic Psychologist* 15:150–166.

———. 1992. Developing an empirical phenomenological approach to schizophrenia research. *Journal of Phenomenological Psychology* 23:3–15.

———. 1994. Phenomenological research in schizophrenia: From philosophical anthropology to empirical science. *Journal of Phenomenological Psychology* 25:104–130.

———. In press. Vulnerability and destiny in schizophrenia: Hearkening to the voice of the person. *L'Evolution Psychiatrique.*

Davidson, L., and L. Cosgrove. 1991. Psychologism and phenomenological psychology revisited, Part I: The liberation from naturalism. *Journal of Phenomenological Psychology* 22:87–108.

Davidson, L., and T. H. McGlashan. In press. The varied outcomes of schizophrenia. *Canadian Journal of Psychiatry.*

Davidson, L., D. A. Stayner, M. Chinman, S. Lambert, R. Weingarten, M. S. Levine, J. K. Tebes, and W. H. Sledge. 1997. Mental illness as a psychiatric disability, II: Innovative outpatient alternatives to engage individuals with serious mental illness in treatment. Address to the First International Conference on the Rehabilitation Process for People with Severe Mental Illness, Bogota, Colombia.

Davidson, L., and J. S. Strauss. 1992. Sense of self in recovery from severe mental illness. *British Journal of Medical Psychology* 65:131–145.

———. 1995. Beyond the biopsychosocial model: Integrating disorder, health, and recovery. *Psychiatry* 58:43–55.

Deegan, P. E. 1992. The Independent Living Movement and people with psychiatric disabilities: Taking back control over our own lives. *Psychosocial Rehabilitation Journal* 15:3–19.

Estroff, S. E. 1989. Self, identity, and subjective experiences of schizophrenia: In search of the subject. *Schizophrenia Bulletin* 15:189–196.

———. 1995. Commentary on "The experiences of long-stay inpatients returning to the community." *Psychiatry* 58:133–135.

Falloon, I. R. H. 1985. *Family management of schizophrenia.* Baltimore: Johns Hopkins University Press.

Fromm-Reichmann, F. 1950. *Principles of intensive psychotherapy.* Chicago: University of Chicago Press.

Giorgi, A. 1970. *Psychology as a human science: A phenomenologically based approach.* New York: Harper and Row.

Goldstein, M. J. 1994. Psychoeducational and family therapy in relapse prevention. *Acta Psychiatrica Scandinavica* 89 (suppl 382): 54–57.

Green, J. 1988. Frequent rehospitalization and noncompliance with treatment. *Hospital and Community Psychiatry* 39:963–966.

Harding, C. M., J. S. Strauss, and J. Zubin. 1992. Chronicity in schizophrenia: Revisited. *British Journal of Psychiatry* 161:27–37.

Herz, M. I., and J. S. Lamberti. 1995. Prodromal symptoms and relapse prevention. *Schizophrenia Bulletin* 21:541–550.

Husserl, E. [1954] 1970. *The crisis of European sciences and transcendental phenomenology,* trans. D. Carr. Evanston, IL: Northwestern University Press.

Kent, S., and P. Yellowlees. 1995. The relationship between social factors and frequent use of psychiatric services. *Australian and New Zealand Journal of Psychiatry* 29:403–408.

Klinkenberg, W. D., and R. J. Calsyn. 1996. Predictors of receipt of aftercare and recidivism among persons with severe mental illness: A review. *Psychiatric Services* 47:487–496.

Leff, J. A., and C. Vaughn. 1981. The role of maintenance therapy and expressed emotion in relapse of schizophrenia: A two-year follow-up. *British Journal of Psychiatry* 139:102–104.

Lin, K. M., and A. M. Kleinman. 1988. Psychopathology and clinical course of schizophrenia: A cross-cultural perspective. *Schizophrenia Bulletin* 14:555–567.

McGlashan, T. H. 1988. A selective review of recent North American long-term followup studies of schizophrenia. *Schizophrenia Bulletin* 14:515–42.

North, C. 1987. *Welcome silence: My triumph over schizophrenia.* New York: Simon and Schuster.

Pfieffer, S. I., D. S. O'Malley, and S. Shott. 1996. Factors associated with the outcome of adults treated in psychiatric hospitals: A synthesis of findings. *Psychiatric Services* 47:263–269.

Rogers, E. S., and V. Palmer-Erbs. 1994. Participatory action research: Implications for research and evaluation in psychiatric rehabilitation. *Psychosocial Rehabilitation Journal* 18:3–12.

Schilder, P. 1976. *On psychoses.* New York: International Universities Press.

Strauss, J. S., C. M. Harding, H. Hafez, and P. Lieberman. 1987. The role of the patient in recovery from psychosis. In *Psychosocial treatment of schizophrenia,* eds. J. S. Strauss, W. Boker, and H. Brenner, 160–166. New York: Hans Huber Publishers.

Wasylenki, D. A. 1994. The cost of schizophrenia. *Canadian Journal of Psychiatry* 39 (suppl 2): S65–S69.

Weiden, P. J., and M. Olfson. 1995. Cost of relapse in schizophrenia. *Schizophrenia Bulletin* 21:419–429.

Wertz, F. J. 1983. From everyday to psychological description: Analyzing the moments of a qualitative data analysis. *Journal of Phenomenological Psychology* 14:197–241.

Whyte, W. F. 1989. Advancing scientific knowledge through participatory action research. *Sociological Forum* 4:367–385.

———. 1991. *Participatory action research.* Newbury Park, CA: Sage Publications.

B. Participatory Action Research Methods

12

■ ■ ■ ■ ■ ■ ■ ■ ■

Activist Participatory Research and the Arts with Rural Mayan Women

Interculturality and Situated Meaning Making

M. Brinton Lykes

IN 1992 I AGREED to accompany a friend to her community of origin in the highlands of Guatemala. She had known of my previous work in Guatemala and had asked me to join a group of women in Chajul who sought to respond to some of the psychosocial effects of more than thirty-six years of war.[1] I have experienced some of the personal effects of living within a society deeply traumatized by war in the context of my more than fifteen years of community-based work in Guatemala. But, as a white, educated woman from the United States, whose government overthrew the democratically elected government of Guatemala in 1954, I am always aware of my situated "otherness" as I live and work among the Maya. My position as "situated other" within a praxis of solidarity informs my ongoing efforts to develop alternative methodologies for making meanings of these realities and participating with local actors in responding to problems in daily living (see, e.g., Lykes 1996).

In this chapter I analyze selected aspects of my experiences of living and working among these women as this work informs my questionings about participatory action research (PAR) strategies as resources for work among survivors of war and political violence. I draw upon these experiences to discuss some of the strengths and limitations of PAR practices within rural Guatemala. I conclude with a brief discussion of proposed criteria for evaluating participatory strategies in PAR that inform my ongoing work in Guatemala and more recent projects in the United States and South Africa. Throughout I strive to question these methods *in situ*, as well as my praxis as an activist researcher.

Living within Contexts of Ongoing War: Silence and Silencing

Researchers and human rights activists have documented the shifts from military to civilian victims characteristic of modern warfare. Seventy states were involved in more than ninety-three wars between 1990 and 1995 in which 5.5 million people were killed (Smith 1997). Many of these wars, such as the war in Guatemala, are internal struggles between popular revolutionary forces and a military that defends gross inequities in the distribution of economic resources within the country. The terror of war and state-sponsored violence creates a situation of "normal abnormality" (Martín-Baró 1989; Taussig 1987) or "terror as usual," in which "one moves in bursts between somehow accepting the situation as normal, only to be thrown into a panic or shocked into disorientation by an event, a rumor . . . something said or not said" (Taussig 1987, 8). The state thereby silences the population by exploiting their fear through terror. Yet, as I have argued elsewhere (see, e.g., Lykes 1996), silence has multiple meanings in the context of terror. State-imposed silencing is often met by the silence of the people (Lykes and Liem 1990). A Guatemalan Mayan educator reflected on this face of silence when she told me:

> We realize that the suffering [of the people] has been compounded by the effects of having to live in silence. By living in silence, I refer to how a Guatemalan is prohibited to talk about his/her suffering and is forced to keep his/her suffering secret. Anything to the contrary is not well accepted by others, and is, in fact, discouraged. For example, even we as teachers contribute to maintaining the silence when we say to our children: "Quiet, do

not talk about it; quiet do not comment on it," because these are the very topics that fill us with fear.[2]

As a response to counterinsurgency, silence is often an adaptive survival strategy. However, at the same time, it exacerbates people's feelings of isolation. It also interferes with Mayan communities' traditional forms of organizing and makes it difficult to develop and sustain social ties or to develop a community-based response. A deep lack of trust is evident in the individual, the family, the community, and the state. The self-silencing within the population complements and reinforces the government's "official story," making it nearly impossible to recognize what one "knows" has happened, for example, that one's child or spouse has been "disappeared." The signing of the Peace Accords between the Unidad Revolucionaria Nacional Guatemalteca, or National Revolutionary Union of Guatemala (URNG), and the Guatemalan government in December 1996 has created political and social spaces in which many who suffered the extreme terror described above have dared to tell their stories.

Narratives and storytelling have been significant resources for facilitating breaks within these multilayered silences. Since 1997, the Office on Human Rights of the Archdiocese of Guatemala (ODHAG 1998) and, more recently, the Commission for Historical Clarification (CEH 1999), established within the context of the Peace Accords and supported by the United Nations, have gathered thousands of testimonies from rural and urban Guatemalans who responded to invitations to speak about the unspeakable, in part because they hoped that by speaking out, they might help prevent such acts from recurring.

As a complement to these "official" testimonies, I have sought to make meaning about this terror and its effects by accompanying survivors in their struggles to encounter their embodied voices. These efforts draw heavily on PAR and on the creative arts. As a method, PAR facilitates the exploration of the complex relationships among silencing, silence, and voice. My work in Guatemala suggests that one cannot understand war and its effects there without approximating an understanding of its symbolic meanings as they resonate through a sense of time in which past and future converge, that is, in the seemingly never-ending present (see e.g., Lykes 1996; Melville and Lykes 1992). Hearing a survivor's testimony into speech (for the expression "hearing into speech," see Morton 1985) one enters into relationship, and what emerges is co-constructed dialogically, in time. That construction then becomes part of a shared story that both constrains and facilitates future storytelling. Other, more traditional, research methods, such as symptom checklists or structured interviews, often fail to capture both the particularity of each person's experience and the collective nature of loss within the Mayan context. As importantly, they miss the fact that decades of war have destroyed not only individual material bodies capable of symbolizing their reality, but also Mayan cultural symbols. The very process of making meaning is thereby at risk. The reality of war and the symbolic meanings of terror have necessitated a reconceptualization of trauma and, as importantly, an alternative methodology for "studying" its effects and multiple responses to it.

Responding to Violence through Participatory Action Research

Given the political, economic, and ethical realities of war and the criticisms of the adequacy of positivist social science for studying war and its effects, I proposed an activist participatory research model or "passionate scholarship" (see DuBois 1983; Lykes 1989) as a more adequate strategy for understanding and responding to the effects of war. Most simply, this is a process through which the researcher accompanies the participant or subject over time, participating and observing while providing resources to the participant and his or her community who, in turn, facilitate the researcher's understanding. (See Lykes 1996 for a more extensive comparison and critique of different research models for studying the effects of violence.) The relationship itself constitutes an action that is then constitutive of the survivor's multiple versions of survival. And, in relationship, I, as participant-researcher, am repositioned and challenged to re-vision myself as "other." This process reflects one's willingness to risk entering another's life and allowing him or her to enter one's own. Understanding and one's possibilities for continuing engagement are thus shaped by an experience of shared subjectivity. As importantly, one's self-understanding as researcher is re-framed.

I situate this model within the broader context of PAR as it has developed within Latin America, Asia, and Africa (see, e.g., Fals-Borda 1988; Fals-Borda and Rahman 1991) and the emancipatory pedagogical practices of Paulo Freire (see, e.g., Freire 1970), both of which were known within Guatemala when I began my work there. However, decades of war and state-sponsored violence had suppressed many Guatemalan communities' capacities to respond to their needs and organize on their own behalf. As significantly, many women in rural communities had little experience in identifying their needs or in participating as active spokespeople within the local community. Although the small group of women I joined in my initial work in Chajul shared a desire to enhance their skills and capacities for survival and resistance through educational and change-based practices that benefited themselves and their wider communities (see, e.g., Hoare, Levy, and Robinson 1993, for a discussion of PAR within native communities), they were less certain about the possibilities of engaging a wider group within the town. We relied heavily on local or indigenous knowledge systems in developing an activist research strategy to respond to the articulated desire of these leaders to "break the silence" enshrouding those affected by the ongoing war and create alternative resources for some of the many women and children forced to survive on their own as a consequence of the war.

"Creative Workshops for Children" constituted the core of an earlier action research program in rural Guatemala developed with health promoters, child care workers, and educators. We accompanied child survivors over the course of several years and developed a firmer knowledge base from which to make meaning of children's experiences of war and its effects (see Lykes 1994). The model emerged gradually, from several years of exchange, practice, and reflection with Argentines experienced in creative techniques for work with child survivors of "disappeared" parents, and with Guatemalan community leaders experienced in traditional and preventive health strategies.

The workshops were designed in part to facilitate communication and to help break silence. The initial commitment was to create a bounded space in which children and youth could begin to integrate theater, bodily movement and expressivity, the plastic arts, music, and words as resources for recovering their natural capacities to play (Winnicott 1982). We sought to create a context in which participants could project themselves and share thoughts, feelings, and fears or anxieties. The group is a context in which these techniques can be appropriated as means of communication. They enable one to take advantage of one's own resources, and of "the other" as resource. In this co-created group-space, creativity is a resource for developing the possibility of modifying one's relations, reestablishing previously destroyed social ties, symbolizing one's experiences of the terror through which one has lived, recuperating or reconstructing one's story, and searching for one's truth (Lapierre 1977; Pavlovsky, Martinez Bouquet, and Moccio 1985).

The group context enables the participant to move from the individual, personal tragedy toward a shared experience with the other, toward a sense of truth in the face of the effects of an organized violence that seeks to annul individual and collective identity. The group also enables me, as situated other, to be in relationship with survivors in this social space of Mayan collectivity. Creative productions from the group—which include art work (drawings, collages), creative storytelling, dramatizations, and masks—provide texts that serve as important resources for further analysis for the group, its coordinators, and me, the situated other and participant-researcher. For example, the group's coordinators read these texts and develop multiple understandings of the affective and cognitive lives of the participants and of themselves. A more systematic reading of the texts of multiple workshops creates a gestalt that moves beyond words and linear thinking to re-present some of the frequently silenced aspects of survivors' lives.

Engendering a Shift in Participatory Action Research

The Creative Workshops were an important resource for my work with women in Chajul. The initial group of six women grew to more than sixty, with participants ranging in age from sixteen to sixty-five. Most women were accompanied by at least one child, so we often worked with fifty women and more than a hundred children. Topics included women's fears about speaking Spanish, the "language of the oppressor," and desires to initiate economic development projects coupled with anxieties about adopting what were considered "men's work roles" within their town. Underlying much of the work were stories, still mostly unspoken, about what it had been like to live in a town occupied by the military, surrounded by the ruins of villages that some of the women had fled as soldiers burned them to the ground, sometimes in the wake of skirmishes with guerrilla organizations, other times having massacred all who had been caught in the town when the military arrived.

During 1993–1994, this group of Ixil women incorporated itself as the Asociación de la Mujer Maya Ixil—AK' SAQB'EB'AL (ADMI: the Association of Mayan Ixil Women—New Dawn) and coordinated a number of economic development and psychosocial assistance projects (see Lykes et al. 1999 for a description of the Association and its work). The Association now comprises a diverse group of women between the ages of sixteen and sixty-five, including members of every political party as well as some who are unaffiliated, and women whose first languages are Ixil or K' iché as well as those who speak one or two indigenous languages and Spanish. In terms of formal education, some participants have completed sixth grade, but most have attended school two years or less. The women's religious affiliations include Mayan traditionalists, several streams within Catholicism, and many Protestant and Evangelical churches and sects. Their work represents a tentative re-threading of community among a religiously, linguistically, politically, and generationally diverse group of women that has as one of its fundamental principles that all women are welcome to organize on behalf of themselves and their community.

I have served as a consultant to the organization, coordinating training workshops and collaborating in supervision of these ongoing community-based interventions. This work combines creative arts and traditional Mayan practices of drama and storytelling with the goal of providing contexts and opportunities for telling one's story of survival and analyzing one's social realities. The workshops have also served as contexts wherein older women within the group have remembered traditional practices, including, for example, rituals surrounding marriage proposals and childbirth, and shared them with young women for whom they were largely unknown. Many of this latter group had been raised during the war, when silencing and physical repression submerged many Mayan cultural practices.

The end of more than thirty-six years of war in Guatemala has afforded some women and men within the country opportunities to voice multiple versions of their survival of massacres, military occupation, internal displacement, extreme poverty, and exile. As these stories have begun to emerge, I have grown increasingly self-conscious about previous attempts at "recrafting" Mayan stories for "consumption" by "others" in English- or Spanish-language professional journals and books.

Although these stories were co-constructed over a dozen years of living and working in community-based projects using the participatory methods described above, their dissemination to a wider community inevitably gives my white, educated, U.S. academic voice precedence over the voices of the indigenous, less formally educated leaders with whom I have worked. This is particularly problematic in the conjuncture of historical forces in Guatemala today, wherein silences are being ruptured and indigenous Mayan leaders are reweaving the fabric of life in rural communities (see Warren 1998, for one analysis of these processes).

As one strategy for responding to my growing concern about voice and re-presentation and the women's articulated desires to share their stories with communities beyond Chajul, we decided to complement the use of indigenous creative resources such as weaving, dramatization, and storytelling (see, e.g., Lykes 1994; Zipes 1995) with a community photography project. Because the group consisted primarily of Ixil-speaking women, very few of whom speak Spanish and even fewer of whom can read and write in any language, we sought methods for working together that would facilitate the participation of all yet enable us to communicate within and beyond our borders. Inspired by the work of Chinese rural women, *Visual Voices: 100 Photographs of Village China by the Women of Yunnan Province* (1995), the women of ADMI decided that they wanted to use photography to develop a public record of their lives, to "tell the story of the violence" and also their story as women responding to the war and its effects. They hoped to prevent future violence by speaking out, and, through storytelling, to build connections with other women in Guatemala and beyond who were engaged in similar processes. As important, they sought new skills to develop economic and psychosocial resources for their communities.

We incorporated two research methods that used photography, "photovoice" (Wang 1999; Wang and Burris 1994; Wang, Burris, and Xiang 1996; see also Lykes in press) and "talking pictures" (Bunster and Chaney 1989), into our existing group processes to consolidate a PAR method that fit the needs articulated within the group. We developed an iterative process of data collection and analysis; women "analyzed as they photographed." Photographers recorded their own life stories, sometimes assisted by a facilitator, through paired interviews among the twenty participants. They photographed life in Chajul and traveled to neighboring villages, photographing women and their families. Through recording multiple stories of daily living, including indigenous cultural and agricultural practices, war and its effects, and ongoing poverty, the participants developed sensitivities to the various forms of violence experienced in the wider municipality, as well as analyses of the complex challenges facing the region as it develops recovery strategies in the wake of war's trauma.

Photographic images provide a powerful and unique tool for documenting women's concerns from their own perspective. The visual image is quite unlike any other form of communication because it is universally apprehended and can be used to facilitate discussion, documentation, and analysis of social issues by the photographer and by those who view the "objects of her gaze." Furthermore, virtually everyone can easily learn how to use a basic camera and begin documenting what he or she deems important and worth capturing on film. The photos have served as generative images or codes (see Freire 1970) through which small groups of participants have been able to co-construct stories about their experiences. The group analytic sessions have been particularly mobilizing and motivating. Through careful planning and the structuring of levels of analysis within the group discussions (Rogoff 1990; Vygotsky [1962] 1986), women have developed strategies for clustering ideas, identifying similarities and differences between and across photos, and constructing holistic analyses of clusters of photographs. They have explored possible proximal and distal causes for the problems represented in any given picture and hypothesized causal sequences. Based on these analyses, the women have identified priorities for future work and, with the resources of the wider community, have begun to generate strategic community-based programs to address these needs.

Participatory Methods as Continually Developing Processes

My experiences to date suggest that using traditional practices of dramatization and storytelling, such as those described briefly above and in my earlier publications, and more "contemporary" resources such as photography has contributed significantly to participants' capacity to "break silence" and affirm multiple and heretofore hidden dimensions of their experiences. In a workshop in Chajul in the summer of 1997, a subgroup of six women dramatized their experiences during wartime of journeying to their family agricultural plots at midday to bring their husbands their lunch. They enacted the experiences of being accosted by members of the Civilian Patrol, often their neighbors, and accused of collaborating with the guerrillas. The dramatization included re-presentation not only of the civilian patrollers but also of the guerrillas. It was followed by a discussion involving all fifty workshop participants, some of whom had not spoken of these experiences for a decade. Women began to externalize, re-present, and then analyze their feelings then and now, and to contextualize these experiences within their present situation, which they characterized as "working towards peace." Those who were not ready or able to verbalize the experiences or their feelings about it participated through experiencing the dramatic representation of a shared history that ritualized past experiences, enabling them to pass the story on to their children despite their hesitancy to speak personally about it. The rupturing of these silences and secrecy afforded the women and their children new opportunities for community participation.

However, those who were either not present for the initial dramatization or not able to engage in conversation about these experiences when they were presented had no easy access to the experience. Efforts to record the dramatization in words and re-present it to others have not always been successful. The words representing the actions frequently presume a level of abstract thinking in the individual listener that is not characteristic of many of these women. This particular "textualizing" of the ritual prioritizes a form of knowledge construction better known to the academy than to rural women, rendering the experience less accessible to this rural population.

The photovoice method offers an important alternative at the level of the creation of the photograph, at the level of "storying the photograph," at the level of analysis, and at the level of sharing the pictures, stories, and analyses beyond the immediate context. The photograph re-presents the photographer's perspective or point of view, but then becomes a stimulus for her to tell the story "behind the picture," and then for the group's reflections, discussions, analyses, and re-representations. The fixed image offers a visual stimulus to ever-widening circles of women that can also be widely "read," providing the opportunity for a discussion of the differing views of reality within the communities of Chajul. The women have traveled from their town to neighboring villages, taken photographs and completed interviews at the sites of recent exhumations of those massacred almost twenty years earlier, and thereby deepened their understandings of the violence in their communities and its effects. Just as significantly, they are developing an understanding of the differing effects of violence and poverty within their town and more rural, smaller village communities. These initial contacts have generated new possibilities for participation by women in these villages who are seeking to improve their lives, responding to the desires of Chajulense women to extend local women's networks as well as to create new opportunities for the generation of knowledge about Mayan women in their own voices.

As we enter this new phase of participatory research, I have several concerns about the method that we have co-developed. We continue to discuss these concerns in Chajul and to strategize in ways that will minimize risk to participants and enhance broad-based participation. I briefly discuss several of these concerns here as examples of the processual nature of the development of any PAR experience as well as an indicator of how any "methodological solution" creates new challenges.

First, the particular history of photography in Central America and, more specifically, in Guatemala suggests a preference for formal rather than informal photographic representations. A picture is something very special for which one must dress appropriately and take on a serious demeanor. Photovoice assumes a spontaneity and informality on the parts of those being photographed that may not be common among members of these rural communities.

A second concern is the cost of developing film and reproducing pictures, particularly in a subsistence economy where the funding for this project could support the annual survival needs of many within the community. Relatedly, this is clearly a time-limited project that lacks local sustainability without continued outside funding.

Third, women photographers are unknown in rural Guatemala. Participants' feedback about the photovoice project confirms that this rupturing of traditional gender roles has contributed positively to their self-image and self-esteem. This is evident in their self-descriptions as researchers and photographers. Not surprisingly, it has also generated various responses among men in the community. Some have responded with respect and enthusiasm, proud that women in Chajul are telling the community's stories beyond its borders. Others have jealously guarded their wives' time, hesitating to allow them to participate in the project because it "distracts" them from their fulfilling their family and household obligations. Others are distressed or angered to see their own roles shifting as a consequence of women's newfound skills. These multiple and varied responses underscore the importance of incorporating a gender-sensitive perspective when approaching community-based work with women. Future work with men in this community would importantly complement this ongoing project.

Fourth, the strength of the photograph is also a weakness. Because photographs can be "multiply read," once presented to ever widening communities, the story of the women in Chajul will be multiply interpreted. Although each photograph is yoked to a story developed within the group (hence "photo-voice"), those who view them will remember or create "other stories." For women who have been isolated in a rural community, this presents new challenges for which they are preparing themselves. As a Euro-American researcher, I have found multiple interpretations to be resources for working through a process of meaning making, but the local realities of these communities place other kinds of constraints on that process. Years of war and armed conflict have created rigid ways of thinking that are frequently accompanied by dualisms and rigid attachments to dichotomous thinking (see Martín-Baró 1994). Although the analysis workshops with project participants have helped them develop greater openness to and interest in "multiple interpretations," they have also contributed to the development and appropriation of a "collective story" that has been "owned" by all project participants. It is this collective story that will be presented to a wider public in book form and become the source for re-storying by those who hear it.

Finally, and most importantly, I share with some local residents a deep concern about the threat posed to them for having photographed and critically analyzed the realities of poverty and violence within their communities and re-presented them to others. The peace process within Guatemala is extremely fragile, and presidential elections in December 1999 solidified the political power of Rios Montt, a former dictator found to be responsible for many of the massacres of the early 1980s (see CEH 1999), and his political party. Such political realities could threaten the well-being of any who speak about past or present repression.

Generating Criteria for Evaluating
Participatory Methods

The group participants, coordinators and I have discussed each of the concerns expressed above on numerous occasions and continue to seek ways to integrate our responses through adapting the PAR methodology to local realities. As importantly, we have developed processes for reflecting upon problems and challenges as they emerge. Among the multiple outcomes of this project has been the further development of local leadership within this women's organization. Eighteen of the twenty women who began the project are active in it twenty-four months later. Some of these women have developed skills to facilitate other similar projects with women in the villages surrounding their town with whom they have established contact through the photovoice process. We walk carefully and thoughtfully as the Chajulense themselves take new risks that could jeopardize their future safety.

Reflecting upon my experiences in Chajul and my previous years working in Guatemala, I have generated several preliminary criteria for evaluating the adequacy of the participatory methods I engage with participants in our action research endeavors. These include (1) the method's compatibility and/or complementarity with other existing resources in local communities in which a majority of the population lives in extreme poverty, which affects the sustainability of the project; (2) the ease with which, as participants, we engage the method toward re-presenting our realities, thereby deepening our critical awareness and understanding of existing social problems and our potential as change agents; (3) the method's contribution toward the development of action-based responses to identified problems; (4) the method's viability as a resource whereby we, as participants, can meaningfully re-present our multiple realities to audiences of activists, policy makers, and potential funders whom we seek to engage as collaborators in supporting our responses to the multiple effects of war, state-sponsored violence, and institutionalized poverty; (5) the method's potential for enabling the sharing of multiple, frequently differing indigenous practices (which, in the case of my work in Guatemala, refers to the sharing of Mayan and Euro-American theories and practices); (6) the method's capacity to facilitate an action/reflection dialectic when new ways of thinking and/or alternative cultural practices emerge within and among local participants and their communities in response to the PAR process; and, (7) the method's minimization of risk to the participants, particularly those who live in a context of continuing violence and/or a fragile peace.

These criteria cannot be satisfied equally by any given participatory practice, nor have they been equally satisfied in my more than eight years of collaboration with ADMI in Chajul. Yet they have contributed importantly to our successes in working together to build an integrated program that responds to some of the multiple psychosocial needs of women and their families in Chajul. The photovoice project anticipates the publication of our "collective story" in July 2000, which will be circulated within and beyond the town. ADMI is organizing a traveling exhibit within Guatemala and beyond, fulfilling one of our many objectives—to tell the story of war and its effects, as well as the stories of some of its survivors. As significantly, the photovoice process has included the prioritization of future community-based projects within Chajul and its surrounding villages. The current ADMI leadership has begun a process of fundraising for these health and educational programs.

I hope that the criteria identified here, among others yet to be developed, will serve as reference points for all of us as we choose among various strategies for future engagement in Chajul and its surrounding communities and for my work within the United States, and, most recently, in South Africa. They offer guidelines for concretizing the important tasks of action and reflection that are so necessary for initiating and sustaining long-term social change toward a more just social order.

Notes

Acknowledgments: The research presented in this chapter was partially supported by a grant from the Soros Foundation–Guatemala and by a sabbatical leave from Boston College. Joan W. Williams and M. Luisa Cabrera contributed importantly to different phases of the project described here, and I graciously acknowledge their contributions to my thinking about the photovoice process and to multiple practical aspects of the project. Finally, my deepest thanks to the women, children, and men of Chajul whose lived experiences and meaning making deeply shaped this work.

1. Until December 29, 1996, Guatemala was the site of the longest-running Central American armed conflict, waged between the government and military of

Guatemala and the Guatemalan revolutionary forces, Unidad Revolucionaria Nacional Guatemalteca (URNG: National Revolutionary Union of Guatemala). The URNG sought a more equitable distribution of land and, in more recent years, asserted the rights of indigenous peoples, who constitute more than 50 percent of the population and have been forced to live in situations of extreme poverty and structural marginalization (for a fuller discussion, see Carmack 1988; Falla 1984, 1994; Warren 1998).

2. From an interview for the training video *Trabajando para un futuro mejor: Talleres creativos con niños [Working for a better future: Creative workshops with children]*. Translation by author. Copies of the video may be purchased in the United States from the author. Distribution in Central America is through ASECSA, Apartado Postal No. 27, Chimaltenango, Guatemala.

References

Bunster, X., and E. M. Chaney. 1989. Epilogue. In *Sellers and servants: Working women in Lima, Peru*, eds. X. Bunster and E. M. Chaney, 217–233. Granby, MA: Bergin and Garvey.

Carmack, R. M., ed. 1988. *Harvest of violence: The Maya Indians and the Guatemalan crisis*. Norman: University of Oklahoma Press.

CEH (Commission for Historical Clarification [Comisión para el Esclarecimiento Histórico]). 1999. *Report of the CEH*. Available on-line at http://hrdata.aaas .org/ceh. Guatemala: CEH.

DuBois, B. 1983. Passionate scholarship: Notes on values, knowing and method in feminist social science. In *Theories of women's studies*, eds. G. Bowles and R. Klein, 105–116. Boston: Routledge.

Falla, R. 1984. Vision of an indigenous people who suffer genocide: Permanent tribunal of people. Condensed English version. In *Guatemala: Tyranny on trial: Testimony of the permanent people's tribunal*, eds. and trans. S. Jonas, E. McCaughan, and E. S. Martinez. San Francisco: Publicaciones Sinthesis.

———. 1994. *Massacres in the jungle: Ixcan, Guatemala, 1975–1982*, trans. Julia Howland. Boulder, CO: Westview Press.

Fals-Borda, O. 1988. *Knowledge and people's power*. New Delhi: Indian Social Institute.

Fals-Borda, O., and M. A. Rahman, eds. 1991. *Action and knowledge: Breaking the monopoly with participatory action research*. New York: Apex Press.

Freire, P. 1970. *Pedagogy of the oppressed*. New York: Seabury Press.

Hoare, T., C. Levy, and M. P. Robinson. 1993. Participatory action research in native communities: Cultural opportunities and legal implications. *Canadian Journal of Native Studies* 13 (1): 43–68.

Kennedy, E. L. 1995. In pursuit of connection: Reflections on collaborative work. *American Anthropologist* 97 (1): 26–33.

Lapierre, A. 1977. *Simbologia del movimiento [Symbolism of movement]*. Barcelona: Editorial Científica-Médica.

Lykes, M. B. 1989. Dialogue with Guatemalan Indian women: Critical perspectives on constructing collaborative research. In *Representations: Social constructions of gender*, ed. R. Unger, 167–185. Amityville, NY: Baywood.

———. 1994. Terror, silencing, and children: International multidisciplinary collaboration with Guatemalan Maya communities. *Social Science and Medicine* 38 (4): 543–552.

———. 1996. Meaning making in a context of genocide and silencing. In *Myths about the powerless: Contesting social inequalities*, eds. M. B. Lykes, A. Banu-azizi, R. Liem, and M. Morris, 159–178. Philadelphia: Temple University Press.

———. In press. Creative arts and photography in participatory action research in Guatemala. In *Handbook of Action Research*, eds. P. Reason and H. Bradbury. Thousand Oaks, CA: Sage.

Lykes, M. B., and R. Liem. 1990. Human rights and mental health in the United States: Lessons from Latin America. *Journal of Social Issues* 46 (3): 151–165.

Lykes, M. B., in collaboration with A. Caba Mateo, J. Chávez Anay, A. Laynez Caba, U. Ruiz, and J. W. Williams. 1999. Telling stories—rethreading lives: Community education, women's development, and social change among the Maya Ixil. *International Journal of Leadership in Education: Theory and Practice* 2 (3): 207–227.

Martín-Baró, I. 1989. *La institucionalización de la guerra [Institutionalization of war]*. Paper presented at the Annual Meeting of the InterAmerican Psychological Association, Buenos Aires.

———. 1994. *Writings for a liberation psychology: Ignacio Martín-Baró*. Eds. and trans. A. Aron and S. Corne. Cambridge, MA: Harvard University Press.

Melville, M. B., and M. B. Lykes. 1992. Guatemalan Indian children and the sociocultural effects of government-sponsored terrorism. *Social Science and Medicine* 34 (5): 533–548.

Morton, N. 1985. *The journey is home*. Boston: Beacon Press.

ODHAG (Oficina de Derechos Humanos del Arzobispado de Guatemala [Office of Human Rights of the Archdiocese of Guatemala]). 1998. *Nunca más: Informe proyecto interdiocesano de recuperación de la memoria histórica [Never again: Report of the inter-diocescan project on the recovery of historic memory]*. Vols. 1–5. Guatemala: Author.

Pavlovsky, E., C. Martinez Bouquet, and F. Moccio. 1985. *Psicodrama, cuando y por que dramatizar [Psychodrama: When and why to dramatize]*. Buenos Aires: Ediciones Busqueda.

Smith, D., with the International Peace Research Institute—Oslo. 1997. *The state of war and peace atlas*. London: Penguin.

Rogoff, B. 1990. *Apprenticeship in thinking: Cognitive development in social context*. New York: Cambridge University Press.

Taussig, M. 1987. *Shamanism, colonialism, and the wild man: A study in terror and healing*. Chicago: University of Chicago Press.

United Nations Department for Policy Coordination and Sustainable Development. 1996. *Promotion and protection of the rights of children: Impact of armed conflict on children*. New York: United Nations Department for Policy Coordination and Sustainable Development.

Visual voices: 100 photographs of village China by the women of Yunnan Province. 1995. Yunnan, China: Yunnan People's Publishing House. (Available from Dr. Caroline Wang, University of Michigan, Ann Arbor, MI 48109).

Vygotsky, L. S. [1962] 1986. *Thought and language*. Rev. ed. Ed. and trans. A. Kozulin. Cambridge, MA: MIT Press.

Wang, C. 1999. Photovoice: A participatory action research strategy applied to women's health. *Journal of Women's Health* 8 (2): 185–192. See also http://www.photovoice.com

Wang, C., and M. Burris. 1994. Empowerment through photo novella: Portraits of participation. *Health Education Quarterly* 21 (2): 171–186.

Wang, C., M. Burris, and Y. P. Xiang. 1996. Chinese village women as visual anthropologists: A participatory approach to reaching policymakers. *Social Science and Medicine* 42 (10): 1391–1400.

Warren, K. B. 1998. *Indigenous movements and their critics: Pan-Maya activism in Guatemala*. Princeton, NJ: Princeton University Press.

Winnicott, D. W. 1982. *Playing and reality*. New York: Tavistock Publications.

Zipes, J. D. 1995. *Creative storytelling: Building community, changing lives*. New York: Routledge.

13

■　■　■　■　■　■　■　■　■

Participatory Action Research as a Resource for Developing African American Community Leadership

S. Darius Tandon, James G. Kelly,
and Lynne O. Mock

DURING THE PAST NINE YEARS, the second author (Kelly) and a small group of doctoral students have been involved in a participatory action research (PAR) endeavor at the University of Illinois at Chicago (UIC). Working in tandem with a church-based community organizing group, the Developing Communities Project (DCP), the university staff has focused on documenting the development of indigenous community leaders in the Chicago South Side community where DCP is located. More specifically, university and community members have worked to (a) document the multiple aspects of community leadership and (b) utilize the findings of this documentation to better develop and train indigenous community leaders.

The first aim of this work is to develop an understanding of the role of ordinary citizens as community leaders (Kelly 1999). Previous empirical research on leadership has focused primarily on individual-level characteristics of persons in organizational settings (Chemers 1993; Fiedler 1995;

Hollander 1992; Yukl 1998). Understanding community leadership, however, requires social scientists to take into consideration the markedly different contexts in which leaders are developed. Specifically, community leadership is most often (a) comprised of indigenous community members with no formal leadership training, (b) collective in nature as a result of working with multiple community constituencies, and (c) developed as a strategy for promoting community empowerment and community change (Glidewell et al. 1998; Obama 1988).

The second aim of this work is to facilitate the host organization's development and training of community members capable of working toward community development. This second goal is a byproduct of this project's PAR approach. Whereas much traditional social science research adheres to the philosophy that action lags behind theory and research (Chavis, Stucky, and Wandersman 1983; Merrifield 1993), PAR guides researchers to explicitly attend to producing concrete action steps aimed at producing tangible community change (Park 1993; Selener 1997).

All aspects of this work have been conducted collaboratively between UIC and DCP. The DCP staff, board members, and leaders have been involved in each phase of the research process including selecting topics, creating methods, training interviewers, conducting and coding interviews, and utilizing interview findings. By including DCP representatives throughout this work, the research team made a continuous effort to construct a genuine, trusting partnership between DCP and the UIC research team that would enhance this work's ecological validity (Bronfenbrenner 1979; Chavis, Stucky, and Wandersman 1983; Kelly 1971), or the degree to which the constructs and products of this work are relevant to DCP.

Changing Research Paradigms

Considerable social science research exists that includes the active involvement of research participants in assessing social phenomena. In fact, the phrase "collaborative research" has become a buzzword of sorts, with government bureaucracies (Centers for Disease Control 1997), private foundations (Amherst Wilder Foundation 1992), and university institutes (see Ainsley and Gaventa 1997 for a review) all conducting research that involves citizens in the research process.

While some of these collaborations promote education and action aimed at social change, many do not. Rather, many "collaborative" partnerships simply include participants in symbolic ways such as eliciting reactions to an already developed research instrument. In fact, much social science that labels itself "collaborative" limits its interaction with research participants to the initial conceptualization or design stages of a research endeavor.

This limited interaction with research participants differs from PAR's ubiquitous interaction with participants throughout the entire research process. Further, by limiting participation solely to the initial steps of a research endeavor, such studies largely remove the education and action elements characteristic of PAR that ultimately lead to community and social change (see Brydon-Miller, this volume; Park 1993). As a result, few examples of how to collaboratively analyze and interpret data are available as reference points.

With this in mind, in this chapter we provide one example of a university/community collaboration to analyze and interpret data aimed at benefiting the host community. Specifically, we illustrate how this work facilitated DCP's efforts to develop its community leaders. Simultaneously, we highlight how data analysis and interpretation also produced significant new knowledge on community leadership.

Collaborative Analysis, Interpretation, and Utilization of Research Data

DCP requested funding from the Illinois Department of Alcohol and Substance Abuse (DASA) to fund drug prevention programs in the geographic area served by the community group. Interested in DCP's model of community organizing and leadership development in preventing substance abuse, DASA agreed to fund DCP with the requirement that the group's organizing and leadership development processes be evaluated. DCP was subsequently introduced to Kelly as the potential evaluator. Given Kelly's interest in understanding the process of community organizing and leadership development, he recommended that the evaluation document the experiences of DCP leaders rather than record incidence and prevalence rates of substance abuse that would reflect DCP's community efforts. DCP agreed to this approach, realizing the potential to gain substantive information about its leadership development processes in addition to fulfilling its evaluation requirements (Tandon et al. 1998).

Planning between the UIC research team and DCP began soon thereafter, and a member of DCP was selected by the executive director to serve as the liaison person between the two parties. At the same time, a Community Research Panel (CRP) of eight community leaders was selected by DCP staff to work with the UIC research team in proposing topics for the documentation of community leadership and selecting a method for the documentation. (For a more detailed description of the CRP, see Glidewell et al. 1998). With those objectives in mind, the CRP held nineteen meetings over the course of a year and a half.

The CRP's desire to allow leaders to tell their unique stories about community work led to the selection of a semi-structured interview as the primary data collection method. The CRP felt that a semi-structured interview would establish trust and rapport with community members, leading to more honest, descriptive responses. The semi-structured interview guide was developed by the CRP and the UIC research team during their nineteen meetings.

Interviews were conducted with eighty DCP members over the course of the next eighteen months. The interview guide consisted of questions in each of four sections pertaining to different aspects of performing community work: (a) The nature of the respondent's community activities, (b) social support required to engage in these community activities, (c) relationships established with other individuals and organizations, and (d) goals and visions for the surrounding community. Several community residents, trained in interviewing, conducted the first twenty interviews; however, due to various job and family conflicts, a trained social science interviewer conducted most of the remaining sixty interviews. On average, each interview lasted ninety minutes. Interviews were conducted in a location specified by the community leader—often his or her home or the DCP office. Upon completion of each interview, a transcript was made from the taped session and interview notes.

A large body of data was elicited by interviewing eighty community leaders. Given the sparse existing literature on community leadership, this information is significant for social scientists interested in the development and training of indigenous community leaders, and the results have been analyzed and published in scientific journals and books (Kelly 1999; Kelly, Mock, and Tandon in press; Tandon et al. 1998).

Equally important in PAR, however, is utilizing research findings to benefit the host community pragmatically. In the present work, this meant enhancing DCP's community organizing efforts—namely, its development and training of community leaders. Given PAR's dual emphasis of generating new scientific knowledge and initiating action (Park 1993; Selener 1997), producing these dual outcomes was a fundamental goal of the present work.

The CRP's efforts were important in ensuring that this work was directed toward benefiting DCP. However, after data were collected from DCP leaders, a more difficult task of collaboratively analyzing this data presented itself. Data analysis is vital in PAR, as community members must continuously reflect upon the ongoing work to ensure that the final outcomes will be maximally beneficial to the host community/organization. In the following section, we describe DCP members' involvement throughout various steps in the data analysis process.

Data Analysis: A Participatory Challenge

The UIC research team undertook the initial step in data analysis. The first two authors (Tandon and Kelly) and another member of the research staff examined each interview and reached consensus on approximately sixty codes pertaining to key themes, issues, and concepts related to various aspects of performing community work. For example, the code "DCP-act" was assigned to all instances in which a respondent mentioned involvement in a DCP-sponsored activity. Other codes included the following:

Resource: Identifies DCP as a resource or possible resource to the community

Reason-act: Reasons for becoming active in DCP

Support: Personal social support or lack thereof for their community work

In accordance with grounded theory (Glaser and Strauss 1967), these codes reflected concepts that best fit the emerging data on community leadership.

Because this process was labor intensive, the UIC research team did not ask DCP members to assist in coding the eighty interviews. Cognizant of the time demands placed upon DCP staff, board, and members, the UIC research team felt that continuous dialogue with the DCP executive director and the UIC/DCP liaison person was a more prudent approach in discussing the initial data analysis. The executive director and liaison person actively undertook two responsibilities. First, they examined each of the sixty codes for clarity. Specifically, they reviewed codes' definitions and suggested alternate wordings to accurately reflect the nature of the codes in the larger context of DCP. Second, the codes were examined for their potential relevance and utility for DCP. Further, the executive director and liaison person identified codes of particular interest to DCP. Codes relating to DCP's church-based organization were among those strongly supported by DCP's executive director, as she was interested in understanding the role that religion had in the work of DCP members.

Working with DCP's executive director and liaison person, we created a set of fifty-six mutually agreed upon codes. Thus, DCP and the UIC research team jointly shaped the building blocks for future data analysis and interpretation. Furthermore, these preliminary data analysis steps attempted to acknowledge both parties' unique skills and expertise. UIC research team members were responsible for the technical aspects of generating codes from interview transcripts, as they were more skilled in executing data analytic techniques; DCP members employed their knowledge about the host organization and the potential utility to clarify and refine various codes.

The underlying importance of the data analysis stage of PAR is to stimulate research participants' thinking about the potential utility of collected data. The degree to which participants are involved in the actual mechanical aspects of coding interviews or running statistical analyses will vary across projects, but the notion that research participants should understand key findings and their relevance is central. To this end, the present work's generation of fifty-six unique codes presented community members with a somewhat incomplete view of the phenomenon of community leadership.

To help illuminate the meaning and potential relevance of these fifty-six codes, the first author prepared a quotebook that presented examples of various coded statements in a unified document (Tandon 1995). This quotebook highlighted several codes pertaining to skills required to perform community work. For example, one community leader discussed the important skill of building relationships:

> I think when I first came to DCP, I thought I had what it took to make things happen. Subsequently, I realized the more we build relationships the more we can organize our community. I thought I had to do things myself, but there are others who have the same common goals and concerns.

Another community member indicated the importance of learning about the political power structure that influences DCP's geographic community:

> You must find out who the politicians are and who are the community shakers, the people [who] are out front, involved in community affairs. And that's something you learn by experience, you have to walk through, you can't be a spectator. You must participate.

In addition to this quotebook, the UIC research team grouped the fifty-six codes into five general themes of community leadership to better facilitate discussion of the potential utility of the interview data. This grouping of smaller, more specific codes into larger, integrated concepts represents grounded theory's "constant search for configurations in the data that suggest that certain pieces of data belong together" (Miles and Huberman 1994, 69). The five community leadership dimensions are: (a) community involvement of DCP leaders, (b) DCP's impact on leaders, (c) factors promoting DCP leaders' continued and active involvement, (d) religious influences affecting DCP leaders' commitment to community work, and (e) DCP leaders' personal visions for their community. These themes were presented to DCP in the form of five conceptual "leadership trees" that simultaneously displayed and analyzed the five discrete dimensions of community leadership. The translation of coded data into a visual format such as leadership trees highlights the importance of "data display" in qualitative research (Miles and Huberman 1994).

Figure 13.1 presents the second leadership tree: "DCP Impact on Leaders." This tree encompasses several codes related to the multifaceted ways that DCP impacts its members. Pertaining to skills necessary to perform community work, this leadership tree further analyzes interview data by indicating in parentheses how many DCP members commented on several

Figure 13.1. *Community Leadership Tree: DCP Impact on Leaders*

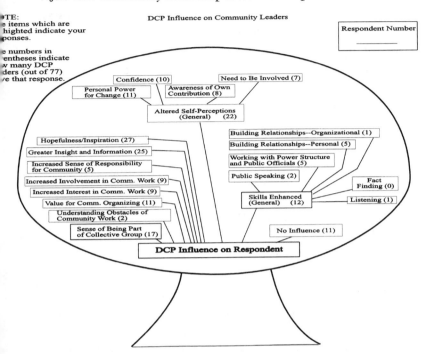

skills that have been enhanced through their involvement with DCP. For example, five DCP members mentioned during their interviews that they were now better able to work with power structure in their neighborhood.

These leadership trees promote concrete action steps aimed at benefiting DCP's efforts to develop and train its membership. Specifically, the leadership trees were thought to better enable DCP staff and membership to understand and draw conclusions from the interview data because of their straightforward, accessible presentation. Moreover, these leadership trees fairly easily stimulated dialogue with DCP staff and membership about the nature of community leadership. For example, a pastor of one of DCP's member churches commented on the potential utility of the leadership trees in bolstering the skills and experiences of his congregation (Shears 1998). Another DCP member commented on the potential to view growth and development in DCP members by creating follow-up leadership trees with the same eighty community leaders (Thomas 1998).

The act of interpreting data is usually denoted as the final step in the data analysis process (Miles and Huberman 1994). The following section describes a specific setting created to focus on this final analysis step. Included in this discussion are specific examples of how the interpretation of various data sources, such as the DCP quotebook and leadership trees, facilitated concrete action steps aimed at enhancing DCP's ability to develop and train its membership.

Data Interpretation and Potential Utility of This Work: The Community Action Task Force

A ten-person Community Action Task Force (CATF) was established with the explicit purpose of helping DCP use the various data sources collected by the UIC research team for its efforts to develop and train community leaders. DCP's executive director selected the CATF, comprised of two pastors, two church deacons, and six laypersons. This group of individuals, in the estimation of the executive director, possessed various skills, competencies, and experiences that would allow them to reflect and act upon the data collected during this research project.

The CATF has met semi-regularly over the past two and a half years to review and discuss the implications of various data sources for DCP. The majority of these meetings have been two-hour dinner meetings at the offices of DCP, where work and socialization among DCP and UIC research staff take place. A half-day retreat was also held at a hotel near DCP. As a catalyst for these CATF meetings, UIC research team members prepared one-page summaries giving an overview of each data source. These documents also highlighted preliminary themes from each body of data. For example, the one-page report pertaining to the leadership tree "DCP Impact on Leaders" (see Figure 13.1) provided a synopsis of how DCP has nurtured community leaders' development and facilitated their community work. The research team also prepared a series of short statements highlighting notable pieces of data, such as the finding that twenty-nine community members had altered their self-perceptions about their role in performing community work because of their involvement with DCP.

Additionally, demographic data obtained during the interview were juxtaposed with interview data to present more analytic themes for this leadership tree. For example, respondents who had been involved in DCP for one to three years showed an interesting cluster of characteristics: (a) greater hope/inspiration for the community, (b) greater insights and information about the community, and (c) greater altered self-perceptions. Based on this finding, the UIC research team noted, "It seems as if DCP leaders who have been involved between 1–3 years have learned a great deal about the community and feel as if they can affect change, even after a relatively short amount of time in DCP."

The one-page documents created by the UIC research team were not intended to serve as the final step in analyzing the community leadership trees and DCP quotebook. Rather, these documents were products that facilitated the CATF's interpretation and recommendations. In other words, the CATF was the setting in which analyzed data were turned over to DCP for its reactions and, ultimately, recommendations for action steps. Because the data from this project were explicitly aimed at benefiting DCP's efforts to develop and train its community leaders, the CATF assumed responsibility for determining what pieces of data were of greatest salience and utility in meeting this goal. Furthermore, in this process, the UIC research team did not focus discussion on particular findings; rather, we served as resources for the CATF.

The CATF was responsible for deciding how much time was spent reviewing each set of findings prepared by the UIC research team. For example, the leadership tree described above, "DCP Impact on Leaders," warranted significant discussion. Each of the four main sections of the DCP quotebook was also met with great enthusiasm by the CATF. Specifically, CATF members recommended that they break into subcommittees to closely review quotes found in each section, as these quotes reflected direct, authentic examples of community leaders' experiences in conducting community work. These subcommittees not only extracted quotes they felt had the most bearing on DCP's efforts to develop community leaders, but they also created two- to three-page reports articulating the perceived utility of these quotes for the organization. For example, the subcommittee that focused on the quotebook section discussing "how DCP functions as a resource to developing community leaders" gave the following recommendations (Turk, Woodson, and Roberts 1997):

1. The information gathered should be used to develop a training manual for DCP.

2. The information should be instrumental in keeping the guiding principles of DCP alive.
3. The information should set forth a relationship for creating active community activists.
4. Training should be ongoing.

Data Utilization: The Creation of Multiple Organization Tools

Discussions of the DCP quotebook and DCP leadership trees, as well as other discrete pieces of work conducted by graduate students (Leopold 1998; Martin 1998; Mock 1999; Tandon 1997), took place during the first seven CATF meetings. In addition, significant review of these data sources was conducted between CATF meetings, such as the subcommittee work described above that further analyzed the quotebook. Whereas the earlier CATF meetings were more analytical, more recent CATF meetings have been more action-oriented. Starting with the half-day retreat in November 1997, the CATF focused explicitly on brainstorming and executing concrete action plans to facilitate DCP's attempts to develop and train its leaders. As a result of these action-oriented meetings, the CATF sanctioned three specific proposals for utilizing the multiple data sources presented to them: (a) The creation of a brochure to highlight the host organization's mission, accomplishments, and strengths; (b) the creation of a training manual to better develop and train organization members as community leaders; (c) the creation of videos that present oral histories of selected organization members.

The organizational brochure was deemed important by the CATF, as DCP did not have a current document that described the organization's mission and accomplishments. It was decided that the brochure would utilize qualitative data from the DCP quotebook in order to describe the organization's mission and accomplishments through the voices of its members. This strategy was viewed as an authentic manner in which to represent the organization. The brochure will also contain basic quantitative statistics describing DCP's membership, such as the average length of time individuals have been involved with DCP. The organizational brochure will be used for fundraising, membership recruitment, and professional presentations.

The training manual recommended by the CATF would present a comprehensive portrait of the various skills, competencies, and knowledge necessary to conduct community work. During their interviews, community members mentioned interpersonal skills and knowledge of community resources, among other items, as facilitating community work. The DCP leadership trees, by virtue of presenting how many individuals gave certain responses (see Figure 13.1), also indicated certain aspects of community leadership that were not as fully developed in DCP members. Based on these observations, the CATF proposed that the training manual should (a) highlight comments made by DCP leaders about various aspects of community work and (b) address areas of community work that were underrepresented in DCP members' interview responses, as compared to the CATF's notions of integral components of conducting community work. Thus, the training manual will be a useful tool to highlight the strengths and competencies of current leaders through their own words and to provide less active and less developed leaders with information on multiple aspects of performing community work.

The third recommendation of the CATF was to create videos that present the oral histories of selected DCP leaders. In examining the five leadership trees created for the eighty DCP members interviewed, the UIC research team communicated to the CATF that a diversity of community leaders existed within the organization. Some of these leaders had been involved in community work for several years; others had only recently become involved. Given DCP's desire to develop and train both *new* and *current* leadership, the CATF recommended that a cross-section of community leaders be interviewed in an attempt to provide a "video library" for recruitment and training purposes. For example, a new DCP recruit could be shown the video of an individual who had recently joined DCP, whereas an existing DCP member who was interested in expanding his or her role in the organization could be presented with the video of an accomplished DCP leader.

The creation of the CATF was vital to this work in several regards. First, it transferred ownership of the data analysis process to DCP. While the UIC research team conducted the bulk of the initial data analysis, the concrete recommendations, implications, and action steps emanating from this work were proposed by the CATF. Because the CATF represented an array of DCP members, it was cognizant of the organization's various strengths, weaknesses, and needs. Thus, the three specific proposals detailed above reflect the CATF's understanding of how the data collected from eighty DCP leaders could best be translated into products that facilitated DCP's attempts to develop and train its membership.

Summary

Data analysis is a complex task for PAR. Engaging participants in data analysis requires research staff to think creatively. We have illustrated how one project has worked with community members to analyze and subsequently interpret and act upon collected data. Moreover, the engagement of research participants during data analysis is vital in ensuring that the interpretation and utilization of data are anchored to the interests of the host community.

Additionally, we have highlighted the importance of creating processes (i.e., the CATF) and products (i.e., DCP quotebook) to facilitate the data analysis, interpretation, and utilization stages of a PAR endeavor. The concluding sections further reflect on the importance of involving research participants in these phases of PAR.

Conclusions from the Present Work

This work, conducted in accordance with guiding principles of PAR, has attempted to produce insights that further develop social scientists' understanding of community leadership while also helping DCP develop leaders capable of working toward community change. Specific to the first goal, this work has yielded substantial knowledge related to the skills, competencies, experiences, and barriers related to conducting community work at the grassroots level. These insights, largely reflected in the presentation and analysis of the five community leadership trees, are presented in greater detail elsewhere (Kelly 1999; Tandon et al. 1998). This chapter has focused instead on explicating the processes and products that have facilitated concrete action steps aimed at enhancing the host organization.

The overarching aims for PAR are to (a) provide opportunities for disenfranchised individuals to become empowered so that (b) they will facilitate social change in their communities. The ongoing collaboration with DCP members has attempted to address the first point. In terms of facilitating social change, Selener (1997) makes an important link between organizational change and development and social change, noting that "an array of outcomes related to social change depend on the group's increased organizational capacity and on community development" (43).

The present work concurs with this philosophy. We believe that the immediate outcomes of this work are critical in further developing DCP's capacity to recruit, develop, and train community leaders. The creation of an organizational brochure will help DCP garner funds and spread its organizational mission in the surrounding geographic community. A training manual will facilitate DCP's ability to systematically train its members to conduct a variety of tasks related to addressing community issues. The creation of several videos highlighting the experiences of different DCP members will assist DCP in recruiting and training leaders. Once DCP's infrastructure is solidified, it will be able to tackle more effectively and comprehensively the host of economic, social, and health ills plaguing the community it serves.

Facilitators and Challenges of the Present Work

This work has benefited from several factors. First, the second author, as lead investigator of this project, was at the time a tenured full professor at UIC. This status largely freed him from the pressures and requirements often placed upon researchers by their academic institutions. In order to gain promotion, tenure, and/or positive peer reviews, researchers become cognizant of the need to publish and present scientifically rigorous research adhering to conventional criteria at a fairly rapid pace. Further, given the norms and demands of many academic settings, social scientists may be deterred from conducting PAR for fear that their methods, analyses, or findings will not appear "scientific" enough (Isreal, Schurman, and Hugentobler 1992; Nyden and Wiewel 1993).

A second factor was the financial and ideological support this project received from its funding agency. Given that PAR's ultimate aim is to produce social change, the question arises as to what extent funding sources, which typically represent the "powerful," will fund such endeavors. MacClure (1990) notes that two yardsticks by which traditional social science projects are selected for funding are (a) the rigor of design and methodology and (b) the expertise of professional researchers. Thus, participatory action researchers who adhere to the philosophy that community members will guide research design are left in a quandary when attempting to procure funding. This work, to the contrary, was supported by the executive director of the Illinois Department of Alcohol and Substance Abuse, who was sympathetic to understanding a community organizing model of promoting community change through this form of research.

Although the UIC research team has established trust and rapport with DCP members during this work, the issue of how to actively maintain community members' interest and participation is relevant across PAR endeavors. Given the pressing time demands facing community organizations, as well as the job and family constraints faced by individual members (Nyden and Wiewel 1993), it is imperative that university collaborators do not burden community members with excessive time demands. In the case of the present work, the CATF has taken close to two years to begin implementing action steps based on the data presented to them. Conducting weekly or biweekly meetings would have greatly facilitated this process; however, the family, job, DCP, and other community responsibilities of CATF members prohibited a faster pace for this work.

Final Reflections

Participatory Action Research is becoming more widely utilized by social scientists in North America (Brydon-Miller and Tolman 1997; Selener 1997). This volume is an important contribution in legitimizing these postpositivist methodologies. One of the key forces fueling the increasing number of PAR endeavors is the recognition that a traditional, logical positivist approach does not provide all of the necessary social change focus that is increasingly needed in our society.

Both independently and as a whole, PAR's key characteristics—joint participation in the research process, education of participants, and an explicit orientation toward action—can facilitate immediate social change. The work described herein highlights one attempt to incorporate these characteristics into a research project in one particular disenfranchised community. Therefore, the conclusions and implications of the present work are not to be taken as "truths"; rather, these statements should serve as reflexive tools for social scientists who are currently utilizing PAR, as well as those who are not.

Ultimately, collaborating with DCP helps shift power in designing programs and policies from researchers or government officials to the communities themselves (Maguire 1987). This shift in power clearly validates the indigenous knowledge and experience of community members. However, this shift must be accompanied by providing community members with skills, competencies, and knowledge necessary to design effective programs and policies. This project has been successful in accomplishing both of the above goals. Members of the Community Research Panel, in reviewing existing literature on research methods, gained a greater understanding of how certain methods promote or silence individuals' voices. DCP's executive director and liaison person became familiar with the process of coding interview data. Most recently, CATF members translated social science data into specific recommendations for improving their organization's attempts to train and develop community leaders. Several CATF members have also commented to DCP's executive director that they are now comfortable writing brief reports.

The UIC research team has also benefited from this work by our increased appreciation of the rewards of PAR. PAR not only expands the quality of obtained information, but also increases the practical benefits of the data for the host community. In viewing how this project has yielded practical benefits for DCP, the UIC research group has experienced closure in seeing that research can indeed be useful.

References

Ainsley, F., and J. Gaventa. 1997. Researching for democracy and democratizing research. *Change*, January/February, 46–53.

Amherst Wilder Foundation. 1992. *Collaboration: What makes it work: A review of research literature on factors influencing successful collaboration.* St. Paul, MN: Amherst H. Wilder Foundation.

Bronfenbrenner, U. 1979. *The ecology of human development.* Cambridge, MA: Harvard University Press.

Brydon-Miller, M., and D. Tolman. 1997. Transforming psychology: Interpretive and participatory research methods. Special issue, *Journal of Social Issues* 53:597–604.

Centers for Disease Control. 1997. *Selected bibliography on community participation.* Atlanta: Centers for Disease Control.

Chavis, D., P. Stucky, and A. Wandersman. 1983. Returning research to the community: A relationship between scientists and citizen. *American Psychologist* 38:424–434.

Chemers, M. 1993. An integrative theory of leadership. In *Leadership theory and research: Perspectives and directions*, eds. M. Chemers and R. Ayman, 293–319. San Diego: Academic Press.

Fiedler, F. 1995. Cognitive resources and leadership performance. *Applied Psychology: An International Review* 44:5–28.

Glaser, B., and A. Strauss. 1967. *The discovery of grounded theory: Strategies for qualitative research*. Chicago: Aldine.

Glidewell, J., J. Kelly, M. Bagby, and A. Dickerson. 1998. Natural development of community leadership. In *Social psychological applications to social issues: Theory and research on small groups*, eds. R. S. Tinsdale, L. Heath, J. Edwards, E. J. Posavac, F. B. Bryant, Y. Suarez-Balcazar, E. Henderson-King, and J. Myers, 61–86. New York: Plenum.

Hollander, E. 1992. Leadership, followership, self, and others. *Leadership Quarterly* 3 (1): 43–54.

Isreal, B., S. Schurman, and M. Hugentobler. 1992. Conducting action research: Relationships between members and researchers. *Journal of Applied Behavioral Science* 28 (1): 74–101.

Kelly, J. G. 1971. The quest for valid preventive interventions. In *Issues in community psychology and community mental health*, ed. G. Rosenblum, 109–140. New York: Behavioral Publications.

———. 1999. Contexts and community leadership: Inquiry as an ecological expedition. *American Psychologist* 54 (11): 953—961.

Kelly, J. G., L. O. Mock, and S. D. Tandon. In press. Collaborative inquiry with African American community leaders. In *Handbook of action research*, eds. P. Reason and H. Bradbury. Newbury Park, CA: Sage Publications.

Lather, P. 1986. Research as praxis. *Harvard Educational Review* 56 (3): 257–277.

Leopold, C. 1998. Supportive relationships among African-American adult and adolescent women. Unpublished master's thesis. University of Illinois at Chicago.

MacClure, R. 1990. The challenge of participatory research and its implications for funding agencies. *International Journal of Sociology and Social Policy* 10 (3): 1–21.

Maguire, P. 1987. *Doing participatory research: A feminist approach*. Amherst: Center for International Education, University of Massachusetts.

Martin, A. 1998. An examination of self-realization in members of a Christian community-based organization. Unpublished master's thesis. University of Illinois at Chicago.

Merrifield, J. 1993. Putting scientists in their place: Participatory research in environmental and occupational health. In *Voices of change: Participatory research in the United States and Canada*, eds. P. Park, M. Brydon-Miller, B. Hall, and T. Jackson, 65–84. Westport, CT: Bergin and Garvey.

Miles, M., and A. Huberman. 1994. *Qualitative data analysis: An expanded sourcebook*. Newbury Park, CA: Sage Publications.

Mock, L. O. 1999. The personal visions of African American community leaders. Unpublished doctoral dissertation. University of Illinois at Chicago.

Nyden, P., and W. Wiewel. 1993. Collaborative research: Harnessing the tension between researcher and practitioner. *American Sociologist* 23 (4): 43–55.

Obama, B. 1988. Why organize? Problems and promise in the inner city. *Illinois Issues*, Fall, 36–40.

Park, P. 1993. What is participatory research? A theoretical and methodological perspective. In *Voices of change: Participatory research in the United States and Canada*, eds. P. Park, M. Brydon-Miller, B. Hall, and T. Jackson, 1–19. Westport, CT: Bergin and Garvey.

Reardon, K., J. Welsh, B. Kreiswirth, and J. Forester. 1993. Participatory action research from the inside: Community development practice in East St. Louis. *American Sociologist* 24 (1): 69–91.

Selener, D. 1997. *Participatory action research and social change*. Ithaca, NY: Cornell Participatory Action Network.

Shears, A. 1998. Personal conversation. April 9.

Tandon, S. D. 1995. *Sample responses from the DCP Interview*. Unpublished manuscript. University of Illinois at Chicago.

———. 1997. The views of community leaders: A multimethod approach to assess personal strengths and community resources. Unpublished master's thesis. University of Illinois at Chicago.

Tandon, S. D., L. S. Azelton, J. G. Kelly, and D. Strickland. 1998. Constructing a tree for community leadership: Contexts and processes in collaborative inquiry. Special issue, *American Journal of Community Psychology* 26 (4): 669–696.

Thomas, M. 1998. Unpublished meeting minutes, July 25.

Turk, G., J. Woodson, and A. Roberts. 1997. DCP as a resource to developing activists. Unpublished technical report.

Yukl, G. 1998. *Leadership in organizations*. 4th ed. Englewood Cliffs, NJ: Prentice-Hall.

14

■　　■　　■　　■　　■　　■　　■　　■　　■

Re-inhabiting the Body from the Inside Out

Girls Transform Their School Environment

Niva Piran

IN HER BOOK *The Second Sex*, Simone de Beauvoir (1974) addressed women's experiences of their bodies and described the way in which a girl during puberty "feels her body is getting away from her, it is no longer the straightforward expression of her individuality; at the same time she becomes for others a thing" (346). A girl's changed experience of her body during puberty may be expressed in different behaviors. In the Western world, the maturational process of puberty among girls is associated with a dramatic increase in preoccupation with body weight and shape (Pike and Striegel-Moore 1997). While body weight and shape preoccupation (BWSP) has been described as "normative" due to its high prevalence among women (Rodin, Silberstein, and Striegel-Moore 1985), it is associated with significant medical, social, and psychological complications even in partial behavioral syndromes (Bunnell et al. 1990; Herzog and Burns 1993). The dramatic increase in BWSP during puberty is one indication that the disruption in girls' sense of self during puberty (Gilligan and Brown 1992) is paralleled by a disruption in young women's experience of their bodies.

Similar to the professional treatment of "hysteria" in the Victorian era, most research work and funding toward understanding eating disorders has been channeled to the study of biological and intra-individual psychological factors, while the social domain has remained relatively unexplored (Piran 1997; Striegel-Moore 1994). To date, the relatively limited research on social factors has followed mainly the positivistic paradigm, which is widely accepted within the field of psychology (Fine and Gordon 1992). These positivistic studies have focused on a social factor labeled "pressures for thinness," which has been hypothesized to be transmitted through the media and to have intensified during the past four decades (for a review, see Levine, Piran, and Stoddard 1999). According to this social theory, the increased incidence of eating disorders relates to the greater discrepancy between widely disseminated media images of thin models and women's actual body weight and shape. School-based programs aimed at primary prevention of eating disorders have been guided by knowledge derived from this positivistic research and the social theory associated with it (Piran 1995, 1997).

This chapter describes a participatory action project aimed at addressing body weight and shape preoccupation in a school. Specifically, it examines the processes of inquiry and knowledge development undertaken by the girls and adolescent women of that school in their quest to understand and change their own body dissatisfaction. The knowledge that emerged in this study about BWSP among the students in the school, anchored in their explorations of their life experiences and in their activism to change their school environment, diverged significantly from the knowledge arrived at through the use of positivistic paradigms. Further, the participatory action project was associated with a dramatic decrease in BWSP, as well as a decrease in the incidence of eating disorders at the school over the past decade, a powerful effect not achieved by didactic programs aimed at prevention (Piran 1999b). These results lend support to the special role in psychology of critical qualitative approaches to theory construction, knowledge generation, and social change.

The chapter is divided into three main parts: the background and initial phase of the project, the process of knowledge construction, and the development of action. Each of these parts begins with a brief methodological and theoretical section and continues with a description of the project itself. The chapter ends with a discussion of the implications of this study for the role of qualitative research in the development of knowledge in psychology.

Background and Initial Phase

Theoretical and Methodological Considerations

One of the crucial components of participatory action research (PAR) is the formation of strong rapport with the community that desires change (Brydon-Miller 1997; Maguire 1987). The processes of knowledge construction and change rely on intensive dialogues, interpersonal connections, and team work. During the rapport-building phase, the community and facilitator/researcher have the opportunity to examine issues of compatibility regarding relevant world views, values, commitment, sincerity, interest, and openness to mutual change through dialogue. Rapport, however, is not a static concept and, once achieved, has to be renegotiated as challenges arise.

The establishment of the working and researching agreement in a particular PAR project may affect both its process and its findings. In this particular project, the working contract had different components. First, it was established from the outset that the location of expertise was with the students, anchored in their life experiences, a central tenet of PAR (Park 1993). Second, as far as knowledge construction, the students chose reflexive explorations in the dialogical space of focus groups as the place to arrive at critical and subversive knowledge and action. This mode of work has been described by Paulo Freire ([1970] 1993) as "conscientization." Third, the link between knowledge production and power, another key aspect of PAR methodology (Brydon-Miller 1997; Gaventa 1993; Maguire 1993), was explicit in this project in that its stated goal was to initiate changes in the school system. Exploring a phenomenon for the sake of activism and change is also in line with feminist research (Fine and Gordon [1989] 1992) and may lead to unique knowledge and insights (Freire [1970] 1993). Fourth, my role was established as a facilitator first and researcher second. (For a description of the fine line between activist and researcher, see Brydon-Miller 1997; Fine 1992).

Description

The participatory action project took place in a competitive, residential, co-educational dance school for students ages ten to eighteen, located in a large urban center in North America. I first entered the school community as a facilitator/researcher in 1985. During the initial phase of the project, I spent a great deal of time meeting all members of the school community, especially the students. In these meetings we explored the issues at hand and decided on goals and ways of working together. The meetings also allowed us to examine, mutually, issues of compatibility.

As an adult woman working in a school setting, I felt a sense of tremendous responsibility for the welfare of the students who were working in this project to implement changes related to the sensitive domain of the body. The maintenance of rapport with all stakeholders of the school community allowed for the system, including the administration, to respect students' explorations and activism and respond favorably to their requests. Students' insights and demands were therefore associated with success, experiences that enhanced their sense of authority in knowledge construction and of power.

When I met with the girls and adolescent women in focus groups to explore their concerns, and their thoughts about addressing these concerns, they expressed extreme preoccupation with body shape, strong denigration of mature women's bodies, and a determination to control and manage their bodies. These initial meetings seemed to be associated with the emergence of several processes in the groups. First, group participants became interested in securing time to explore and develop an understanding of these issues together as a group. Second, the personal preoccupation with deficiencies and inadequacies of the body started to shift toward the examination of shared adverse social conditions. Third, in a few of the groups, the initial emotional tone of dysphoria began to shift toward one of protesting adverse experiences. Fourth, it seemed that a certain hope was emerging in a number of groups that these difficulties could be understood and possibly changed. This process resembled Catharine MacKinnon's (1989) description of consciousness-raising groups for women: "Consciousness raising, through socializing women's knowing, transforms it, creating a shared reality that clears a space in the world within which women can begin to move" (101).

Group participants felt strongly that focus groups worked best for them because nowhere else did they have the opportunity to talk (or stage little spontaneous scenes, or sing, or draw) about their body-anchored experiences. Aside from the occasional comment about how fat one was, the body was usually a silent domain in their school. The girls felt that it would be best to organize separate focus groups for each age group and that they should set the agenda for each group and determine the number of groups needed. I shared with them my belief that through their life experiences in and outside of the school they had the knowledge to understand BWSP and to guide constructive changes within the school system. I described my commitment to work with them by listening, facilitating, and taking part in focus groups and by supporting their work to change the school. I also described how little was known about BWSP based on girls' own experiences. I told them that, as a women's health researcher, I wanted to learn about this issue from them by studying what they said was important to them and by observing the way they worked to change the school. We decided that at the end of each focus group, the group would discuss and summarize what happened in the meeting, agree on what actions they may want to pursue, and decide what they wanted to share with others at the school or in research and what they wanted to keep in confidence within the group. We also discussed the importance of safety to all members of the groups.

The Emergence of Critical Understanding about Body Weight and Shape Preoccupation

Theoretical and Methodological Considerations

The process of generating new knowledge in this PAR project involved community members in groups exploring their own body weight and shape preoccupation with the stated goal of changing their school environment. The process of critical reflection by community members about their social realities and the critical knowledge that emerges in that process have been described by different authors. Freire ([1970] 1993) used the term "conscientization" to describe the transformation of knowledge embedded in life experiences of community members to critical consciousness about the forces that affect the community's realities, through a process of critical reflection in groups. MacKinnon (1989) similarly described the feminist consciousness-raising movement as a group-based process by women that "socializes women's knowing. It produces an analysis of woman's world which is . . . collective and critical" (101). In her discussion of standpoint epistemology, Nancy Hartsock (1983) highlighted the advantaged epistemological position that oppressed members of a social system have in understanding their social system. She also described the special importance of processes such as group reflection and group-based consciousness-raising in allowing oppressed members of a community to reinterpret reality from their own perspective.

The body has been a rich domain for theoretical discussions. Critical social theorists such as Michel Foucault (1979) have contended that individuals' experiences of their bodies are tied to their social power, worth, rights, and privileges. Rich (1986), like other feminists, similarly described the body as a politically inscribed entity when she suggested that "the repossession by women of our bodies will bring far more essential change to human society than the seizing of the means of production by workers" (285). The examination of the critical interpretation derived by young women in a dance school regarding their body weight and shape preoccupation may provide an opportunity to examine their understanding in relation to these theoretical constructions.

Description

The emergence of critical knowledge through focus groups can be best understood by including a few short excerpts from three group meetings with young women. In total, just over three hundred group meetings occurred at the school over a ten-year period. I recorded these excerpts immediately following group meetings, in line with the summary agreed upon by the group at the end of the meeting. In reading these excerpts, note that while each group process was unique, the focus groups usually started with a descriptive stage, moved on to an interpretive critical stage, and, when relevant, ended with an action-oriented phase. Over time, the participants in the project developed a critical

Table 14.1. *Content and Action Themes Generated by Young Women Discussing Body Weight and Shape Preoccupation*

Core Category	Content Categories	Content Themes	Action Themes	Action Categories	Core Category
INEQUITY Expressed in the body domain	Ownership	External dictations of food intake External dictations of appearance Objectification of the body Sexualization of the body External monitoring of natural processes Disrespect of privacy Harsh physical training	Change cafeteria style, no staff pressure No teaching staff comments accepted; body diversity in school performance No evaluation accepted by peers/teachers Sexualization is not accepted Change routines to disallow interference Provision of locked places & privacy New training curriculum that enhances safety & health	Students guide changes toward a respectful and safe **ownership** of the body at the school	Towards body—anchored **EQUITY**
		Sexual harassment Sexual and physical assault Sexual and physical abuse	Anti-harassment new peer group & school policies/norms New peer group & school policies/norms; enhancing safety procedures Where relevant, student approach services		
	Prejudicial Treatment	Weightism Sexism Racism Ethno-cultural immigration	Established new peer & staff norms to cease body-anchored expression of societal prejudices; Address staff and administration when norms breached	Students work toward arresting the use of the body as a medium to express **societal prejudices**	
	Social Construction of Women	Powerless/smaller/nonmuscular woman Disowned of sexual desire/sexual to others Bodily functions embarrassing Nurture others, not self Good/compliant/controlled Unopinionated/nonchallenging/quiet Anger free/not physical Always responsible, in cross gender situation, for failed endeavors	Mutual support for exhibiting attitudes & practicing behaviors that challenge societal restraints among peers & in school; Challenge peers & staff who disallow such changes	Students challenge **socially constructed** images of women	

understanding of disruptive events in the body domain that guided multiple changes in the school environment.

Example A: "I Felt That My Body Was Public"

Meagan starts speaking in a group of thirteen-year-olds about her discomfort with her body, especially with menstruation, a new experience for her: "I resent having to tell resident staff why I need to go to the pharmacy when I get my period. I feel that this is a private thing." Mary: "One time last year I was asked to prove that I had my period so I could go out. When I came to the staff room, there were three staff there; I felt that my body was public." Cindy: "Aaron told me that all the boys' washrooms have condoms, but we don't have Tampax machines in our washrooms. How come?" . . . The group seems struck by this comparison. Elizabeth: "I don't think that they respect the bodies of girls as much as boys." Rebecca: "It's the same thing when we change. Residence staff feel comfortable getting into my room any time, even when I change. A week ago, [a staff member] came with a guest and I was changing in the room, and she did not even leave the room or apologize. I did not feel comfortable saying 'will you please leave the room right now?'" . . . Elizabeth: "We should go together to the staff and demand that they install Tampax machines in all washrooms. We should also demand that they respect our privacy."

This plan was carried through successfully.

This group discusses different issues related to the right for a private and respectful ownership of their (female) bodies. The events alluded to in this excerpt are but a few examples of many types of events participants described as disrupting their experience of respectful ownership of the body (see Table 14.1). Participants repeatedly indicated that these disruptive experiences intensified during and following puberty and made them feel uncomfortable in their changing bodies.

Example B: "My Father Put My Mother Down. . . . You Need to Have Power to Feel OK about Yourself"

Sarah says in a group of twelve-year-olds: "I am so fat I hate my body, I am so scared I will look like my mother." "No, you're not fat," responds the group. Sarah continues, "I hate my body. My father always puts my mother down because of her weight. She is fat now but she used to be skinny." Says

Mary, "My father also puts my mother down because she is fat but I am not worried about it." Sarah: "My father is also fat now. My mother is at home since we came here [North America] from [Eastern Europe] and she does not have a job. My father has a good job. He puts my mother down all the time." Mary: "When my father puts my mother down she could not care less. She has a really good job and she loves it so she just does not care. She likes going out with her girlfriends." . . . A group member asks, "Why does your mother feel bad [to Sarah] and your [Mary's] mother feel good?" The group begins a process of comparison of different factors such as ages, weights and other appearance measures, and education. They discuss Sarah's mother's immigration and her being alone and jobless at home. . . . "It is power," they say, "Mary's mother has power so she can feel good about herself the way she is, and that makes Mary feel good about herself," "You need power to feel OK about yourself," and "Girls need power."

This group analyzes the contrast between the experiences of two mothers and their daughters and arrives at an understanding of the relevance of two intersecting social issues to body image. One issue involves the prejudicial treatment of women; the other involves the impact of social worth and social power on body acceptance. In many focus groups the girls and adolescent women discovered that, in the prejudicial treatment of women and minority group members, the body was used as an avenue to express prejudicial attitudes. They noted that demeaning allusions to natural bodily processes of women (e.g., premenstrual syndrome [PMS]), women's body characteristics and body shape (e.g., "cow," "bitch," or "cunt"), or women's appearance (e.g., "dumb blondes") were commonly used to devalue women's views, constrain their power, belittle their way of seeing things or their contribution, discount their anger or their rights, or control them through embarrassment (see Table 14.1).

Example C: "Girls Can't Have Too Much Power"

A group of girls requests an "emergency" focus group meeting. A group of fourteen-year-olds sits together and discusses how bad they feel about teasing a girl at the school by calling her a "butch." They notice that she has stopped eating with them and they are worried that she may develop an eating disorder. They say that she is a very good dancer and they are jealous of her. I ask where the term "butch" comes from and what it is about. They explain that she is very athletic and muscular. "We call her 'butch' because she has such strong muscles, she can lift a guy." Another girl says, "So what if she is strong?" Several girls answer, "A girl is not supposed to be stronger than guys, she is supposed to be smaller." I ask whether this comment is only about physical strength. "Everything," answers one girl, "Guys don't like it when you are too strong, like too opinionated or something." Another says, "Girls can't have too much power." . . . A period of quiet settles in the room after this last statement. A girl talks at last, "I can't believe what we did. We wanted to take her power away." Another girl adds, "Remember how [a staff member] says I am too loud, that I should be more quiet and polite, that's the same thing." The group is shaken by their collusion with destructive stereotypes about women. They work out a plan of action: they will approach the girl collectively, apologize to her about their teasing, and explain that they did not realize how prejudiced they were about "girl power."

This plan was followed through and carried out successfully.

In this group the girls examine their own construction of femininity and masculinity, in particular their constraining image of femininity as weaker and powerless. Their collusion with the image of the powerless woman shocks them. The powerless, polite, quiet, woman is associated with a thinner, smaller, and nonmuscular appearance. Other constraining images of femininity were expressed in other groups (see Table 14.1). They often felt limited and controlled by these constraining constructions of women.

These three excerpts exemplify the emergence of critical understanding among the girls and young women in the school about their own body weight and shape preoccupation. As can be seen from these excerpts, the concepts of social power, worth, and equity were key elements repeatedly alluded to in the girls' and young women's interpretive understanding. As a researcher recording and studying the developing discourse around BWSP at the school, I completed an ongoing thematic analysis of the group process that I recorded after each group. The final analysis involved material collected from more than three hundred groups. All themes were readily classified into three main content categories: body ownership, societal prejudices, and the social construction of women (see Table 14.1). It seemed that, for the young women who participated in the project, BWSP worsened when their sense of ownership over their body was disrupted, when their bodies were used as a medium to express pervasive societal prejudices, and when the social construction of women constrained and demeaned ways of being in the body that did not comply with perceived societal expectations. In line with the young women's in-group interpretive understanding, the categories of body ownership, societal prejudices, and the social construction of women were found to be subsumed under the core category of "social power and equity."

In the critical understanding of BWSP that emerged in the groups, body ownership, societal prejudicial treatment, and the social construction of women were the domains in which inequitable treatment of women was expressed. The girls and young women perceived that the intensification of these expressions of inequity in the body domain during puberty was related to their increased preoccupation with body weight and shape. Their interpretive understanding is strikingly different from the professionally derived social theory of eating disorders, which focuses on media-generated "pressures for thinness." The understanding generated by the young women not only highlights the relevance of the core issue of social equity to BWSP, it also articulates the expression of social inequity in their daily experiences of living in their bodies. Whereas social theory based on media-generated "pressures for thinness" places the blame "out there," the "body equity" theory of BWSP challenges young women's immediate social environment.

The Emergence of Critical Action in Body Weight and Shape Preoccupation: Transforming the School Environment

Methodological and Theoretical Considerations

Social transformation and emancipation from oppression are among the basic tenets of PAR (Brydon-Miller 1997). Freire ([1970] 1993) emphasized the role of action in adding to the process of knowledge construction. In the process of emancipation, critical knowledge leads to action. In turn, action and the ensuing change lead to new knowledge (see Figure 14.1).

In this participatory action project, the inextricable connection between critical knowledge and action has enriched the process of knowledge construction in two ways. First, in line with Freire's description, the dialectic process of action and reflection guided transformations in the school sys-

Figure 14.1. *Facets of the School System Transformed through Participatory Action Project*

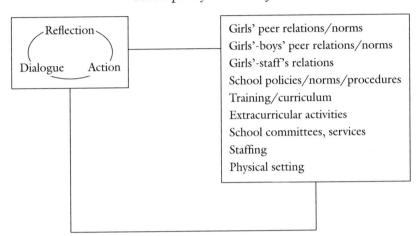

tem. Second, in terms of theory development, categories that emerged in the analysis of action served to confirm categories that emerged in the thematic analysis of focus groups.

Description

In a PAR project, the goal involves change and social transformation. The critical understanding that emerged in the project regarding BWSP—namely, the relevance of social equity, power, and worth to girls' and young women's experience of the body, especially during and following puberty—guided wide-ranging changes in the school environment.

This section includes a description of some of the changes that occurred in the school. I ground this description in three excerpts from group proceedings, based on the verbal summaries of group members.

Example D: "True Partnerships Are Mutual"

A distressed, self-deprecating, silent group discovered to their surprise that they all were affected similarly by the same dance class, a pas-de-deux class. Finding the class difficult, the young men had blamed a few of the young women, claiming they were "too heavy" or "too fat" to be lifted, and the young women were feeling hurt and ashamed. Also, a few of the women had been injured during the exercise, either by the way they were held or because they were dropped.

As the young women started to relate their personal experiences, they discovered that these experiences were shared. They questioned the prejudice that the woman dancer's weight, rather than her stamina (to jump and thus help with the lift, and to hold her posture), prevented successful exercises. They questioned their silence about their right to safety. They questioned the pattern whereby they were attacked by the young men for failed pas-de-deux exercises. They also questioned their acceptance of responsibility for failed exercises.

The group decided to unite during and after classes to confront the young men about their prejudice regarding weight and women dancers, their placing responsibility exclusively with the women, and their attacking style. They were firm that "true partnerships are mutual," and that they "would not settle for less, not only in dance, but also in real life," and that "dance is like a metaphor for life." The group also decided to demand that the school administration provide the men with safety training ("I have a right to be safe") and partnership training ("I am not going to take it any more") before starting the pas-de-deux classes. The group asked me to convey these requests to the school administration. Prior to my meeting, I received a phone call from the director that the women had stopped attending pas-de-deux classes as a protest, until all these issues were rectified.

This summary exemplifies (1) the young women's process of exploration and discovery of the nature of disruptive events in the domains of body ownership (injurious training), prejudicial treatment (women dancer's weight), and social construction of women (silent, responsible for failed endeavors) that impacted negatively on their body and self image, and (2) the way these women planned transformative action in response to these events. The young women decided to address the challenges that arose in the domain of "respectful ownership" by requesting a change in the training curriculum (training male partners in safety prior to pas-de-deux classes), as well as changes in their partners' behavior. They directly confronted and addressed their male partners about the men's misperceptions and prejudices about women's bodies and expressed their view of mutuality in partnerships.

They resisted stereotypic images of women as silent and passive by vocally demanding changes in the curriculum, and by confronting and informing their partners about their refusal to take responsibility for failed exercises and about their view of mutuality in partnerships. In their demand for safe ownership of the body and nonprejudicial treatment, and in their vocal and powerful quest for change, the young women worked toward equitable treatment at the school. All these changes toward greater equity have been incorporated successfully into the school life. The school changed its curriculum to assure young women safety and shared partnership practices. Male partners are well aware of school-wide partnership norms of never making comments about partners' body shape or blaming one side for failed shared exercises. The young men now say to me: "You think I am crazy? I will never make a comment about body shape" or "I never blame my partner when we can't do an exercise in class."

Example E: "They Rate Us on the Slut List"

> This middle-school age group was agitated, angry, and hurt. They started to talk about their male peers. Sarah: "I am afraid to walk by the guys in the corridor." Nancy: "I got punched and grabbed." Rebecca: "I got tripped." Tal: "They rate us on the 'slut list.'" Chelsea: "They said I was five on the 'cunt' list." . . . Jennie: "This is sexual harassment. What is the definition of sexual harassment?"
>
> I define sexual harassment, and we discuss the definition in the group.
>
> Sarah: "I don't feel safe talking to the boys about this. . . . I feel scared. They will laugh at me. Can we talk to the school about this problem? The school needs laws."

This was one of the first groups at the beginning of the project to talk about the pervasiveness of sexual harassment at the school. Following this and other groups, a committee of students and staff was formed to write a "code of ethics" booklet that included a definition of sexual harassment and the school anti-harassment policy, including relevant penalties. By working on anti-harassment school policies, the girls and young women helped achieve greater equity in the school environment.

Example F: "You Dance from the Inside Out"
In this example, "new student" is a student who just joined the school, and "veteran students" are students who have been at the school for a while; all students are first-year high school students.

New student: " I don't think the school pushes students enough. For example, I think that all our bar classes should be on point."

Veteran student: " But I think that our bodies are not ready for that yet. We still need to strengthen our bodies first. Then when we are ready for longer exercises on point, we could do it without getting injured."

New student: "Yes, I agree that we will have more injuries when we do bar on point, but you have to do what you have to do to become a dancer."

Another veteran student: "But I kind of like that the school is teaching us the basics first and only when we are ready we do more difficult exercises."

New student: "It is true that the school makes sure students learn the basics first. That's not what happened to me in my other school. I was thrown into things before I knew the basics. I was injured a lot, but that's the only way to learn."

Another veteran student: "What I resent is that the school does not individualize the body conditioning program enough. They do build strength in dancers, but everyone's needs are different. I have requested that the physiotherapist plan for me my own program, and she hasn't done it yet."

Several veteran students: "Don't wait for her, just go back and demand the program from her. She has so many students, so you have to fight to get her attention." " I have my own program." "I do too."

New student: "I think they exaggerate the building up of muscles. Sometimes I think that they go too far. When I see a "fat chick" on stage, it really disturbs me. I can't enjoy the dance."

Another veteran student: "It really hurts my feelings and makes me angry when you say 'fat chick.' That really puts me down. I don't care about how much muscle bulk somebody has. I actually like a strong and muscular female dancer."

Another veteran student: "I like the natural look. Everybody is different. It is an art. You can express your feelings no matter what your actual weight is. We have a right to be who we are. I don't want to change my body."

New student: "I have to say, I think that they should not let some girls go on stage; their fat distracts from their movements. My director in [her home city] always told us to lose weight and stay extremely skinny."

Veteran Student: "But how can you dance like that? If your focus is all the time on the outside, how can you dance? Because when you dance, you don't dance from the 'outside in,' you dance from the 'inside out'!"

This group, occurring at a later stage of the project, exemplifies several changes that have taken place as an outcome of young women's actions. The students who have been in the school for a while and have taken an active part in the participatory action project have developed new norms of body-anchored discourse among themselves that are more positive and are strikingly different from that of the new student. This group process suggests that within the context of greater equity, the body becomes a domain of positive experiences, inspiration, care, and connection and is not associated with discourses of deprecation or deficiency.

The examples above mention several facets of school life that changed with this participatory action project (see Figure 14.1). All changes worked toward the creation of a more equitable social system where the young women's bodies were not a site of societal oppression and their voices about their experiences were heard and held social power.

Just as I listed the content themes that came up in focus groups, in analyzing the content of the groups I also listed all plans for actions as well as the actions themselves taken by the girls and adolescent women and examined their interrelationships and categorical classifications. The emergent classification resembled that of the content categories (for examples of the classification of specific actions, see Table 14.1 as well as discussions following examples D, E, and F). Changes in all three domains (body ownership, prejudicial treatment, and social construction of women) worked together toward "creating greater body-anchored equity," the core category underlying all actions taken by the young women. The convergence of content and action themes served as a way to confirm the understanding, or "theory," of body image challenges reported by the young women at the dance school.

Discussion

In exploring body weight and shape preoccupation in their dance school through cycles of reflection and action (Freire [1970] 1993), girls and young women derived an understanding and related action plans that targeted expressions of (mainly gender) inequity in their school environment. The girls and young women found that inequity in the body domain was expressed through violations of their experience of ownership of their body, through the expression of sexist and other social prejudices by deprecating their bodies, and through restrictive and stereotypical expectations of them as young women. During puberty, expressions of inequity through the body intensified, as did their body weight and shape preoccupation.

In discussing the understanding of BWSP derived from this participatory action research, we need to consider the particular school context. The school provides intensive training in dance in addition to a stringent academic program. The challenging dance program may intensify particular body-related experiences. For example, interference with a young woman's sense of ownership over her body may be particularly accentuated in this setting due, for example, to the ongoing monitoring of students' bodies as they practice and perform, as well as the extensive physical demands placed upon the body at the school. Similarly, in the domain of the prejudicial treatment of the body, a young woman may experience greater weightist attitudes, greater gender inequity (there are many women in ballet, while men are scarce), and greater racism since many schools and companies lack role models from diverse racial and ethnic backgrounds. In terms of the third domain, the social construction of the female ballerina may be even more restrictive than that of women in general (Vincent 1979).

To date, no other qualitative study of students' experiences of BWSP has been conducted in a school. The findings of the study are in line with those of a few qualitative studies in the area of body image (Larkin, Rice, and Russell 1999; Steiner-Adair 1990; Thompson 1994) and with the view of social critics in the body domain (Bordo 1993; Foucault 1979; Marx 1963; Rich 1986).

The dance school has been a site for two social science studies examining BWSP and eating disorders using two different methodologies and arriving at two different understandings. In 1980, a positivistic study (Garner and Garfinkel 1980) was carried out at this school that aimed to test the professionally derived social theory of BWSP and eating disorders. According to this social theory, the increased incidence of eating disorders relates to the greater discrepancy between widely disseminated media images of thin models and women's actual body weight and shape. The positivistic study used a quasi-experimental design, using comparison groups assumed by the researchers to differ mainly in the degree of "pressures for thinness" exerted upon students in different school settings. A higher incidence of BWSP in the dance school as compared with two other school settings was interpreted by the researchers as supporting their hypothesis that individuals subjected to stronger "pressures for thinness" are at a higher risk of developing anorexia nervosa.

In contrast, the girls and young women at the school who took part in this participatory action research project, which started in 1985, arrived at a divergent understanding of their own body weight and shape preoccupation through a group-based process of reflection and action. In these groups, they transformed the knowledge embedded in their daily life experiences to critical consciousness about the forces that shaped their social reality (Freire [1970] 1993). This critical consciousness centered on the role of inequity in social power and worth, expressed through the use of the body as a site of societal oppression, in the development of BWSP. Disrupted ownership and prejudicial treatment of the body, as well as constricted ways of living in the body, were all expressions of the use of the body as a site of societal oppression. The young women's action plans aimed at freeing the domain of the body from oppressive forces toward the goal of achieving greater (mainly gender) equity in their school. This necessitated transformation in all facets of the school environment. The understanding derived by the young women in this study is evident in multiple ways.

The divergent understanding that emerged has important implications, not only for expanding the theoretical frame and working toward social transformation, but also for the psychological practice of treatment and prevention. Elsewhere (Piran 1999b) I have documented in detail the way in which the participatory action project was associated with a significant reduction of BWSP and eating disorders in the school, an outcome not achieved by applying prevention programs guided by the "pressures-for-thinness" social theory. Prevention programs not anchored in participants' life experiences are less likely to be effective (Piran 1995, 1997).

While the field of education has sanctioned processes of knowledge production and social transformation associated with PAR projects for a few decades now (Hall 1993), the discipline of psychology is just starting to shift toward acceptance of PAR work (Brydon-Miller 1997). Reflecting about my involvement in the participatory action project described in this chapter, I am poignantly aware that had I practiced prevention work at the dance school according to the widely sanctioned "pressures-for-thinness" theory of eating disorders, I would have actively silenced girls' and young women's voices and knowledge about problematic areas in their lives. Further, I would have stunted their crucial work toward social transformation. I would also have missed an invaluable learning experience, as this research project enriched my understanding of the relationship between body and culture. These thoughts vitalize my commitment to this type of work, even when I observe the tendency in psychology to marginalize knowledge derived from varied qualitative methodologies.

I am also aware that these methods—honoring knowledge that develops in dialogue, critically examining the social forces that contextualize the dialogue, and following the commitment to social transformation—are relevant beyond research. They are also relevant to the practice of therapy, health-promotion activities, teaching, and other activities included in the practice of psychology.

References

Beauvoir, S. de. 1974. *The second sex.* 2d ed. New York: Vintage Press.

Bordo, S. 1993. *Unbearable weight: Feminism, Western culture, and the body.* Berkeley: University of California Press.

Brydon-Miller, M. 1997. Participatory action research: Psychology and social change. *Journal of Social Issues* 53:657–666.

Bunnell, D. W., I. R. Shenker, M. P. Nussbaum, M. S. Jacobson, and P. Cooper. 1990. Subclinical versus formal eating disorders: Differentiating psychological features. *International Journal of Eating Disorders* 9:357–362.

Faludi, S. 1991. *Backlash: The undeclared war against American women.* New York: Crown.

Fine, M. 1992. Preface. In *Disruptive voices: The possibilities of feminist research.* Ann Arbor: University of Michigan Press.

Fine, M., and S. M. Gordon. [1989] 1992. Feminist transformation of/despite psychology. In *Disruptive voices: The possibilities of feminist research,* ed. M. Fine, 1–25. Ann Arbor: University of Michigan Press.

Foucault, M. 1979. *Discipline and punish: The birth of the prison.* New York: Vintage Books.

Freire, P. [1970] 1993. *Pedagogy of the oppressed.* New York: Continuum.

Garner, D. M., and P. E. Garfinkel. 1980. Socio-cultural factors in the development of anorexia nervosa. *Psychological Medicine* 10:647–656.

Gaventa, J. 1993. The powerful, the powerless, and the experts: Knowledge struggles in an information age. In *Voices of change: Participatory research in the United States and Canada,* eds. P. Park, M. Brydon-Miller, B. Hall, and T. Jackson, 21–40. Toronto: OISE Press.

Gilligan, C., and L. M. Brown. 1992. *Meeting at the crossroads: Women's Psychology and girls' development.* Cambridge, MA: Harvard University Press.

Hall, B. 1993. Introduction. In *Voices of change: Participatory research in the United States and Canada,* eds. P. Park, M. Brydon-Miller, B. Hall, and T. Jackson, xiii–xxii. Toronto: OISE Press.

Hartsock, N. C. M. 1983. The feminist standpoint: Developing the ground for a specifically feminist historical materialism. In *Discovering Reality,* eds. S. Harding and M. B. Hintikka. Dordrecht, Holland: D. Reidel.

Herzog, D., and C. D. Burns. 1993. A follow-up study of 33 subdiagnostic eating disordered women. *International Journal of Eating Disorders* 6: 741–747.

Larkin, J., C. Rice, and V. Russell. 1999. Sexual harassment and the prevention of eating disorders: Educating young women. In *Preventing eating disorders: A handbook of interventions and special challenges,* eds. N. Piran, M. P. Levine, and C. Steiner-Adair, 194–206. Philadelphia: Brunner/Mazel.

Levine, M. P., N. Piran, and C. Stoddard. 1999. Mission more probable: Media literacy, activism, and advocacy as primary prevention. In *Preventing eating disorders: A handbook of interventions and special challenges,* eds. N. Piran, M. P. Levine, and C. Steiner-Adair, 1–25. Philadelphia: Brunner/Mazel.

MacKinnon, C. A. 1989. *Towards a feminist theory of the state.* Cambridge, MA: Harvard University Press.

Maguire, P. 1987. *Doing participatory research: A feminist approach.* Amherst: Center for International Education, University of Massachusetts.

————. 1993. Challenges, contradictions, and celebrations: Attempting participatory research as a doctoral student. In *Voices of change: Participatory research in the United States and Canada,* eds. P. Park, M. Brydon-Miller, B. Hall, and T. Jackson, 157–176. Toronto: OISE Press.

Marx, K. 1963. *The poverty of philosophy.* New York: International Publishers.

Park, P. 1993. What is participatory research? A theoretical and methodological perspective. In *Voices of change: Participatory research in the United States and Canada,* eds. P. Park, M. Brydon-Miller, B. Hall, and T. Jackson, 1–19. Toronto: OISE Press.

Pike, K. M., and R. H. Striegel-Moore. 1997. Disordered eating and eating disorders. In *Health care for women: Psychological, social, and behavioral influences,* ed. S. J. Gallant, G. P. Keita, et al., 97–114. Washington, DC: American Psychological Association.

Piran, N. 1995. Prevention: Can early lessons lead to a delineation of an alternative model? A critical look at prevention with schoolchildren. *Eating Disorders: The Journal of Treatment and Prevention* 3:28–36.

————. 1997. Prevention of eating disorders: Directions for future research. *Psychopharmacology Bulletin* 33 (3): 419–423.

————. 1999a. The reduction of preoccupation with body weight and shape in schools: A feminist approach. In *Preventing eating disorders: A handbook of interventions and special challenges*, eds. N. Piran, M. P. Levine, and C. Steiner-Adair, 194–206. Philadelphia: Brunner/Mazel.

Piran, N. 1999b. Eating disorders: A trial of prevention in a high risk school setting. *Journal of Primary Prevention* 20 (1): 75–90.

Rich, A. 1986. *Of woman born*. New York: W. W. Norton.

Rodin, J., L. R. Silberstein, and R. H. Striegel-Moore. 1985. Women and weight: A normative discontent. In *Psychology and gender: Nebraska symposium on motivation*, ed. T. B. Sonderegger, 267–307. Lincoln: University of Nebraska Press.

Shisslak, C. M., M. Crago, and L. S. Estes. 1995. The spectrum of eating disturbances. *International Journal of Eating Disorders* 18:209–219.

Smith, D. E. 1987. *The everyday world as problematic: A feminist sociology*. Toronto: University of Toronto Press.

Steiner-Adair, C. 1990. The body politic: Normal female adolescent development and the development of eating disorders. In *Making connections*, eds. C. Gilligan, N. Lyons, and T. Hanmer, 162–181. Cambridge, MA: Harvard University Press.

Striegel-Moore, R. H. 1994. A feminist agenda for psychological research on eating disorders. In *Feminist perspectives on eating disorders*, eds. P. Fallon, M. Katzman, and S. Wooley, 438–454. New York: Guilford Press.

Thompson, B. 1994. Food, bodies, and growing up female: Childhood lessons about culture, race, and class. In *Feminist perspectives on eating disorders*, eds. P. Fallon, M. Katzman, and S. Wooley, 355–378. New York: Guilford Press.

Vincent, L. M. 1979. *Competing with the Sylph: Dancers and the ideal body form*. New York: Andrews and McMeel.

Wolf, N. 1991. *The beauty myth: How images of beauty are used against women*. New York: Morrow.

15

■　　■　　■　　■　　■　　■　　■　　■　　■

Negotiating the Observer-Observed Relationship

Participatory Action Research

Cynthia J. Chataway

How Do You Do PAR?

I have found it difficult to answer requests for advice on how to do participatory action research (PAR). The dilemma has been to not be too specific, but to suggest a process and boundaries within which useful and acceptable answers will emerge from any particular context. Thus, to a certain extent, principles are the only real direction one can give to a potential participatory action researcher (Brown 1993; Fals-Borda and Rahman 1991; Reason 1993; Whyte 1991). Potential co-researchers need principles on-site to decide whether or not to work with the researcher (the equivalent of informed consent). The operationalization of these principles is then ideally worked out in dialogue with local actors. Thus, PAR in practice can look drastically different from one setting to the next (e.g., Center for Community Education and Action Inc. 1991; Maguire 1987; Smith and Willms 1997; Whyte 1991).

More than anything, PAR is an attitude. It is a commitment to a way of being with people, to be responsive to their needs and concerns (Caulfield

1979), and to accept the vulnerability that comes with full participation in multiple layers of social complexity (Behar 1996; Dreier 1999).[1] In PAR, the needs and interests of the people in the research context are prioritized, and research "subjects" are invited to be full participants in designing research and deciding how the results will be used and represented. The conceptual and methodological boundaries between researcher and subject roles that currently predominates in psychology are loosened, allowing for some of the interchangeability that was more common in the early years of psychological research (Danziger 1990).[2]

Although attitude is most important, the range of skills that the outside researcher brings may also influence how responsive he/she can be to the needs of the people and the context. It is helpful to have some familiarity with a wide range of research methods, including quantitative hypothesis-testing questionnaires (Schuman and Presser 1981; Zimmerman and Zahniser 1991); ethnography (Atkinson and Hammersley 1994); community development (Campfens 1997); and visual experiential methods of inquiry such as mapping, modeling, and video, as used in Participatory Rural Appraisal (Chambers 1997; Mukherjee 1993). In addition to interdisciplinary research abilities, third-party intervention experience can help one include and integrate diverse needs and interests while designing research. Skills such as facilitation (Schwarz 1996), mediation (Moore 1996), dispute system design (Constantino and Merchant 1996), and theater of the oppressed (Boal 1999; Schutzman and Cohen-Cruz 1994) are all useful, although not necessary. Experience with a range of processes can also contribute to the confidence needed to be able to function in a participatory process, as well as the courage to let the content unfold as it will. In many ways, PAR resembles mediation, in that the outsider/mediator makes a commitment to democratic principles of practice, rather than to a particular product, and his/her job is to facilitate the emergence of answers from the system, rather than to provide answers (Gray 1989).

The attitude of the PAR researcher might be described as commitment to full democratization of both content and method (Guba and Lincoln 1989). The distinction between content and method is important because PAR is sometimes misunderstood as standard anthropological research. Anthropological methodology generally democratizes the content of research (e.g., by checking interpretations with informants on-site), while decisions on method remain with the external researcher (Heron 1996,

27). In PAR the "subjects" of research are ideally as engaged as the outside researcher in decisions about both method and content. Just as the insiders share expert knowledge of their context with the outside researcher, the outsider shares expert knowledge of the range and dis/advantages of methods with the insiders. Together they make informed decisions about both content and method.

PAR researchers have not yet, as far as I know, gone so far as to invite members of historically oppressed groups to engage in systematic joint inquiry of the researcher's privileged world. This step would perhaps complete the mutual research relationship and maximize the possibility of overcoming the limitations on understanding and perspective-taking that are inherent when one remains within one's own culture (Merton 1972). In subsequent research, Native people have raised the possibility of coming to study my community.

I have found that academic granting agencies and ethics boards do not tend to understand or support PAR in practice, despite accolades for the value of the method (which far exceeds minimum ethical responsibilities toward research participants) and the potential of the process to make a positive difference in people's lives. Grants and ethics committees tend to decide whether to approve PAR proposals by the same criteria they use for standard research. Namely, they look for specific hypotheses and a detailed research design, in a way that prioritizes content over process. A focus on content undermines and withdraws support from a process-oriented approach like PAR, especially in the early stages. Since PAR research develops over time through a lengthy consensus-building process with people in the context, what can and should be specified in advance are the principles of the process: how participants will be involved, decision rules, and responsibilities to the context. In some cases, the research will not be fully designed until more than a year of intense collaboration has taken place.

Although results in psychology will always be "codetermined by the social relations between experimenters and subjects" (Danziger 1990, 9), the accounting psychological researchers are required to do "is typically limited to purely technical considerations. It is precisely the social aspects of scientific practice that are systematically excluded from practitioners' discussions about methodology" (13). Fine (1994) invites researchers to see how examining "these 'relations between' [self and other] get[s] us 'better' data" by creating occasions for researchers and informants to discuss what is, and is not happening within "the negotiated relations of whose story is being told, why, to whom, with what interpretation" (72). In PAR, participants and researchers jointly examine their relations with each other. To get the process started, the outsider needs to model a willingness to be scrutinized and held to declared standards of practice. Declaring principles will not mean they will never be violated, but that one is accountable for violations and takes public responsibility for them.

Insiders will find PAR significantly different from their assumptions about research and their past experiences with researchers. They will, at least initially, judge this new behavior from within their prevailing set of assumptions. Against a backdrop of authoritarian relationships, inclusive and responsive behavior may be judged as indecisive, uninformed, a waste of time. One may encounter the idea that only students need the input of others to make decisions about their research. Demystifying the research process challenges both the monopoly on knowledge construction and the researcher's own authority. A PAR researcher needs considerable clarity, commitment, and confidence in the principles to avoid becoming defensive during the initial period, as people adjust and test a new kind of research relationship. Some people, particulary the more powerful, may issue subtle ultimatums that unless their wishes are given a predominant place, that they will not contribute, and may even attempt to undermine the research. This is a method within which the researcher cannot escape vulnerability, nor should he or she try, since mutual vulnerability allows the effects of domination to be reflected upon more accurately and safely (Behar 1996). "[R]esearch that does not reflect on and analyze the social context from which it springs serves only the status quo" (Kirby and McKenna 1989, 16).

Of course, principles are cold and lifeless; researchers need examples to be able to picture themselves in a context and make an informed choice about whether to become involved in such a process. I gained the courage to "learn by doing" (Maguire 1993) at a conference listening to stories about doing PAR in a poor district of Caracas, Venezuela.

In the following sections, I discuss some of the details of a three-year PAR project in the Native community of Kahnawake and then offer an analysis of the dialectical process involved in our emergent understanding.

In the past decade, PAR has almost become the standard way to do research in Native communities in Canada (Jackson 1993), but there is a dirth of detailed description and analysis of the many ways this process can manifest.

Overview of Three Years' Work

Over the three years of the PAR project in Kahnawake, we engaged in a lengthy process of consulting to achieve consensus among the factions and between the factions and me on defining the research questions, developing the research tools, collecting the data, interpreting the data, and deciding whether and how to use and communicate new learnings or to move into further research.

I was initially introduced to people in this highly factionalized community of eight thousand just outside Montreal by a Native professor and two Native graduate students on a visit we made together. (See Chataway 1994 for details of factionalism, such as traditional Longhouse and Band Council factions.) Over the three years I made twenty-two trips alone, with an average stay of five days. For most of these visits, I either paid for accommodation in the community or stayed with a respected apolitical family to which I had been introduced during that initial visit. This family was very helpful in explaining the history of the community and suggesting a diverse set of other people with whom I should speak. In my first few visits, I immersed myself in meetings with a wide range of community members and in reading at the Cultural Centre.

Some consultation with research participants was done between community visits, by facsimile and phone. In total I worked with more than 120 community members. The sets of people who participated in each stage of the research overlapped by approximately 50 percent from one stage to the next, in a kind of chaining pattern. Therefore, the participants in the final year (dialogue group) tended to be people referred to me by community members after several months or even a year of working in Kahnawake.

The first step in relationship-building was to find a way to communicate the goals and principles of PAR effectively over coffee, in language that could be repeated as often as necessary. Mutual inquiry and problem-solving (Reason 1993; Whyte 1991) became "I'd like to work with you on research to better understand the kinds of challenges currently facing the community." For traditionally-subordinated groups to experience control and ownership of intellectual property (Fals-Borda and Rahman 1991) became "[m]ost of the logistical work will be done by myself but the direction, process, and design of the project, and the decision regarding what to do with the results, will be made through consultation with the people who wish to participate." To develop self-sufficient motivated local action-researchers (Fals-Borda and Rahman 1991) became "I'm interested in whether there is some issue that people here would like to do research on together. I'd like you to think of the research as your own, and I am just helping you to get it done."

To offer reassurances about the kinds of concerns people raised, I made several commitments to the community regarding who would be included/excluded, how decisions would be made, and how the various goals held by different people would be prioritized. These commitments were: (1) anyone who wished to have input into the research would be included, (2) research decisions would be made by consensus, and (3) community needs would be given priority (i.e., above my research interests/ needs). The elected grand chief was very open to and supportive of this research. The first time I met with him, he mused, "Whenever anyone comes on the reserve to do anything, I am inundated with calls from people asking if that person is really who they say they are, if they are legit. . . . You are obviously doing something right." In my case, he had received only one call.

To demonstrate inclusiveness, I made it a point to meet with people from each political group approximately equally, parking my car in front of each home or office conspicuously, each time I was in the community. Consensus meant that agreement between myself and at least one central person in each political group was a prerequisite for engaging in the research at all, and for moving from one stage of research to another. When a research decision needed to be made, I met with at least one but generally more of my contacts from each political group to discuss the options. I tried to identify any agreement that emerged from these discussions, wrote that up, and contacted each person again. If all those involved could live with the agreement, we proceeded accordingly. If there were objections or substantive additions, then all were consulted again. (See Figure 15.1.)

Figure 15.1. *Participatory Action Research Design in Kahnawake*

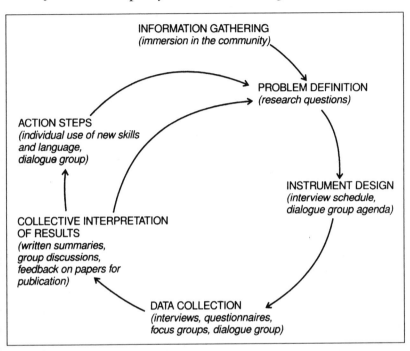

Once I had developed a general level of understanding of the community and a wide base of working relationships, and it became clear that there was an interest in collaborative research, I began collecting suggestions regarding an overarching research question. After three or four weeks I began to distribute draft lists of these suggestions and to compile feedback on them. There was one question that people from across the community said was important, so we focused on that question and moved to the instrument design stage. The question was, "What are the barriers to designing and adopting a new system of government in this community?" I discussed the range of potential research tools that I could make available to them, and they chose initially to have me interview community members with a set of questions they would devise. This interview schedule was developed through a long process during which community members contributed questions and commented upon the questions contributed by others. Names of individuals or groups contributing questions were not listed with their particular contributions.

Even when the set of interview questions was fairly stabilized, we continued to develop it as I carried out the interviews with individuals from each political group. In these interviews I asked for people's answers to the questions *and* their reactions to the questions themselves. The core questions did not change as a result of this process, but the surrounding questions changed considerably.

In interpreting the interview results, at the suggestion of several community members, I wrote a fairly unanalyzed summary of the similarities and differences between responses to the interview questions and added some of my own observations on the decision-making patterns and dilemmas I perceived in the community. Interviews revealed considerable agreement on the ideals that should underlie community decision-making but disagreement regarding how these ideals would look in practice. Questionnaire results suggested that there was wide disagreement on how to apply a central value held within the community, namely, that their government should be culturally legitimate.

The interview summary was discussed in focus groups (with five to twenty-five members of one political group at a time), and each focus group produced a statement about the challenges facing community decision-making. A list of these statements and a summary of the group discussions were provided to all groups and further discussed. These statements concerned the need for more trust, a greater sense of community, and clarity about cultural identity.

After a year and a half, we moved into the action stage.[3] Some of the interviewees had suggested that we bring together members of each political group for facilitated discussion. This suggestion was supported in the focus groups. So I asked each political group to recommend two people to participate in an intergroup dialogue. Once ten people had been recommended and had agreed to participate, I worked with these people to develop mutually acceptable ground rules, goals, agenda, and role of the chair for this dialogue group. At this stage, the focus was defined as a dilemma: "How can we satisfy the need for the community to unite in respect and understanding . . . and at the same time confront the history of betrayal each group feels it has experienced when trusting others?" The group met seven times, approximately monthly, for eight months.

I suggested to this dialogue group that we write something to communicate what we had learned. All group members declined taking responsibility for producing a public product from our work, but several read and responded to articles that I wrote for distribution in the community and for publication. One or more members of each political group read and gave extensive feedback, which was integrated into all papers before publication.

Observer or Observed?

The preceding section offers the "technical" version of what actually took place over those three years. It is a story that can only be told now that the work is complete. I did not predict much of what occurred, nor did I understand as it was taking place. My thoughts on what we accomplished and did not accomplish can be found elsewhere (Chataway 1994, 1997). The rest of this chapter focuses on the quality and challenges of our research relationship (the "social aspects"; see Danziger 1990) that I think were crucial to anything being accomplished at all.

Community members had strong reactions to me as a researcher, and to any research focus on themselves. Fear at being the focus of research was intermingled with satisfaction at engaging actively in and learning from their own inquiry at all major stages of the research. I shared their satisfaction with influencing the research process, as well as their anxiety when I was the focus of scrutiny.[4]

Throughout the research we oscillated between two different foci, each of which offered a different kind of explanation for the community's predicament. The process began with a critical focus on me as a potentially dangerous outsider, later shifting to a critical focus on community members and their responsibilities for their situation, forever punctuated by critical reflection on outsider involvements. In the final year, within the small dialogue group, we were able to hold both of these foci at once, with some level of acceptance, and jointly develop action steps. It may be that the PAR approach, which allowed for analysis of the full research relationship, supported and developed their ability to see their situation more fully, without denying or ignoring the influence of outsiders, the responsibilities of insiders, and their ambivalence about where their focus should be. We were not so much searching for the "truth" of their situation as developing a way of understanding that "fit with" the experiences of all, and thus would allow collective action.

Observing the Outsider

The initial months were crucial to the navigation of our relationship—and to the decision on behalf of at least some community members that it might be safe and valuable to work together. These were also the months in which I was most confused, thinking I was supposed to be an active researcher and facilitator of community decision-making, but instead finding myself constantly under scrutiny, almost as though I was the object of analysis.

From the first research trip I made by myself, I entered into a process of almost-constant self-definition as community members directed their complaints about their previous research experiences at me. For example: "I remember the last dissertation done here. That was the beginning of all the troubles we are having now." "It is not going to help us, just going to help you. Sometimes we feel we're caged in, and people are always coming in. This is the way children feel too. We don't like to feel we're experimented on." Expectations about my motives ranged from consumption ("to take their story") to appropriation ("to adopt Native ways"). Perhaps I opened the floodgates for such observations by asking them if they had an interest in working with me. In the context of bad past experiences, the initial answer was almost entirely negative. Listening skills I had learned as a mediator were helpful as I reflected back people's concerns before reasserting my commitment to their well-being, with statements such as: "I can see how upsetting it would be to feel used for the benefit of people who already have lots of privileges you do not have. Is that part of what you are saying? I would like to work *with* you in a very different way than what you are describing, on a problem or challenge that is identified by the community." As the object of their scrutiny, I experienced what they probably have often felt: as a person I was obscured and in my place was a category, to which the reaction was strong and negative.

I wrote a letter to create a clear permanent record, which I could leave with people, of my goals and commitment to their safety.[5] In this letter I stated openly what I hoped to gain, as well as offering to assist the community in problem solving. "I would like to be sure that the research I am doing will, as much as possible, respond to the expressed wishes of the community while also meeting the requirements of my doctoral dissertation." I explained that I was a student with time and some resources to devote to research, and that I wished to work on something that would be potentially useful to people grappling with major challenges. This was not enough to reduce the tremendous scrutiny immediately. People knew something about dissertations. They knew dissertations had to pass evaluation by senior professors who would be unlikely to prioritize the needs of the community. Fortunately, I had created what I considered an "insurance policy" for this concern: I explained that I had a half-complete laboratory research project that could serve as my dissertation if the work in Kahnawake did not result in a product that was acceptable to my evaluating committee. This information seemed to help mark my presence in the community as somewhat new since I did not *need* them in order to get my degree.

We began to shift from an exclusive and exhausting focus on me and concerns about my hidden agendas to considering their concerns about their community. However, I was never able to forget that I would "offend by [my] very presence," as a representative of the dominant society. For instance, at the beginning of a focus group, after meeting with the leader of that particular group for more than fifteen hours, this man stood in front of me, pointed his finger at me, and said: "You white people think you can just come in here for half an hour, take what you want, and leave!" I met his honest indignation with my own, defending myself by saying: "You know it is not fair to associate me with that, I have met with you at least five times for several hours each." My reaction did not allow him his ambivalence about this outsider who was so involved in his community. In some ways my reaction actually demanded that he protect me from his ambivalence. He looked confused, walked away, and never participated in the research again, although many in his group continued to participate.

Observing the Community

In the beginning, I felt fairly sure that the only appropriate focus for any research we might do together would be on their problematic relationship with the mainstream Canadian society. Many of their comments seemed to confirm my assumption: "Outsiders should not know about us. We have a lot, a lot of problems with the provincial and federal governments. They just use whatever they can find against us." "The ignorance of the white community works to our advantage. They think we are more ferocious than we are. We feel in control of that relationship." On the other hand, many community members stressed that their relationship with the non-Native society was not a concern to them. "They [non-Natives] are irrelevant to us." "We have no relationship with the non-Native system." If I asked questions, they generally went unanswered.

Despite the warnings against focusing on the community, most of the content that people shared with me in those initial meetings focused on internal relations within the community. Confused about whether there was any work we could do together, I wrote up several research questions about the relationship between Kahnawake and mainstream Canadian society and asked for comment. Eventually, a traditional leader told me directly what so many had been telling me indirectly, that their main concerns were about the breakdown of internal relations in the community. Upon reviewing my journal reflections on my interviews I realized that out of my fear of meddling in their internal affairs I had inadvertently steered conversations away from this topic for several months, asking questions and showing more interest in the external relationship. With this revelation, I drafted a research proposal that was of interest to all groups, on their difficulties with collective decision-making.

People's interest in the research grew, but there always remained suspicion about the internal focus. "You may seem trustworthy, but what if someone in government gets this information and uses it against us." "You've been to almost every part of this community asking questions about land, government, and things to do with the sovereignty of the nation. People are wondering what you are doing, asking the same questions as the SQ [police]." When I explained to the second person quoted here that I had wanted to do research on the relationship between Natives and non-Natives, but that the community members had identified internal issues as their central concern, he responded softly, "Yes, those are the issues we are concerned about." Another said, "This is something an outsider can help with, because you have a fresh perspective." So, while the fear remained, the interest in what could come of the research was often enough to counterbalance it.

Developing the interview schedule also evidenced tremendous ambivalence. People told me initially to drop the "irrelevant" interview questions I had added about their relationship with the non-Native society. However, when the list was reduced to one question about the relationship between the community and the larger society, with the rest of the questions being about the community's internal conflict, people remarked that the set of questions made it sound like the situation was "all their fault." So we added back in several questions about outside influences on their decision-making process.

In addition to their concern about an outsider's gaze, members of the community also feared being the target of criticism from each other, and thus felt they needed to protect themselves. Public criticism of others was common in the newspaper, community radio station, and at community meetings. Therefore, I often changed the wording of someone's contribution (such as an interview question) so that the contributor would be less identifiable, or so that the statement would sound less accusatory. The reasons for any changes were discussed with the contributor, and changes were not made without his/her agreement. These efforts to preserve the anonymity of people's contributions protected community members from criticism and allowed people to consider the ideas rather than reacting to the contributor of the ideas.

Community members in Kahnawake also did not want certain aspects of their community to be seen. There were strong sentiments to deny and exclude the more difficult parts of the community system. For example, several community members suggested I ignore members of a "radical group," saying these people would refuse to participate, would "call me down," and would "make no sense." Members of this "radical group" did actively participate by attending long meetings and providing documentation and written responses, but they made demands of their own that I stop including all voices equally. "You have to come to the conclusion about who here is telling you the truth and who isn't." Despite these reactions, I continued to meet with all groups and gradually learned about the essential role played by each in the community system. The "radical group" (like me) turned out to represent both a danger and an opportunity for the community. In private interviews people often told me that although the rest of the community seemed to think that this group was crazy, they felt that it had a lot of knowledge to offer about Mohawk traditions. Unfortunately, the prevailing conception in Kahnawake was that members of this group used their knowledge as a weapon against others in the community. Excluding this group, however, as many had asked me publicly to do, would have excluded an important and influential voice.

Especially in the more powerful and more active community groups, people expressed the hope that the research would reveal the ways in which "we are all saying the same thing." In addition to wanting a clear sense of direction, their desire to demonstrate consensus seemed to be motivated by concern about the outside gaze. For example, the editor of the local newspaper wrote, "In tradition it is said that one should never show two faces to the enemy. The enemy should only see one face, one mind, one people. . . . Not showing division is a discipline" (Deer 1993, 2). In striving for this homogeneity they were prepared to overlook substantial differences in experience and opinion.

Conclusion

Collaboration between Natives and non-Natives can evoke tremendous ambivalence. I was familiar with this kind of conflicted experience because before commencing this community research, I had attempted to write a paper with two Native graduate students. My intended co-authors described this experience as a "dangerous state of liminality." They felt that other Native students were suspicious of them for working with non-Natives, particularly because we were "studying Indians." In reflection papers about the experience, they wrote that it was impossible to complete the paper we were writing and preserve the relationships among ourselves and with the Native student community.

In Kahnawake we were sufficiently able to avoid the danger areas of the research relationship to produce several documents that were widely distributed in the community. But it was a delicate balancing act to generate a collective product about internal difficulties without publicly crediting individual contributions (in order to protect individuals from criticism), and without revealing "the kind of information the police would like to have." In response to the written research analysis, several said, "I was not surprised. I could have written the same thing you wrote, but because it is from an outsider, people will see it with less bias." Even within the dialogue group, community members questioned their ability to act publicly as a group under community scrutiny. This was a painful but enlightened realization. "Sometimes I'm a little disappointed in our behavior, like that we couldn't admit we were part of that group."

Throughout the research, we struggled to see the whole system, with all its internal and external pressures, rather than ignoring the presence and influence of some parts of the system. The value of PAR in coming to terms with the insider-outsider relationship is highlighted by the fact that in the final year, a systemic analysis of their community emerged. The dialogue group articulated the community's difficulties as an almost impossible choice, imposed by Canadian law, between meeting their identity needs through the traditional system, and meeting their pragmatic needs through the imposed band council system.[6] By observing themselves as research participants, and their reactions to me as outsider, we came to better understand the community system and the barriers to change. With this understanding the community was better able to act toward overcoming the barriers by accepting internal responsibility and beginning to work together in the dialogue group and, with the relationships formed there, outside of the dialogue group.

Notes

1. Similar principles underlie the methods used in approaches such as liberation anthropology, active sociology, and feminist research.

2. Early psychologists frequently took the role of research participant, while their students kept records of the responses of their mentors. Early publications also sometimes listed all the names of research participants, since their personal credibility was considered relevant to the quality of the research data they generated.

3. This stage was supported by an Applied Social Issues Internship Award from the Society for the Psychological Study of Social Issues.

4. I thank Catalin Mamali (personal communication, January 25, 1999) for pointing out the dialectical nature of the relationship between observer and observed at the core of these reactions.

5. Krogh (1998) provides a set of very helpful questions to guide the development of a joint partnership agreement, which is a more systematic way to arrive at a clear framework for the working relationship.

6. After the Canadian government required that band councils replace traditional councils on reserves (1890 in Kahnawake; see Alfred 1995), resources were increasingly distributed to the community through these elected bodies, requiring people to make choices between receiving necessary resources and maintaining loyalty to their traditional leadership.

References

Alfred, G. R. 1995. *Heeding the voices of our ancestors*. Don Mills, Ontario: Oxford University Press.

Atkinson, P., and M. Hammersley. 1994. Ethnography and participant observation. In *Handbook of Qualitative Research*, eds. N. Denzin and Y. Lincoln, 248–261. New Delhi, India: Sage Publications.

Behar, R. 1996. *The vulnerable observer: Anthropology that breaks your heart*. Boston: Beacon Press.

Boal, A. 1999. *Legislative theatre*. New York: Routledge.

Brown, D. 1993. Social change through collective reflection with Asian non-governmental development organizations. *Human Relations* 46 (2): 249–272.

Campfens, H. 1997. *Community development around the world: Practice, theory, research, training*. Buffalo: University of Toronto Press.

Caulfield, M. D. 1979. Participant observation or partisan participation? In *The politics of anthropology: From colonialism and sexism toward a view from below*, eds. G. Huizer and B. Mannheim, 309–318. Paris: Mouton Publishers.

Center for Community Education and Action Inc. 1991. *Participatory research: An annotated bibliography*. Amherst, MA: Center for International Education, University of Massachusetts.

Chambers, R. 1997. Whose reality counts? Putting the first last. New York: Intermediate Technology Publications.

Chataway, C. J. 1994. Imposed democracy: Political alienation and perceptions of justice in an aboriginal community. Unpublished doctoral dissertation. Harvard University.

———. 1997. An examination of the constraints on mutual inquiry in a participatory action research project. *Journal of Social Issues* 53 (4): 747–765.

Constantino, C., and C. S. Merchant. 1996. *Designing conflict management systems*. San Francisco: Jossey-Bass.

Danziger, K. 1990. *Constructing the subject: Historical origins of psychological research*. Cambridge: Cambridge University Press.

Deer, K. 1993. About showing divisions. *Eastern Door* 2 (6): 2.

Dreier, O. 1999. Personal trajectories of participation across contexts of social practice. *Outlines: Critical Social Studies* 1 (1): 5–32.

Fals-Borda, O., and M. Rahman. 1991. *Action and knowledge*. New York: Apex Press.

Fine, M. 1994. Working the hyphens: Reinventing self and other in qualitative research. In *Handbook of qualitative research*, eds. N. Denzin and Y. Lincoln, 70–82. London: Sage Publications.

Gray, B. 1989. *Collaborating*. Oxford: Jossey-Bass.

Guba, E., and Y. Lincoln. 1989. *Fourth generation evaluation*. New Delhi, India: Sage Publications.

Heron, J. 1996. *Co-operative inquiry. Research into the human condition.* London: Sage Publications.

Jackson, T. 1993. A way of working: Participatory research and the Aboriginal movement in Canada. In *Voices of change: Participatory research in the United States and Canada*, eds. P. Park, M. Brydon-Miller, B. Hall, and T. Jackson, 47–64. Toronto: OISE Press.

Kirby, S., and K. McKenna. 1989. *Experience, research, and social change.* Toronto: Garamond Press.

Krogh, K. 1996. Ethical issues in collaborative disability research: Applications of the partnership agreement framework. *International Journal of Practical Approaches to Disability* 20 (1): 29–35.

Maguire, P. 1987. *Doing participatory research: A feminist approach.* Amherst: Center for International Education, University of Massachusetts.

———. 1993. Challenges, contradictions, and celebrations: Attempting participatory research as a doctoral student. In *Voices of change: Participatory research in the United States and Canada*, eds. P. Park, M. Brydon-Miller, B. Hall, and T. Jackson, 157–176. Toronto: OISE Press.

Merton, R. K. 1972. Insiders and outsiders: A chapter in the sociology of knowledge. *American Journal of Sociology* 78:9–47.

Moore, C. 1996. *The mediation process.* San Francisco: Jossey-Bass.

Mukherjee, N. 1993. Participatory rural appraisal: Methodology and applications. New Delhi: Concept Publishing.

Reason, P. 1993. Co-operative inquiry, participatory action research, and action inquiry: Three approaches to participative inquiry. In *Handbook of qualitative research*, eds. N. Denzin and Y. Lincoln. Thousand Oaks, CA: Sage Publications.

Schuman, H., and S. Presser. 1981. *Questions and answers about attitude surveys.* Toronto: Academic Press.

Schutzman, M., and J. Cohen-Cruz, eds. 1994. *Playing Boal: Theatre, therapy, activism.* New York: Routledge.

Schwarz, R. M. 1996. *The skilled facilitator.* San Francisco: Jossey-Bass.

Smith, S. E., and D. G. Willms. 1997. *Nurtured by knowledge: Learning to do participatory action-research.* New York: Apex Press.

Stewart, S., ed. 1995. *Participatory rural appraisal, abstracts of sources: An annotated bibliography.* Brighton: Institute of Development Studies.

Whyte, W. F. 1991. *Participatory action research.* London: Sage Publications.

Zimmerman, M., and J. Zahniser. 1991. Refinements of sphere-specific measures of perceived control: Development of a sociopolitical control scale. *Journal of Community Psychology* 19:189–204.

■ ■ ■ ■ ■ ■ ■ ■ ■

Possibilities and Challenges of
Engaging Subjectivities

Part IV

■ ■ ■ ■

16

■   ■   ■   ■   ■   ■   ■   ■   ■

Minding the Gap

Positivism, Psychology, and the Politics of Qualitative Methods

Erica Burman

"MIND THE GAP" appears in large letters on the edge of London Underground platforms, and is often shouted aloud where the trains fail to fit with them. I use this phrase here to designate discussions of actual or potential (or even desirable) similarities and distances between qualitative and quantitative approaches to research. While questions about the nature and extent of the "gap" between these two approaches are currently exercising social science academics and practitioners, minding the gap here may mean eliminating it or, alternatively, recognizing it. What is at issue is less the relative merits of techniques of analysis than the politics of research practice. It is the ethical-political investments of researchers that fuel the current revival of qualitative approaches in disciplines like psychology in which quantitative research has traditionally predominated. However, whether our goal is to undermine the gap or to maintain it, we should be clear about the bases on which we arrive at these positions.

In the current context of academic and applied psychology, qualitative (interpretive and textual) approaches to conducting and analyzing research are increasingly acquiring critical attention (see, e.g., Banister et al. 1994; Burman, Mitchell, and Salmon 1996; Henwood and Nicolson 1995; Henwood and Parker 1994). This popularity in part arises through the calls to do research "with" rather than "on" people that mark a new critical-humanist movement in psychology. The extent to which qualitative research fulfils claims of doing "different" or "better" research urgently requires attention, as does exploration of the models of research that underlie these claims.

Notwithstanding, and perhaps to pre-empt, the backlash that closely follows this delicate and recent revival of interpretive modes of inquiry and analysis in psychology, we need to scrutinize the grounds on which qualitative research is warranted. It is precisely because I welcome these developments that I want to caution against using arguments for qualitative research that dilute its critical edge by allowing it to be assimilated into quantitative approaches. This threatens to occur especially where method and analysis are pried apart, and the conduct and interpretation of the investigation are regarded as amenable to evaluation in equivalent, if not identical, terms to that of quantitative research.

Let me offer two warrants for my focus on method in psychology. First, from my double position as a teacher of psychology and, increasingly, women's studies, I am continuously struck by the gendering of subjectivity in psychology (cf. Hollway 1989), and its subsequent (overt) excision from (but covert maintenance in) research accounts. Second, in teaching developmental psychology to professional health workers, I have reflected upon how ideological assumptions about "normal families" within research provoke contest and debate. And yet, in both contexts the position of psychological researcher and my role as a teacher of psychology carry unquestioned authority and command respect.

Rose's (1985, 1990) and Ingleby's (1985) Foucauldian analyses of psychology suggest that psychology's specificity arises from the administration of methodological devices. As a modern, Western practice of classification, calibration, and control, psychology is a discipline based on administrative technologies of surveillance. While in this psychology has much in common with other social sciences such as sociology, anthropology, and criminology, what gives it its specificity, as well as its compelling hold on both popular conception and institutional practice, is the "psychological complex." This collection of assumptions about individual, personal responsi-

bility and social relations accords psychology a principal role in the policing of relationships and makes self-regulation a key feature of modern, rational subjectivity (Parker 1994a).

Thus, the fact that methods teaching occupies a key role in psychology undergraduate degrees (both in terms of proficiency and the sheer
volume of "practical work" required by professional psychology organizations) makes the study of warrants for particular methodological approaches important. As I elaborate elsewhere (Burman 1996, 1998),
while in North American social sciences (including psychology) the textbook acts as the pedagogical device in terms of the work of "knowledge
filtering and consensus building" that Lubek (1993) outlines, in the
United Kingdom methods teaching performs these functions. Here another gap, the issue of cultural-geographical specificity, becomes apparent. Other countries (and their psychologies) may be less committed to
the positivist model of science that characterizes Anglo-U.S. psychology.[1] Claims to an objective or disinterested science have sometimes
been important to maintain academic (and to support the struggle for
political) freedoms. Since the political uses and functions of qualitative
psychology differ according to the context of intervention, it follows
that the progressive features attributed to qualitative psychology are a
topic for analysis rather than an unexamined presumption.

Shifting or Warding Off the Crisis

It is in this context of mounting criticism of the noxious effects of psychological practices alongside an awareness of the very partial agendas they
serve that qualitative methods are currently enjoying a revival in psychology. But even this use of the term "qualitative approaches" blurs together
a variety of different models that reflect the diverse ingredients of the
"new paradigm" critiques emerging from psychology's "crisis" in the
1970s. After all, the new paradigm in psychology was not a unitary
methodology; rather (to adopt a feminist inflection here), it was inspired
by a different ontology (cf. Stanley and Wise 1993). The "paradigm shift"
was concerned not so much with changes in method as technical devices
(although such changes followed from these), but with a shift from
an ethos of manipulation and instrumentality to one of mutuality and
co-authorship and, in some (more critical and feminist) varieties, from

subjection to emancipation. The crisis in social psychology, therefore, was one of credibility as well as epistemology; the ethic of scientific expertise based on prediction, control, and replicability was resisted on both academic and moral grounds.

Nested within the humanist impulse of new paradigm research to treat people as competent authors and accountants of their actions (Harré and Secord 1972; Reason and Rowan 1981) lay a set of potentially contradictory claims. Is new paradigm work in psychology considered "better" because it is morally superior (however this is evaluated)? Or because it is founded on a more adequate theory of human action and interaction? Or because it provides additional means of investigating phenomena that have eluded quantitative research, of reaching the places no other method can? I suggest that this last reason, whether deployed strategically or as principle, functions as the dominant discursive rationale for qualitative methods in psychology. Moreover, the proliferation of texts on qualitative methods, outside (e.g., Silverman 1993; Denzin and Lincoln 1994) and inside psychology (Henwood and Parker 1994; Banister et al. 1994), as well as the inclusion of qualitative approaches within mainstream psychology methods texts (e.g. Foster and Parker 1995), suggests that this may not be an issue for psychology alone.

The rest of this chapter takes up these questions. It does so at a relatively general level of analysis, the abstraction of which is offset by other detailed accounts in this book. In this analysis, I draw upon textbook accounts, teaching experiences, and versions of qualitative research undertaken by undergraduate and postgraduate students whose work I have supervised.

Humanism under Suspicion

The current impulse toward qualitative research is a humanitarian one: to be "nicer" to people; not to exploit or dehumanize them by treating them as objects. Talking to and with people and treating their accounts as informative (and in some cases authoritative) explanations for their actions, rather than measuring their behavior, was crucial to the humanist rejection of behaviorist psychology. "Being human" is therefore counterposed to an ethic of manipulation. Nevertheless, we would do well to recall the critiques of humanism and person-centered counseling (e.g., Waterhouse

1993). These critiques highlight the dangers of preserving power relations, or rendering them incontestable, when they are shrouded in the rhetoric of egalitarianism. Critical debates in qualitative research have highlighted three areas where the discourse of democracy threatens to obscure the maintenance of the traditional direction of power in researcher-researched relations.

Relationship

First, there is the issue of relationship in research. The early claims to empathy, authenticity, and trust in research, according to which these methods were promoted as feminist or empowering as well as new paradigm, were soon discredited (see, e.g., Oakley 1981). The assumption that being listened to is necessarily a validating experience for the informant, and as such is sufficient reward in itself, has been shown to be patronizing (Ribbens 1989). Beyond this, the facilitation of a positive research relationship could be viewed as a more insidious form of manipulation. Known in the trade by the cosy epithet "rapport," the social features of the research relationship easily become quantified and commodified in some accounts into devices to promote disclosure. Although Finch (1984) illustrates the dangers of inadvertent exploitation in soliciting accounts whose disclosure may later be regretted, both student and professional researchers frequently describe the research relationship as a manipulable device of social lubrication, with the democratizing impulse therefore functioning as a means to elicit unguarded confidences. Further, such is the abstracting imperative of "rapport" that student researchers often write disclaimers about any previous relationships they have with their informants. In a bizarre reversal of Oakley's (1981) account, friendships are, or apparently should be, suspended or irrelevant in the context of research. That research relations could be portrayed as occurring outside history—the history of the relationship, or of the structures that produced this as a research relation—is indicative of the ways the humanist impulse can converge with more mainstream drives toward scientization and naturalization to give rise to such abstraction and reification of the research process. By such means, the research process is abstracted and reified in ways not unlike those that occur in the quantitative approaches against which qualitative work was formulated as a critique.

Equality

Feminist researchers, who have been in the forefront of developing debates about power relations in research, have highlighted the naiveté of earlier claims of equality in research relationships—for example, where feminist research was presumed to be research by women, with women, about women. In part this assumption arose through the tendency for feminists to do research with women in similar structural positions as themselves—mainly white and middle class. But research relationships mobilize and reproduce within their process the structural positions that exist outside research contexts (or indeed may well have motivated the research). Thus researchers have had to confront the fact that—except where the research question is explicitly arrived at by (and not even merely "in consultation with") the researched—the fantasy of democratic research is belied by the basic issue of who gains (materially, symbolically) from the research. Indeed, only by a very unhermeneutic split between process and product could such a proposition have been tenable in the first place.[2]

Participation

Third, claims of "participation" beg the question of the basis on which the co-participant is involved. To participate more often means to join, or be enjoined into, someone else's project. Again, the problem is not, or not only, how to avoid this, but that the humanist discourse invites qualitative researchers to treat structural power relations as dispensable or transcendable. Such discourse thus unwittingly—or, more worryingly, cynically—disguises the exercise of power.

On all these issues, feminist and poststructuralist critiques of humanism are helpful. First, they remind us that "human" (in English at least) is usually understood as "man" or is defined in male-oriented ways. Second, humanism presupposes a separation between individual and society. Third, and correspondingly, it treats the individual as active, unitary, and rational. Research work that is committed to this "new paradigm" is in danger of bolstering precisely the rational unitary subject of psychology it was formulated to disrupt (see Parker 1989; Morss 1995). In practical terms, this can lead to piling up the qualities and identities of the researcher and researched, which leads to such bizarre and decontextualized practices as "matching" on the basis of gender or "race," with scant regard for how these marginalized positions are themselves fractured and intersected by issues of class, age, and sexuality, for example (Phoenix 1990). They thus treat as static, ahistorical entities what are structurally produced and reproduced relations to which the research directly contributes, and from which, in some cases, it directly benefits (as in the researching of designated "social problems").

Qualitative Differences

On what grounds is qualitative research different from quantitative research? Or, to turn the question around, in what circumstances are qualitative studies to be deemed appropriate? What the motley collection of approaches to research that are termed "qualitative" have in common is that they are interpretive; that is, they reject the possibility of arriving at an understanding of actions, events, or objects outside practices of representation. Differing approaches that conflict in other respects—phenomenological, social constructionist, discursive—here agree, and stand against positivism's assumption of an unmediated relation between the world and acts of investigating it. Traditional criteria for evaluating empirical work—validity, replicability, and generalizability—are therefore either irrelevant or in need of redefinition according to this different starting point.

The difficulties that beset quantitative research correspondingly turn into resources for qualitative work. So rather than being methodological horrors, as Woolgar (1988) puts it, problems of indexicality (where explanation is tied to particular occasions and uses, and changes correspondingly), inconcludability (where the meaning of an account is inexhaustible and will continually change as more is added), and reflexivity (where the process of interpretation structures the phenomenon under consideration and this correspondingly changes the ways we view it) become topics for analysis once we accept that research is inevitably contextualized. Thus, the main "gap" that qualitative research "minds," or theorizes, is that between objects and representations. As "an essentially interpretive enterprise, it works with the problems—the gap—rather than against it" (Banister et al. 1994, 4).

Assimilatory Practices in Qualitative Research

While it is difficult to specify an exhaustive set of criteria that will apply to the whole range of qualitative approaches (but see Banister et al. 1994, chap. 1), it is nevertheless possible to identify four inadequate but common rationales for doing qualitative research.

Qualitative Analysis Is Suitable for Studies with Small Sample Sizes

A first inadequate criterion for conducting qualitative research is because the sample size is too small to merit statistical analysis. While this may be obvious, it is nevertheless sometimes forgotten that the qualitative character of a study arises from the nature of its questions and process; the mode of analysis follows from, rather than defines, this nature. The correlative preoccupation of people who attempt to understand qualitative research in quantitative terms is the concern with how many (interviews, informants) or how much (text) is "enough." Enough for what? Statistical tests have prerequisite limits on numbers governing their applicability. The "power" of qualitative research resides not in the quantity of subjects, but in the strength of its analysis—its rigor and meaningfulness in relation to theoretical and practical questions. While this does not mean that the number of participants or interviews involved or the volume of text analyzed are irrelevant to the evaluation of a study, this alone cannot determine its merit or value. Rather than "how much," what is important is what the researcher has done with their material.

Qualitative Work as the Pilot Study

Second, it is common to see qualitative research warranted as preparatory or exploratory inductive research, "pilot studies" to be "followed up" by rigorous hypothetico-deductive inquiries. This, however, maintains a rhetoric of discovery. It is not enough to distinguish qualitative research on the grounds that a hypothesis cannot be specified because the study is not experimental. On its own, this invites the charge of being atheoretical and of failing to acknowledge or theorize guiding presuppositions. We should not try to smuggle qualitative research in as if it were simply a variant of quantitative research. Rather, we should be open about why and how a research problem may elude absolute specification at the outset—for example, because of the ways in which the nature and focus of the research can change over time, acquiring new meanings in the precise context, or because it is explicitly negotiated with the participants. By doing this, we can illustrate the rigor and systematicity of qualitative research, rather than muffling it in a cloud of atheoretical apology.

The Extent of the Truth: "Finding More"

Third, both advocates and critics of qualitative research make the same error when they claim to find out "more." The difference between qualitative and quantitative research is not quantitative, but arises from subscription to a different interpretive framework. That is, contrary to claims that it reaches places no other method can, qualitative work does not extend the armory of psychological methods (I use the battle metaphor advisedly), but creates a different representation of the phenomenon at issue. Claims that qualitative research extends quantitative research run the risk of undermining the integrity of the former. This additive-extension model creeps back into accounts of qualitative work in several ways. One subtle way is when the focus on the flexibility and responsiveness of the interview as a research tool is shifted away from concerns of uniqueness and non-replicability to extend the range of contexts amenable to investigation.

However, the consequences of the drive to "find more" is most evident in claims of arriving at a "full response," of capturing an elusive, unguarded reaction, or of revealing (previously hidden) truths. It is precisely where claims about "finding the truth" arise that the foundationalism of positivist psychology returns. This development is facilitated by the incipient naturalization to which varieties of qualitative research have sometimes subscribed, as where analytic material is said to be "gathered" or "collected" like ripe corn. Rhetoric of discovery or revelation returns us to a conception of knowledge (whether as "facts" or "findings") as existing outside the practices that produce it. Along with the purportedly "soft, feminine" status accorded qualitative analyses within essentialized gender binaries, we can also discern the machismo of the traditional scientific ethos of control and manipulation: that of the pioneer exploring previously uncharted territories (Morgan 1981).

Cosy Complements

Fourth, it is inadequate to treat qualitative and quantitative approaches as simply complementary. This liberal discourse has been convenient in allowing qualitative approaches to claim some curricular space and legitimacy (and we used it in Banister et al. 1994). However, it offers too friendly or harmonious a rendering of the qualitative/quantitative relation—one that positivists are right to recognize as disingenuous.

Two aspects warrant mention in this regard. First, qualitative research provides competing as well as complementary interpretations that challenge positivist psychology, rather than simply adding to it. The interpretive tradition in psychology has its roots in just such a challenge, and we do both the tradition and ourselves a disservice if we sanitize such conflicts in the pursuit of legitimacy. Second, the complementary position implies the mistaken assumption that the two approaches operate within an equivalent topography.

In contrast, I want to argue for the noncommensurable character of the relation between qualitative and quantitative research—that is, they are not necessarily competing or complementary. Such a formulation, rather than being epistemological, highlights the political nature of claims to knowledge, along with the corresponding legitimating strategies of particular knowledge-generating practices. Thus, qualitative research has been used to highlight the limits (and sometimes the abuses) of positivist research. It has done this by (1) presenting alternative interpretations of the "same phenomena" and (2) demonstrating that there are arenas that positivist research does not know, cannot theorize, or fails to recognize.

This is why it is so important that qualitative research is not merely regarded as adding to the repertoire of quantitative methods, since this threatens to extend the gaze of psychological regulation to areas previously considered absent or ineffable. It is also why the issue of documenting absences (another kind of "gap") that is so central to the value of qualitative methods in psychology is so politically charged. Does such research usher in new territorializing and colonizing practices that objectify its rare, exotic subjects further? Or does it point a critical finger at the speculating discipline, indicating previously unrecognized features of the framework according to which we pose research questions? In other words, is the discipline put under scrutiny by such investigations?

Reflexivity

Highlighting issues of subjectivity and partiality in research in these ways indicates how reflexivity has acquired such importance in recent methodological debates. Reflexivity also underscores how the aim to document absences always involves analyzing the unmarked presences—just as feminist and postcolonial critics (Ware 1992; Frankenberg 1993) have pointed out that (the traditional research focus on) blackness presupposes (a usually implicit) whiteness, with particular significance for research practice in psychology (Howitt and Owusu-Bempeh 1994; Phoenix 1990; Ullah 1996).

Reflexivity refers to the practices of actively reflecting on one's own experience as a researcher in accounting for the interpretive resources brought to bear in arriving at interpretations, and including the experience of the process of the research in one's account of it. Reflexivity has been theorized and developed in important ways within feminist research.

Psychology students often expect that writing reflexively about qualitative studies they have conducted will constitute a transgression of the scientized code of detached, depersonalized, supposedly objective narrative style that characterizes the pseudoscientific model of their training. In my experience, this expectation often generates some incredulity, and occasionally resistance from students who have absorbed disciplinary codes too well. However, most students experience the transition as a relief, and even as an emancipation. . Putting objectivity in its place as a particular, and particularly deluded, form of subjectivity (Hollway 1989) continues to be one of the most powerful interventions in psychology prompted by qualitative work (see also Parker 1994b; Wilkinson 1988). Nevertheless, we need to be clear about why and how it is worthwhile being reflexive.

While reflexive accounts of researcher processes and participation in research strengthen rather than weaken claims to its value, the focus on experience and investments should not turn into a process of retrospective laundering or sanitization of subjectivity after which the data emerges scientifically pure and squeaky clean. Nor should a reflexive analysis take the form of a set of disclaimers that proscribe any claims to valuable, coherent, and perhaps generalizable analyses. As discussed elsewhere in more detail (Burman 1991; Parker and Burman 1993), too often student researchers treat reflexivity as a requirement to confess (their mistakes, the limits of their analyses), or to dismiss or explain away the relevance of their work because it fails to conform to the positivist research criteria of comparison and standardization. We need to move beyond the binary of being "only subjective" (rather than objective) to consider the varieties of forms of reflexivity that different qualitative approaches allow or promote (e.g., discursive versus feminist varieties—see, respectively, Potter 1988; Stanley and Wise 1993). Moreover, we also should beware of allowing the impetus to theorize the ways we narrate aspects of ourselves in our representations of others to immobilize us or prevent us from doing work that aims to affect or comment upon people and their practices. Otherwise we are in danger, as feminists and black critics have pointed out, of reproducing the traditional exclusions governing research topics and processes (Wilkinson and Kitzinger 1996).

And So?

I have been arguing that qualitative approaches are vulnerable to recuperation according to a positivist agenda that privileges research as an "empirical" rather than interpretive matter.[3] We need to attend to the disciplinary-specific character of rhetorics of knowledge and the hegemony of science within notions of research.[4] My focus in this chapter has been to caution against the incipient drift to cast qualitative work within terms amenable to quantitative evaluations. I have suggested that this development both undermines the project of interpretive inquiries and works to limit or contain the critique of quantitative work that qualitative approaches invite. However, there is a certain paradox in making the case for the independence of qualitative from quantitative research, since the descriptor "qualitative" spans an assortment of approaches from diverse disciplinary, epistemological, and political backgrounds that are only assembled together in relation to "quantitative" work. By definition, therefore, they are identified according to their (non)quantitative status—reproducing that familiar opposition.

I conclude with a set of five interrelated claims aiming to exaggerate and exacerbate the gap between qualitative and quantitative work in order to maintain the radical potential of the former, as well as that of progressive research in general. First, the progressive (empowering, transformative, enabling, action-oriented) character of research is always ultimately a matter of politics, not technique. Thus, while some approaches to research, or even techniques, may be useful (e.g., research contracts for "informed consent," or sharing of transcript material with informants), they alone cannot guarantee properly ethical practice. Nor should ethics be promoted on instrumental grounds to prompt a "good" response.

Second, both qualitative research and the debates about its credibility stand as examples of the intimate relations between knowledge and power. The dangers of exploitation arise where qualitative research is treated as (only) a method divorced from wider structures of power.

Third, it follows that qualitative research is no more invulnerable than quantitative research to abuses of power. Indeed, there is a long tradition of qualitative research in the form of case histories in medicine and psychiatry that are central to its practices of surveillance and evaluation. As Rose (1985) points out, clinical and scientific models work together as complementary practices of psychological regulation. It is the strategic, corrective status of current accounts of qualitative work that lend them their efficacy and moral superiority.

Fourth, notwithstanding the ways knowledge and power connect, we would be mistaken to regard specific methodological practices as determining in a wholesale way particular epistemological frameworks. Following Harding (1986) and other feminist researchers, we should treat methods as relatively autonomous from frameworks (e.g., positivist-instrumentalist), and thus focus on the particular purposes, interventions, and effects of particular research projects. Hence a quantitative study may in some circumstances be more appropriate to address certain research questions—either because in this situation it is worth harnessing the legitimacy and persuasive power of numbers, or because the mode of investigation and (lack of) research relationship limits the intrusiveness and sensitivity of the study.[5] Thus, we need to move beyond varieties of methodological fetishism that promote qualitative research as intrinsically "better" or more appropriate than quantitative (see also Kelly, Regan, and Burton 1992).

Fifth, and finally, while moral-political criteria are often deployed to justify qualitative research, the politics arises from our commitments and conduct with these research methods, rather than flowing in some unmediated way from them. Just as it is important in qualitative research not to lapse into the incipient naturalization that abstracts the products from their relations and practices of production, so it is also vital not to play into the scientizing game by treating moral-political features as either entirely external to or reducible to the methods of qualitative research.

Notes

1. There are, for example, both European and South American traditions that are much closer to hermeneutics and explicit political engagement, respectively, (e.g. D'Adamo et al. 1995). Further, they function within a different history of state-academy relations. For example, in countries with current or recent experience of authoritarian regimes, discussions of the self-regulation so beloved by Foucauldian critical psychologists may be redundant or irrelevant.

2. I should emphasize here that I in no way wish to discredit consultative work, nor to fall prey to the converse problem of romanticizing the informants' account and treating this as the only authentic or legitimate analysis. (See Maynard and Purvis 1994, for an exploration of these issues.)

3. I was recently powerfully confronted with the fallout from such a positivist hegemony on definitions of "research" when co-teaching a women's studies class on "research methods." During the class, my co-tutor, a literature specialist, exclaimed, "But I don't do real research, what I do is only scholarship." From our mutual puzzlement over such definitions developed an important discussion about the different forms of research expertise within different disciplines.

4. Related to this issue of specificity, it is worth recalling that some disputes and distinctions of method or framework in the social sciences are matters of irrelevance or banality elsewhere. The current flourishing of (I am tempted to say "invention of") discourse analysis in psychology is a case in point. This analysis (sometimes explicitly) imports debates from literary theory and cultural studies. In so doing, it systematizes and scientizes what is largely a very general mode of analysis, so that the work appears bizarre and unrecognizable to those in its supposedly "host" disciplines. Yet psychology discourse work, because of those who have taken it up, has been assumed to be equivalent to critical and explicitly political research, especially around gender issues (see, e.g., Wilkinson and Kitzinger 1995). Like the partiality and situatedness of qualitative analyses, we need to evaluate the purposes and value of qualitative research in relation to particular arenas of intervention.

5. As Sieber (1993) points out, notwithstanding the calls to allow people to frame their experiences in their own terms within qualitative research, in some circumstances the prior and explicit structuring of response categories of questionnaires and other quantitative techniques may be experienced as helpful.

References

Banister, P., E. Burman, I. Parker, M. Taylor, and C. Tindall. 1994. *Qualitative methods in psychology: A research guide.* Milton Keynes: Open University Press.

Burman, E. 1991. Power, gender, and developmental psychology. *Feminism and Psychology* 1 (1): 141–154.

———. 1994. *Deconstructing developmental psychology*. London: Routledge.

———. 1996. The crisis in modern social psychology and how to find it. *South African Journal of Psychology* 26 (3): 135–142.

———. 1998. Disciplinary apprentices: "Qualitative methods" in student psychological research. *International Journal of Social Research Methodology* 1 (1): 25–46.

Burman, E., S. Mitchell, and P. Salmon, eds. 1996. *Changes: Journal of Psychology and Psychotherapy* 14 (3).

Burman, E., and I. Parker, eds. 1993. *Discourse analytic research: Repertoires and readings of texts in action*. London: Routledge.

D'Adamo, O., V. Garcia Beaudoux, and M. Montero, eds. 1995. *Psicologia de la accion politica*. Buenos Aires: Paidos.

Denzin, N., and Y. Lincoln, eds. 1994. *Handbook of qualitative research*. London: Sage.

Finch, J. 1984. "It's great to have someone to talk to": The ethics and politics of interviewing women. In *Social researching: politics, problems, practice*, eds. C. Bell and H. Roberts, 70–87. London: Routledge and Kegan Paul.

Foster, J., and I. Parker. 1995. *Carrying out investigations in psychology*. Leicester: British Psychological Society.

Frankenberg, R. 1993. *White women, race matters*. London: Routledge.

Griffin, C., and A. Phoenix. 1994. Qualitative methods and feminist psychology. *Journal of Community and Applied Social Psychology* 4:287–299.

Harding, S. 1986. *Feminism and methodology*. Buckingham: Open University Press.

Harré, R., and P. Secord. 1972. *The explanation of social behaviour*. Oxford: Basil Blackwell.

Henwood, K., and P. Nicolson, eds. 1995. Qualitative research. *The Psychologist* 8:109–129.

Henwood, K., and I. Parker, eds. 1994. Qualitative methods. *Journal of Community and Applied Social Psychology* 4.

Henwood, K., and N. Pidgeon. 1994. Beyond the qualitative paradigm: Framework for introducing diversity within qualitative methodology. *Journal of Community and Applied Social Psychology* 4:225–238.

Hollway, W. 1989. *Subjectivity and method in psychology: Gender, meaning, and science*. London: Sage.

Howitt, D., and J. Owusu-Bempeh. 1994. *The racism of psychology*. Lewes: Harvester Wheatsheaf.

Ingleby, D. 1985. Professionals as socializers: The "psy complex." *Research in Law, Deviance, and Social Control* 7:79–109.

Kelly, L., L. Regan, and S. Burton. 1992. Defending the indefensible? Quantitative methods and feminist research. In *Working out: New directions in women's studies*, eds. H. Hinds, A. Phoenix, and J. Stacey, 149–160. London: Falmer Press.

Lubek, I. 1993. Social psychology textbooks: An historical and social psychological analysis of conceptual filtering, consensus formation, career gatekeeping, and conservatism in science. In *Recent trends in theoretical psychology*, vol. 3, eds. H. J. Stam, L. P. Mos, W. Thorngate, and B. Kaplan, 359–378. New York: Springer Verlag.

Maynard, M., and J. Purvis, eds. 1994. *Researching women's lives from a feminist perspective*. London: Taylor and Francis.

Morgan, D. 1981. Men, masculinity, and the process of sociological inquiry. In *Doing feminist research*, ed. H. Roberts, 83–113. London: Routledge and Kegan Paul.

Morss, J. 1995. *Growing critical*. London: Routledge.

Oakley, A. 1981. Interviewing women: A contradiction in terms? In *Doing feminist research*, ed. H. Roberts, 30–61. London: Routledge and Kegan Paul.

Parker, I. 1989. *The crisis in social psychology and how to end it*. London: Routledge.

———. 1994a. Reflexive research and the grounding of analysis: Social psychology and the psy complex. *Journal of Community and Applied Social Psychology* 4: 239–252.

———. 1994b. Reflexive social psychology: Discourse analysis and psychoanalysis. *Free Associations* 32 (4): 527–548.

Parker, I., and E. Burman. 1993. Against discursive empiricism and imperialism: Thirty-two problems with discourse analysis. In *Discourse analytics research*, eds. E. Burman and I. Parker. London: Routledge.

Phoenix, A. 1990. Social research in the context of feminist psychology. In *Feminists and psychological practice*, ed. E. Burman. London: Sage.

Potter, J. 1988. What is reflexive about discourse analysis? The case of reading readings. In *Knowledge and reflexivity: New frontiers in the sociology of knowledge*, ed. S. Woolgar. London: Sage.

Reason, P., and J. Rowan, eds. 1981. *Human inquiry: A sourcebook of new paradigm research*. Chichester: Wiley.

Ribbens, J. 1989. Interviewing: An unnatural situation? *Women's Studies International Forum* 12 (6): 579–592.

Rose, N. 1985. *The psychological complex*. London: Routledge and Kegan Paul.

———. 1990. *Governing the soul*. London: Routledge.

Sieber, J. 1993. The ethics and politics of sensitive research. In *Researching sensitive topics*, eds. C. Renzetti and R. Lee, 14–26. London: Sage.

Silverman, D. 1993. *Interpreting qualitative data: Methods for analysing talk, text, and interaction*. London: Sage.

Stanley, L., and S. Wise. 1993. *Breaking out: Again: Feminist consciousness, feminist research*. Routledge and Kegan Paul.

Ullah, R. 1996. Black parent governors: A hidden agenda. In *Challenging women: Psychology's exclusions, feminist possibilities*, eds. E. Burman, P. Alldred, C. Bewley, B. Goldberg., C. Heenan, D. Marks, J. Marshall, K. Taylor, R. Ullah, and S. Warner. Buckingham: Open University Press.

Ware, V. 1992. *Beyond the pale: White women, racism, and history.* London: Verso.

Waterhouse, R. 1993. "Wild women don't have the blues": A feminist critique of "person-centred" counselling. *Feminism and Psychology* 3 (1): 55–71.

Wilkinson, S. 1988. The role of reflexivity in feminist psychology. *Women's Studies International Forum* 11 (5): 493–502.

Wilkinson, S., and C. Kitzinger, eds. 1995. *Feminism and discourse.* London: Sage.

———, eds. 1996. *Representing the other: A feminism and psychology reader.* London: Sage.

Woolgar, S. 1988. *Science: The very idea.* London: Tavistock.

17

▪ ▪ ▪ ▪ ▪ ▪ ▪ ▪ ▪

The Congruency Thing

Transforming Psychological Research and Pedagogy

Patricia Maguire

"You didn't teach me anything! I had to learn it myself!" [After a short pause, in a quieter voice:] "Can I get a copy of your overheads?"

These angry words from a participant in the final session evaluating an institute on participatory action research (PAR) reveal some of the challenges of teaching about and learning to do PAR. Identifying and facing these challenges is a critical component of the project to transform human inquiry and human inquirers (Brydon-Miller and Tolman 1997; Meulenberg-Buskens 1996; Lincoln and Reason 1996; Kerlin 2000; Levin and Greenwood 2000). In this chapter I describe one short-term effort to train participatory action researchers, identify lessons for training researchers, and explore implications for the transformation of psychological research.[1] I contend that it will remain difficult to transform how psychological research is done "out there" without simultaneously transforming how it is taught "in here"—in the academy and in community-based professional development.[2] It's the congruency thing.

The explosion of work piercing the dominance of orthodox, positivist research and its conceptualization of science bears witness to the momentum for dismantling the entrenched privileging of quantitative research in the social sciences (Reason and Bradbury 2000; Tolman and Brydon-Miller 1997; *Forum Qualitative Sozialforschung* 2000; Lincoln and Reason 1996; Denzin and Lincoln 1994). This development is concurrent with a dismantling of androcentric privileging in the sciences, natural and social, and a recognition of the contributions of feminist principles to the transformation project (Devault 1999; Fonow and Cook 1991; Schiebinger 1999; Bleier 1986; Morawski 1997; Maguire 2000). Psychology's acceptance of the methodological and epistemological sea change may be slow, contentious, and fraught with heated debate (Tolman and Brydon-Miller 1997; Marecek, Fine, and Kidder 1997). However, the exemplars showcased in this book demonstrate that the transformation of psychology through the use of interpretive, qualitative, and participatory action research (qualitative and quantitative) approaches, frequently grounded in feminist principles, is underway and unstoppable.

To further advance the project of transforming human inquiry, we must question and transform the pedagogical practices and underlying philosophies used to teach human inquirers. The positivist juggernaut is vulnerable. However, if positivism remains the dominant paradigm that organizes psychology (Tolman and Brydon-Miller 1997, 599), it is likewise the dominant paradigm that organizes and shapes the teaching of psychologists, indeed most social scientists and educators. This is seen, for example, in the fragmentation of knowledge into disconnected disciplines; the dichotomizing of knowing and doing, and of thinking and feeling; the presumption of context and time-free generalizations; the contention that knowledge and knowers should and can be value-free; and the endless quantification of knowledge and experience (Lincoln and Reason 1996, 6). I wish to emphasize that I am referring to teaching methodologies, philosophies, and contexts, not merely content. Positivist research approaches are essentially congruent with the pedagogical practices used to teach research, and even the knowledge base, of most social science disciplines. While increasingly effective challenges to this dominance continue to emerge, much of the hidden curricula, methodologies, and values of teaching replicate an unquestioned positivist grounding.

Humanizing and democratizing knowledge creation requires humanizing and democratizing the institutions in which we teach (Levin and

construction and organizational redirection, it was already decided that the organization's resources would be made available to historically black universities. The contested question was for what purposes these resources would be shared. Other units were using funds to shore up the positivist research paradigm. There was little recognition from the organization's top echelon of the value of qualitative research approaches or need to promote them, but the unit was allowed to proceed for the time being.

The PAR institute staff was composed primarily of unit members and a few outside consultants, mostly South Africans. The unit was an unusually multiracial group within the larger organization, primarily due to newly created internship positions. For the institute, deliberate staffing choices achieved racial and gender diversity. Some of the institute staff, black and white, women and men, had been active in the struggle against apartheid, and a few had survived detentions. Many institute staff had concrete experiences with state-sponsored degradation, threats, abuses, and psychological and even physical torture. While institute staff might be risking their "professional lives" by promoting participatory research in a very pro-positivist, quantitative research organization, some had risked their real lives in the struggle against apartheid. This put the initial bureaucratic intrigues and infighting about qualitative research, indeed participatory action research, in perspective for them and me. Institute staff were also willing to undertake the challenges of working across color and gender lines.

The training was initially conceived of as a participatory, experiential institute for thirty-five to forty participants in which we would teach and learn about PAR by going through the phases of a scaled-down PAR project, albeit in a compressed time frame, on an issue of genuine concern determined by the group. The goal was to make our pedagogical practices congruent with the values and practices of PAR. How could anyone learn about PAR through the nonparticipatory methods of most traditional education?

Astonished when enrollment swelled to nearly two hundred,[3] we tenaciously clung to our participatory intentions and design, enlisting additional unit staff to facilitate smaller groups for activities, reflection, and processing. It was a daunting task. The physical configuration of the institute site worked against participatory pedagogy. The plenary auditorium, the only place big enough to hold two hundred participants, had, like those in many universities, stadium-style seats, overlooking a stage where an instructor could stand with a microphone and overhead projector.

Nonetheless, in break-out rooms and even in the auditorium's bolted-down seats, participants worked in creative small groups, presented and posted flip-charted reflections and applications up and down aisles, took turns at facilitation, and increasingly took control of the institute. We believed that if we helped the institute community create "a space" and climate that would honor all voices and experiences, participants would "get in it, use it, and take control of it." They did, though active participation was not always comfortable for themselves as learners. Some participants ended up using the institute to organize an advocacy group that challenged the organization's reorganization process. As active participation moved from theory to practice, it became increasingly uncomfortable for the larger organization. There were risks and consequences. Recognizing that people have differing preferences for and comfort levels with varied approaches to learning, referred to as learning styles (Kolb 1985; Gregorc 1979; Cole 1995), we integrated, although to a lesser degree, more traditional teaching methods and materials. We included short content lectures complete with overhead transparencies and a course reader.

Overall, however, pedagogical practices favored active participation; challenged traditional student–teacher power relationships; honored participants' diverse experiences, voices, and multiple identities; supported developing relationships; and promoted action taking. Both the feedback sessions (aimed at responding to evolving needs) and the final evaluation indicated that the institute was a mixed experience for many participants. As the angry words of the participant quoted at the beginning of the chapter suggest, the expectations and processes of democratizing and humanizing pedagogy created tensions. Certainly we made design and facilitation errors. We probably erred on the side of too much attention to process and too little to lecture "delivery" of content about PAR. But something deeper was going on. If the institute participant was angered at not being "taught" anything, what happened? What are the lessons and implications for transforming research?

> For all your degrees in psychology, you still don't know shit about dealing with your mother. —My father, around 1975

Twenty-five years ago, my high-school-educated father clearly articulated the chasm between theory and practice, between knowing and doing, and between thinking and feeling. I don't recall that he ever uttered the words "dichotomy" or "binary." Yet his experience taught him to question the Cartesian dichotomy that has influenced Western philosophy for centuries (Toulmin 1990). He realized that years of university education, if primarily theoretical and abstract, distant and rational, are inadequate preparation for understanding lived experience and taking theoretically informed concrete action. A series of binaries and dichotomies shape and are further nurtured by Western pedagogical practices that separate and privilege theory over practice, knowing over doing, thinking over feeling, and masculine over feminine. Years of positivist-influenced university training can make one suspicious, distrustful, and discounting of experiences, feelings, relationships, and collegial learning.

Participants had come expecting to learn about a research approach which contended that marginalized or ordinary people should take control of knowledge creation through empowering, participatory practices. Yet some had come expecting to "be taught" about this approach by experts in the usual, top-down, one-way lecture, teacher-as-expert model. Learning by doing, through active, collaborative techniques, created a tension reflected, for example, in the comment of the angry participant. Rather than "damning with faint praise," this comment might be construed as praise with not so faint damnation. The participant acknowledged what is hoped for in participatory, experiential learning: that is, participants will take an active role in the learning process, co-creating a collaborative, potentially empowering learning community. It is the Freirian antithesis of banking education.

The participatory, experiential expectations and practices of the institute were well advertised in advance. We allotted considerable time to build the climate collaboratively, clarify the underlying pedagogical philosophy, and negotiate and agree upon expectations for participants and staff. Yet the concrete enactment of abstract principles created tensions. Many institute participants were not only university trained, they were university faculty. As Vita Rabinowitz and Susan Weseen (1997, 607) observe, they did not come tabula rasa. Advance advertisement and up-front negotiation about participatory processes came up against years of personal, institutional, and national experience of and socialization to student–teacher roles and expectations.

Certainly the historical context of South Africa influenced their expectations of and experience with education. However, my years of educational experience, formal and informal, as student or faculty in a wide variety of settings, cultures, and time periods, suggest to me that many student–teacher expectations cross time, class, cultural, and national boundaries. Although expressed in culturally unique ways across time, all too often Dewey's contention that democracy stops at the schoolhouse door, and all that this implies, appears nearly universal. Tensions resulted when we tried to counter socialization to the expectations and roles of hierarchical, dualistic, fragmented, context, and value-free learning.

Relationships

In recognition that research is an inherently relational process (Bleier 1986, 3; Way 1997, 704), we used pedagogical processes that supported and promoted relationship building. Small-group work, in which some groupings remained consistent while others rotated through the institute, mirrored the belief that people learn and develop "in relationship" (Jordan et al. 1991). The residential nature of the institute, in which participants shared meals and dorm rooms, also supported interpersonal relationships. Staff spent several days prior to the institute beginning to build a sense of team and trust. It took time for us to get through institute agenda devoted to relationship building. For some participants, this detracted from the time available for "content." In the classic tug of war between task and process, some saw the attention to relationship building as a waste of time, better spent on the task of learning about the content of PAR. Relating and working across gender and color lines, particularly in the post-apartheid context, also created discomfort as deep divisions surfaced. We tried to create space and support for naming and exploring these deep divisions. It was no easy task.

Student–Teacher Power Relationships

By using pedagogical practices that honored and built on diverse experiences, created space for all voices, supported participants' increasing control of the process, and openly shared facilitation tasks, we tried to unsettle traditional student–teacher power dynamics. We openly named this and worked to draw linkages between unsettling student–teacher power dynamics and unsettling the "researcher–researched" power dynamics of positivist research. Ongoing and final feedback comments indicated that participants, like most people, come to every encounter with a lifetime of expectations. Expecting to be taught in a top-down way by the expert, in-charge teacher, participants knew how to keep their end of that bargain. Tensions surfaced when that was challenged, causing all of us to acknowledge feelings, values, and varied expectations.

Time

Developing relationships takes time. The increased time demands of qualitative research result in part from this dynamic. It is not that one gets "better data" from such time, but perhaps very different data about human experiences (Way 1997). We wanted to demonstrate that the time needed to share and listen to lived experience and to develop relationships was not wasted or frivolous. Similarly, one does not necessarily learn "more" through participatory pedagogical practices, which take longer than lectures. Rather, one might learn very different things. The insights gained from collaborative, participatory practices often reveal different lessons, implications, and applications than those gained from regurgitating the teacher or text. A commitment to PAR takes a patience that respects the potential benefits that come from working together over time.

Honoring Lived Experience

Early climate-building activities allowed participants and staff to discuss and share their pre-institute experiences of and as researchers. The small-and large-group work gave participants opportunities to listen, talk, and report on their work, and thus created space for and validation of the lived experience of those often silenced, ignored (Rabinowitz and Weseen 1997, 606), or endangered by voicing their beliefs.

Honoring and discussing lived experience through group work presented challenges as the dynamics of gender, color, class, and culture expressed themselves overtly and covertly. As a facilitator, I often found myself trying to make "airtime" equally available to women participants. Despite efforts to shift power dynamics, participants often look to facilitators to "give permission" or name the elephant in the room. I named "airtime" as an issue for all participants and facilitators alike by posing questions for reflection. Who's talking, how often, and for how long? How could we collectively encourage and create "space" for quieter participants? Why bother? What are the implications for doing PAR? Participants named the notion of "community" as an issue for exploration. What did "community" mean in post-apartheid South Africa? What were the implications of this definition for doing PAR?

Reflecting on and Learning from Lived Experiences

For ten years before teaching in a university setting, I was a training consultant to international development agencies, often facilitating workshops in which other trainers were trained—that is, training people in the facilitation skills and values of participatory, experiential education or nonformal education for empowerment (Kindervatter 1979; Freire 1970, 1973). It was difficult for my father and me to find mutually understandable terms to discuss what I did. He wondered why anyone would pay his daughter to train those already skilled, for example, in "appropriate technology" when he thought I knew little about technology, appropriate or otherwise. After many frustrating conversations about the purposes and processes of experiential education, he observed, "OK, you can live and learn. Or live and stay stupid." He concluded that experiential education was about trying to not "stay stupid." It's also about not remaining powerless. It's not enough to have experiences. We have to find ways to learn from them and to take control of conditions that shape future experiences. Participatory, experiential processes are aimed at helping people learn from experience through reflection on and critique of the structural and personal influences on experience. The goal, short and long term, is to take control and action, which ultimately contributes to the co-creation of more just, loving, democratic, and equitable institutions, structures, and relationships.

In the institute, our pedagogical practices and considerable time were committed to reflecting on the experiences people brought to the training as well as the experiences we were having of and at the training. Reflecting on experience and identifying feelings, learning experiences, implications, and applications placed many participants on unfamiliar ground. Authoritative lectures, textbooks, and teacher-designed tests train students to ignore and discount personal insights, reflections, and feelings. The expert teacher will tell us what's worth knowing and how it can be applied, if that's even covered on the test. If a goal of PAR is to include ordinary and marginalized people in the knowledge-creation process, we have to unsettle the notion that anything worth knowing comes from the expert teacher or text. It's the congruency thing.

> Is it asking too much of human nature and of psychology to seek to neutralize power differentials and foster collaboration?
> —Baker's Dozen 1997, 242

So what does any of this imply for the ongoing project to transform psychological research? Jill Morawski (1997, 677) argues that the greatest challenge to, and contribution of, feminist scientists lies in changing the environment in which science is generated, or, as she puts it, "modifying the near environment." In the South African PAR institute, we focused on that very thing, modifying the near environment. In a very deliberate, self-conscious way, we strove to make the process of learning about PAR congruent with the process of doing PAR. Ultimately, to change the conditions within and methods by which researchers create socially significant knowledge, we have to change the pedagogical conditions within and methods by which researchers learn new research practices. Just as political, social, and psychological forces shape psychology researchers' methodological choices (Rabinowitz and Weseen 1997, 607), pedagogical choices by those teaching research reflect political, social, and psychological forces.

Although participants expressed discomfort, even anger, with the demands and expectations of participatory practices, they also took incredible action, which is the goal of PAR. Participants made use of the space, structure, and climate of the institute to protest the process of the organization's reorganization effort. Many participants, particularly those from historically black universities, believed they were systematically and intentionally being left out of the organization's supposedly public and participatory reorganization process. The organization's rhetoric espoused a transparent consultation process that was to include all research stakeholders. The participants themselves initiated the forming of a group to take political action that significantly affected the reorganization effort in a way unforeseen and uncontrolled by the organization's hierarchy. As it became clear that political action would result from the participants' organizing during the PAR institute, unit staff were given the opportunity to distance themselves from the bureaucratic fallout, which might affect them professionally within the organization. Few took that option. Perhaps partially as a result of the participants' actions, within a year after the PAR institute, the small unit, unable to defend itself against a series of bureaucratic maneuvers, was dissolved. My relationship with the larger organization was also dissolved. Neither action was a surprise. Some of the unit staff and I took pride, however, that despite consequences and tensions the congruency thing worked.

The "near" environment of much psychology education, graduate or undergraduate, privileges practices and conditions that are the antithesis of interpretive or participatory research. It is difficult for researchers-in-training to learn to value listening to people's stories when the near environment privileges the professor's voice. It is difficult for researchers-in-training to value "experience" when the near environment privileges abstract theory. It is difficult to learn to make sense of and give meaning to lived experience, when the near environment supports hiding and ignoring one's own experience, feelings, and thoughts, in order to "survive" personally or professionally (Baker's Dozen 1997; Bernardez 1997; Rabinowitz and Weseen 1997). It is difficult to learn to equally value nonquantitative ways of making sense of experience, when the near environment privileges assessment techniques and admission standards that quantify all learning. It is difficult for researchers-in-training to learn to name and explore the intimate connections between thoughts and feelings, when learners are expected to leave their "limbic systems" at the classroom door and proceed as if it were possible, indeed preferable, to teach to a disconnected prefrontal lobe. It is difficult to learn to value diversity and multiple identities when the composition of the literature, texts, faculty, students, and staff do not reflect these qualities.

To support the production of new, valid, credible knowledge (Tolman and Brydon-Miller 1997, 602), we must simultaneously create spaces, climates, and pedagogical practices that support new ways of knowing, decision-making, and resource allocating. We must challenge what we consider as "evidence" of knowing. And we must be willing to work through the discomforts, tensions, and risks involved. Transforming psychological research by transforming the education of psychology researchers may seem like a formidable task. However, concerned educators and researchers are already building on similar work in other disciplines. The task of identifying skills and competencies essential to new human inquiry has begun (Lincoln and Reason 1996). The exploration of participatory pedagogy consistent with feminist and social justice agendas is ongoing. The effort to challenge and abandon the false dichotomies between theory and practice, knowing and doing, thinking and feeling, masculine and feminine is underway. In the end, how we come to know about the universe, be it through education or research, must strive for congruency with why we want to know. To create knowledge for empowerment and social transformation requires us to change how we teach researchers to create such knowledge. There's no way around it.

Notes

1. Although this chapter describes non-university-based training, I have used similar pedagogical practices in graduate-level psychology courses over the past twelve years in a rural, multicultural university program. Use of the term "we" is contentious. These are my interpretations, but they were reached through discussion, notes, and faxes throughout the collaborative design, facilitation, and evaluation of the PAR institute. For reasons discussed later, the "we" has long been dispersed.

2. This is particularly timely given the recent embracing of participatory research, evaluation, and appraisal by multinational and international donor agencies. There is a danger that participatory rhetoric has been hijacked, leaving behind the underlying values and skills and leaving intact non-participatory, non-democratic practices and structures.

3. I believe this interest in PAR reflected the post-apartheid hunger for democratic processes. Also, despite the fact that PAR was known to have originated partly in Africa (Hall 1993), there has been little exposure to and availability of materials in South Africa.

References

Baker's Dozen. 1997. Feminist student voices. In *Shaping the future of feminist psychology*, eds. J. Worrell and N. Johnson, 227-244. Washington, DC: American Psychological Association.

Bernardez, T. 1997. Feminizing psychoanalysis: the process and experience of integrating feminist thinking and practice in a new psychoanalytic institute. In *Doing feminism: Teaching and research in the academy*, eds. M. Anderson, L.

Fine, K. Geissler, and J. Ladenson, 91–102. East Lansing: Women's Studies Program, Michigan State University.

Bleier, R., ed. 1986. *Feminist approaches to science.* New York: Pergamon Press.

Bradbury, H., and P. Reason, eds. 2000. *Handbook of action research.* Thousand Oaks, CA: Sage.

Brydon-Miller, M., and D. Tolman. 1997. Engaging the process of transformation. *Journal of Social Issues* 53 (4): 803–810.

Cole, R. 1995. *Educating everybody's children: Diverse teaching strategies for diverse learners.* Alexandria, VA: Association for Supervision and Curriculum Development.

Denzin, N., and Y. Lincoln, eds. 1994. *Handbook of qualitative inquiry.* Thousand Oaks, CA: Sage.

DeVault, M. 1999. *Liberating method: Feminism and social research.* Philadelphia: Temple University Press.

Fonow, M. M., and J. A. Cook, eds. 1991. *Beyond methodology: Feminist scholarship as lived research.* Bloomington: Indiana University Press.

Forum Qualitative Sozialforschung (Forum: Qualitative Social Research). 2000. Concept. On-line journal, cited 26 January 2000. Available at: http://www.qualitative-research.net/fqs/fqs-e/kinzept-e.htm

Freire, P. 1970. *Pedagogy of the oppressed.* New York: Continuum.

———. 1973. *Education for critical consciousness.* New York: Continuum.

Greenwood, D., and M. Levin. 1998. *Introduction to action research: Social research for social change.* Thousand Oaks, CA: Sage.

Gregorc, A. 1979. *Student learning styles.* Washington, DC: National Association of Secondary School Principals.

Hall, B. 1993. Introduction. In *Voices of change: Participatory research in the United States and Canada,* eds. P. Park, M. Brydon-Miller, B. Hall, and T. Jackson, xiii–xxii. Westport, CT: Bergin and Garvey.

Jordan, J., A. Kaplan, J. B. Miller, I. Stiver, and J. Surrey. 1991. *Women's growth in connection.* New York: Guilford Press.

Kerlin, B. 2000. Qualitative research in the United States. *Forum Qualitative Sozialforschung (Forum: Qualitative Social Research)* On-line journal, cited 26 January 2000. Available at: http://qualitative-research.net/fqs.

Kindervatter, S. 1979. *Nonformal education as an empowering process.* Amherst: Center for International Education, University of Massachusetts.

Kolb, D. 1985. *Learning style inventory.* Boston: McBer and Company.

Levin, M., and D. Greenwood. 2000. Pragmatic action research and efforts to transform universities into learning communities. In *Handbook of action research,* eds. P. Reason and H. Bradbury. Thousand Oaks, CA: Sage.

Lincoln, Y., and P. Reason, eds. 1996. Editor's introduction. *Qualitative Inquiry: Special Issue on Quality in Human Inquiry* 2 (1): 5–11.

Maguire, P. 2000. Uneven ground: Feminisms and action research. In *Handbook of action research,* eds. P. Reason and H. Bradbury. Thousand Oaks, CA: Sage.

Marecek, J., M. Fine, and L. Kidder. 1997. Working between worlds: Qualitative methods and social psychology. *Journal of Social Issues* 53 (4): 631–644.

Meulenberg-Buskens, I. 1996. Critical awareness in participatory research: An approach towards teaching and learning. In *Participatory research in health: Issues and experiences,* eds. K. de Koning and M. Martin, 40–49. London: Zed Books.

Morawski, J. 1997. The science behind feminist research methods. *Journal of Social Issues* 53 (4): 667–682.

Perry, B. 1996. Incubated in terror. In *Children, youth, and violence,* ed. J. Osofsky. New York: Guilford Press.

Rabinowitz, V. C., and S. Weseen. 1997. Elu(ci)d(at)ing epistemological impasses: Re-viewing the qualitative/quantitative debates in psychology. *Journal of Social Issues* 53 (4): 605–630.

Schiebinger, L. 1999. *Has feminism changed science?* Cambridge, MA: Harvard University Press.

Reason, P., and H. Bradbury, eds. 2000. *Handbook of action research.* Thousand Oaks, CA: Sage.

Tolman, D., and M. Brydon-Miller. 1997. Transforming psychology: Interpretive and participatory research methods. *Journal of Social Issues* 53 (4): 597–604.

Toulmin, S. 1990. *Cosmopolis: Hidden agenda of modernity.* New York: Free Press.

Way, N. 1997. Using feminist research methods to understand the friendships of adolescent boys. *Journal of Social Issues* 43 (4): 703–724.

Worell, J., and N. Johnson, eds. 1997. *Shaping the future of feminist psychology.* Washington, DC: American Psychological Association.

18

■ ■ ■ ■ ■ ■ ■ ■ ■

Discursive Approaches to Studying Conscious and Unconscious Thoughts

Michael Billig

IN RECENT YEARS, an increasing number of psychologists have been contending that psychology has historically ignored the extent to which psychological phenomena are socially constructed (e.g., Gergen 1994; Shotter 1993a, 1993b; Sampson 1993). One part of the social constructionist movement in psychology has been discursive or rhetorical psychology. Discursive psychologists contend that many of the phenomena, such as attitudes, remembering, and thinking, that psychologists have traditionally studied are constituted in discourse. Consequently, rather than searching for hidden, internal processes, psychologists studying these phenomena should be adapting the micro-sociological and rhetorical methods that have been used to investigate the social practices of talk (for presentations of the discursive approach, see, e.g., Billig 1996; Edwards 1997; Harré and Gillett 1994; Parker 1992; Potter 1996). In particular, discursive psychologists have used the techniques of that branch of sociology known as Conversation Analysis (Drew 1995; Nofsinger 1991; Psathas 1995), as well as forms of ideological analysis (Billig et al. 1988; Billig 1992; Edley and Wetherell 1995; Wetherell and Potter 1993). So quickly has discursive psychology grown in Britain that it has arguably become the dominant trend in British social psychology.

It would be wrong to characterize the turn to discursive psychology merely in terms of using qualitative methodologies. The methodological techniques stem from a philosophical position regarding the nature of mental processes. This philosophical position, rather than methodology per se, distinguishes discursive psychology from more orthodox forms of psychology, especially cognitive psychology. Discursive psychologists have paid much attention to the nature of thinking and have stressed the social and rhetorical bases of thought, recasting conscious thinking in terms of dialogic processes. A further step can be taken. As I have emphasized in recent work, unconscious thinking—and unconscious emotions—can also be understood in terms of dialogue (Billig 1999). By taking this extra step, psychologists can construct a deeper, more nuanced image of the individual by emphasizing that we are formed not only by the discourses we utter, but also by those that we unconsciously and routinely avoid.

Philosophical Background

By and large, cognitive psychologists have taken a Cartesian position regarding the nature of human thinking. They assume that the subject matter of psychology comprises internal states or processes, which are themselves unobservable and must be inferred from outward behavior. As Potter and Wetherell (1987) showed in their path-breaking book, *Discourse and Social Psychology*, social psychologists have tended to study "attitudes" by seeking the internalized "attitudinal systems" of individuals. An attitudinal system is always a hypothetical construct: it does not, and cannot, exist in the same way as a table or chair. It is presumed to be hidden within the individual's head, governing the way that the individual organizes thoughts, experiences, and reactions. In consequence, for much of social psychology, especially cognitive social psychology, the objects of study—whether attitudinal systems, social identities, or cognitive schemata—are unobservable. Similarly, when cognitive psychologists study "memory," they search for internal, unobservable systems of information storage, postulating hypothetical entities such as "engrams," "memory-traces," and "memory-organization packets." These are ghostly essences, lying behind and supposedly controlling what can be directly observed.

Discursive psychology, by contrast, does not locate "memory" and "attitudes" within the head of the isolated individual. Rather, it sees them as constituted through social activity, especially through conversation. Ludwig Wittgenstein addressed the question, How can we have a psychological language? (Harré and Gillett 1994; Shotter 1993a, 1993b). By psychological language, Wittgenstein was not referring to the technical concepts of psychologists, but to everyday psychological terms, such as "thinking," "hoping," and "feeling." Again and again, he criticized the naive Cartesian theory that such words denoted internal, private states. For instance, if someone says "I feel happy," then, according to Wittgenstein, they are not merely, or even principally, describing an internal state. Wittgenstein's great insight was that we could never have a public psychological language if its constructs only labeled inner states. Our psychological language, Wittgenstein claimed, must function in much the same way as our language of physical objects does. We learn how to use words such as "table" and "chair" by observing how these words are used; in this way, we learn to play the appropriate language-games. Wittgenstein stressed that precisely the same happens with the use of psychological words. Their sense must be understood in terms of the social practices of their usage. Children learn to use language such as "I remember" or "I have a pain" in the same way that they learn other concepts; and children can be corrected if their usage is incorrect, even if they are ascribing the words to themselves. Thus, the criteria for using psychological words cannot be internal, private states, which are only known to the speaker. As Wittgenstein stated in *Philosophical Investigations*, "an 'inner process' stands in need of outward criteria" (1953, 580).

In his criticism of Cartesianism, Wittgenstein developed a further point. By and large, our use of language is not confined to describing the external world or internal states. We do things with words: "words are deeds" (Wittgenstein 1980, 46). To understand our psychological language, therefore, we should investigate what we are doing when we are using such language in talk (Wittgenstein 1953, 190). Wittgenstein was, in effect, proposing a pragmatic view of language: the meaning of utterances was to be understood in terms of their usage. While Wittgenstein illustrated his arguments with hypothetical examples, the development of recording devices has made possible the empirical investigation of naturally occurring talk. The micro-sociological work of Harvey Sacks and other Conversation Analysts has shown that even the apparently simplest snatches of conversational interaction involve the practice of complex codes of turn-taking and interaction (e.g., Heritage 1984; Psathas 1995; Sacks 1987; Silverman 1998).

By and large, Conversation Analysts have come from a sociological, rather than psychological, background, and have investigated the micro-processes of talk, in order to show how social order is reproduced through talk. Potter and Wetherell (1987) and Edwards and Potter (1992) had the insight to apply the techniques of Conversation Analysis to show concretely how our mental lives are constituted and reproduced through talk. Analysis of actual talk confirmed Wittgenstein's argument: statements using psychological words, such as "I believe," "I think," and "I feel," are not used in conversation as simple reports of inner states, as if they were outward manifestations of internal structures of belief, cognition, or feeling (Edwards 1997). Such phrases are part of outwardly observable social interaction, opening up the possibility that the supposedly inner, individual, and hidden psychological world is theoretically and methodologically directly observable through examining the practice of talk.

Thinking and Remembering

Examples of this theoretical and methodological transformation can be briefly given. Discursive psychology does not assume that thinking is something distinct from speech, as if thought must lie behind each act of speech. Of course, this position does not imply that all the contents of experience are language-based. Clearly perceptual experience, of the sort which nonhumans can also have, is not rooted in language. Rather, the distinctively human forms of thinking or deliberation—such as thinking about what to do next, about other people's characters, about morality, injustice, and so on—are constituted within social life and within language.

Important methodological implications follow from this position. If thinking is a form of inner dialogue, then children learn to think by being immersed in a world of dialogue. They acquire the rhetoric of justification and criticism, which is so crucial for conversational debate (Billig 1996; Edwards and Potter 1992). These skills can then become internalized, so that the developing child learns to debate with him/herself. The skills of individual thinking, or inner speech, are, therefore, acquired through dialogic skills. In this respect, the basic skills of deliberative thinking are not mysterious, hidden processes. They can be outwardly observed in conversation, when speakers debate together.

Conventional psychology tends to assume that conversational utterances are manifestations of more basic cognitive processes, which the psychologist should *really* be studying. Discursive psychologists, by contrast, stress that utterances are not necessarily *signs* of internal processes, as if the cognitive process occurs first, and then the speaker finds words in which to clothe the thoughts. Instead, thinking can be performed in dialogue and, thus, the psychologist can study thinking directly by studying the outward processes of dialogue in their own right (Billig 1996).

There are good reasons for making such a claim. Every day, people produce utterances neither they nor anyone else have made before. Conversationalists are not merely following codes of conversation or externalizing an internal schema. They react to the novelties of each conversational situation, producing utterances designed for each rhetorical occasion—or, to use the jargon of Conversation Analysis, they formulate "occasioned utterances." Discursive novelty can particularly be seen in argumentative discussions, where the rhetoric of justification and criticism comes into play (Billig 1991, 1996; Edwards and Potter 1992). In the business of argumentation—that is, argument-as-discussion, rather than argument-as-quarrel—new utterances are continually formulated. We often discover what we think about an issue by hearing ourselves talk it, as we find ourselves saying new things. Even those who are speaking on topics they have often spoken about will be responding in conversation to new rhetorical challenges.

Discursive psychologists stress that utterances should be understood in relation to their sequencing in interaction. Thus, in studying "attitude-talk" a discursive psychologist does not consider utterances as if they are decontextualized reflections of an inner attitudinal statement. Typically, statements of opinion involve justifications and criticisms and are designed to counter or support other views that have been raised in the particular conversation. The meaning of such utterances is derived from the interactional argumentation. As I observed in debates in which English families talked about the British Royal Family, even those who held strong views and continually argued for a particular position would subtly alter their formulations as they supposedly repeated themselves in the course of conversation (Billig 1991). Careful examination of the talk shows how speakers shift their articulations to deal with the moment-by-moment demands of argumentative discussion. Seldom, if ever, is talk exactly repeated.

In discussions, exchanges are often too quick and too discursively complex to be considered secondary, as if they are the mere reflection of prior inner thoughts. Instead, the utterances can be treated as the thinking itself. Thus, the formulation of criticism and justification in argumentation constitutes the thoughtful activity of criticizing and justifying. We need look no further than the transcript of the talk to find the thinking. Conversationalists are jointly engaged in the activity of thinking, which psychologists can directly study by attending to the details of interaction.

Remembering and Memory-Talk

Discursive psychologists have paid considerable attention to the topic of memory (see, e.g., Edwards 1997; Edwards and Potter 1992). Instead of treating memory as an internal process, discursive psychologists examine the memory-claims that people make. The activity of explicitly remembering or forgetting typically takes place in interaction, as someone claims to have remembered a forgotten piece of information, apologizes for forgetting a birthday, and so on. There is not space here to go into the variety of actions that speakers can perform with memory-claims, but the results have shown the complexity of memory-talk. Edwards (1997), for instance, has analyzed couples in family therapy making claims about past events in their relationship. The participants do not merely tell stories, as if they are accessing an internal store of engrams. They rhetorically fashion their stories in order to justify their current presentation of their selves and to undermine their partner's competing presentations. For instance, Edwards cites the case of a couple disputing how the woman's behavior should be described: was she being friendly or flirtatious when she was speaking to another man in a bar? The business of moral blaming is achieved by constructing such versions of the past. In this respect, memory-claims are part of wider arguments (Antaki 1994; Buttny 1993).

The collective and social nature of remembering is illustrated by my study of an English family reminiscing about the royal wedding of Prince Charles and Princess Diana (Billig 1992, 1997c). The daughter-in-law claimed that she watched the wedding on television and that it was so memorable that she would "never forget" it. However, as the family discussed what they did upon that unforgettable day, a dispute arose about the name of the singer who participated in the service. The daughter-in-law claimed it was the popular singer Elaine Paige. The others disputed the claim. The convincing evidence, which settled the argument, was provided by the father, who said that he had not watched the event. In this way, the memory-story can be jointly constructed in conversation; even those who do not claim to have personally experienced the past can contribute to this construction.

The basic principle of Conversation Analysis is to analyze how the utterance is being "heard" by other respondents, so its meaning is recoverable with respect to the subsequent turns in the conversation. What matters is not so much the analyst's hunch about the meaning of the utterance, but how the participants display their understanding. For instance, in Edwards's analysis of couples talking in therapy, the analyst does not seek to judge whether or not the speaker really was flirtatious or friendly, but to understand what the participants meant by their various claims and counterclaims.

All this has a direct bearing on the nature of what cognitive psychologists have called "explicit" or "declarative" memory (Schacter 1993, 1996). Explicit remembering involves making claims, which can be disputed. The skills to make such claims, like other rhetorical skills, must be acquired. Children have to learn what count as culturally acceptable and convincing memory-claims. Discursive psychologists studying mother-child interaction have shown how adults verbally instruct children as to what is memorable and how memory-stories should be "properly" told (Edwards and Middleton 1988; Fivush and Kuebli 1997; Middleton and Edwards 1990). Tessler and Nelson (1994) have provocatively claimed that "all adult–child talk is . . . a form of memory talk or memory instruction" (see also Billig 1999, chap. 6).

The discursive research suggests that in making memory-claims, speakers are typically engaging in a variety of interactional business (Edwards and Potter 1992). By the same token, claims to have forgotten something are not simple reports of inner failures to access memory. As Lynch and Bogen (1996) and Potter (1996) have shown, the claim "I can't remember" can be used as a means of forgetting. It can be employed to foreclose the type of conversation that does memory-work through collective talk about the past. Just as children have to learn the rhetoric of memory-talk, so too they must acquire the rhetoric for making claims to forget. In this regard, explicit forgetting is an acquired skill. One might say that children must learn how to remember and to forget.

Repression and Unconscious Thought

Conversation Analysis typically concentrates on linking the utterance to the immediate discursive context, addressing the question, Why was that utterance made at that particular time in that particular sequence of talk? in terms of the structure of the conversation itself, rather than in motivational assumptions about speakers (Drew 1995). Discursive psychologists suggest that this approach results in too de-psychologized an image of the actor. Accordingly, some discursive psychologists have been reexamining, and reclaiming, the psychology of emotions (Edwards 1997; Harré and Parrott 1996). This work stresses the social and discursive aspects of emotions and examines the rhetorical function of emotion-talk. Claims about "being happy" or "being angry" involve a social display of the conventions associated with the relevant categories. Again, such claims should not be taken as an unmediated reflection of inner states. Frequently, claims to be happy or angry are made in disputes about social relations. Thus, the arguments of couples in therapy are filled with disputes about how each other's emotions should be characterized. Discursive psychologists, above all, wish to examine the use of emotion terms in social interaction.

In recent work, I have attempted to take the discursive position a step further by applying it to the topic of unconscious thinking and emotions (Billig 1997a, 1998, 1999; Parker 1998a, 1998b). To do so, I have recast Freud's depth psychology in terms of conversational action and reinterpreted Freud's classic case histories, such as those of Dora, the "Rat Man," and Little Hans. In these reinterpretations, I have shifted the focus away from the "big" symbolism, to which Freud himself paid great attention, and onto the "little" words of dialogue, which Freud often considered less important but which Conversation Analysts have shown to be crucial in the conduct of conversation. As I will argue, the small words of dialogue are crucial for acquiring and practicing the skills of repression.

At the root of this discursive reinterpretation of Freud lies the question, How can repression occur? In Freudian theory, repression is the key construct: unconscious thoughts are those that have been repressed, or pushed aside, from conscious awareness. Surprisingly, Freud in his writings paid little attention to the actual mechanics of how people might go about the business of repressing shameful thoughts. Most importantly, Freud does not face the issue of how we *learn* to repress. A discursive approach, by contrast, links the skills of repression to those of rhetoric, claiming that language is inherently both expressive and repressive. I present a brief outline of my view of this process below (for a full discussion of my position, see Billig 1997a, 1999).

Speakers possess a rhetoric that enables them to change topics of conversation and push embarrassing topics from the conversational agenda. This is the rhetoric of performing what Conversation Analysts have called "topic shifts" (Drew 1995). From an early age, caretakers can be heard attempting to distract young children and change topics that are considered socially inappropriate (Dunn 1988). Consequently, children are provided with models of the rhetoric of closure. In adult conversations, this rhetoric can be employed to ensure that some topics are avoided, so that a form of repression can be collectively maintained in dialogue. In one of my studies, I analyzed a conversation in which speakers could be heard collectively to avoid embarrassing issues of race and to project racial motivations onto "unnamed others" (Billig 1997b, 1992). A smoothly practiced rhetoric, possibly without conscious awareness, permits dangerous questions from being asked. For this rhetoric, the little phrases (such as "yes, but . . .") can be crucial for changing the focus of dialogue (Billig 1998).

What can be practiced outwardly in dialogue can be internalized and used for inner speech. The rhetoric of closure can be applied to inner speech in order to push away, or repress, troublesome thoughts. The patient Freud referred to as the "Rat Man" provides a classic example (Freud [1909] 1991). The patient was a young lawyer who was troubled by inner voices commanding him to perform bizarre actions. He believed that if he did not obey the commands, awful things would happen to those whom he loved. He devised formulae to drive the inner voices away. The formulae often used the typical rhetoric for changing topics of conversation. In effect, the patient was saying "yes, but . . ." to himself. The patient's "defensive formulae" were, by and large, unsuccessful: the compulsive voices kept returning. Yet, the formulae show how the driving out of consciousness can be accomplished: smooth changes of inner topic, paralleling outward conversational moves, can be used as an early warning device of avoidance. The process of repression can thus be understood in rhetorical terms (see Billig 1999 for more details).

In this rhetorical reinterpretion of repression, I have proposed three criteria for making an interpretation of someone's action in terms of an unconscious emotion, such as unconscious love (Billig 1999). These criteria can be illustrated by the case of Elisabeth von R., a young woman with hysteria, described by Freud in *Studies on Hysteria* (Freud and Breuer [1895] 1991). Freud believed that Elisabeth's case rested on her repressed love for her brother-in-law. The hypothesis of a repressed emotion, such as "repressed love," is reasonable if the following three criteria are fulfilled:

1. The person in question is acting in the conventional ways that someone said to have the emotion in question acts. Thus, Elisabeth was showing the conventional signs of love for her brother-in-law: she enjoyed going for long walks with him; she seemed to have sparkled in his company; and she constantly wished to please him.

2. The emotion in question would be shameful to admit. The shame provides the motivation to repress the emotion. As Freud described, Elisabeth's whole moral being revolted against the idea that she could be in love with her sister's husband, especially after her sister died in childbirth.

3. The person denies vehemently that they have the shameful emotion. Such denial represents what Freud and subsequent psychoanalysts have called "resistance." The denial, according to Freudian theory, is made with a force that seems inappropriate. When Freud told Elisabeth his hypothesis, not only did she accuse him of making a wicked accusation, but her pains suddenly returned, necessitating the end of the session. Thus, she was repressing not so much an inner sensation of love, but the judgment that she was in love. The shame would come, not from the internal sensations themselves, but from labeling these sensations as those of love, for shame provides the motive to deny and thereby to repress (see Billig 1999, for extended argument of this point).

The third criterion ensures that any judgment that someone has a repressed emotion must necessarily be contestable. At the minimum, the judgment is contested by the person who is said to have the repressed emotion. If the patient readily accepted the judgment, then the emotion would not be repressed. The labeling of an emotion as unconscious is a matter of interpretation, not scientific exactitude. Yet, according to the discursive perspective, this contestability is also a feature of emotions, for there often is debate about which emotion words to use. Thus, couples in therapy argue lengthily, and without resolution, about how to describe their own and their partners' emotions (Edwards 1997). As Edwards and other discursive psychologists point out, it is the nature of emotion terms that they are contested and that there is no objective way of determining whether someone "really" should be described as "unhappy," "grumpy," "fed up," or "always complaining."

The psychoanalytic notion of resistance, however, continues to be a troubling concept. Some critics have seen it as a way in which (mainly male) analysts justify discounting the denials of their (mainly female) patients (see, e.g., Forrester 1990). However, the micro-analysis of talk may help to rescue this important concept of psychoanalytic theory. Denials can accomplish actions. "I can't remember" may be a means of achieving the forgetting, closing down discussion about the past. Elisabeth's denial, with her returning pains and accusations against Freud, could be seen as a means of changing the focus of the conversation, keeping the issue of her supposed love for her brother-in-law from the conversational agenda. In short, this type of denial accomplishes an avoidance of certain topics. On the other hand, claims not to remember can be made in such a way that they open up the conversation to talk about the past. In the conversation about the singer and the royal wedding mentioned earlier, participants talked about the past, seeking to fill in the forgotten elements.

What counts, then, is not the claim to have forgotten, or the denial that one might have a particular feeling, but the mode of denial within the context of talk. For instance, Elisabeth's forcible denial was very different from that of another patient described in *Studies on Hysteria*, Lucy R. When Freud suggested to Lucy that she was really in love with her employer, the patient denied his diagnosis, but not in the manner of Elisabeth. Lucy, by contrast, phrased her denials in such a way that she opened up the discussion, so that Freud was invited to justify his position, and the two could discuss the possibility further (see Billig 1999). A denial that accomplishes resistance should be made with a rhetorical force that stops the conversational flow, rather than opening up discussion of the topic. In order to sustain this thesis, however, much future work needs to be conducted on the ways denials are made by the patient and received by the therapist in therapeutic dialogues.

In this abbreviated discussion, we have seen some of the ways in which discursive analysis can reveal how the details of language are involved in both conscious and unconscious thinking. The discursive reworking of psychoanalytic ideas will require more direct investigation of contemporary psychoanalytic dialogues. This reclamation of ideas about the unconscious is in line with Wittgensteinian assumptions (Billig 1997a), demonstrating that discursive psychology, which is still at a comparatively early stage of development, holds the promise of being a detailed, nuanced psychology, grounded in a specific interpretive methodology.

References

Antaki, C. 1994. *Explaining and arguing*. London: Sage.

Billig, M. 1991. *Ideology and opinions*. London: Sage.

———. 1992. *Talking of the royal family*. London: Routledge.

———. 1996. *Arguing and thinking: A rhetorical view of social psychology*. 2d ed. Cambridge: Cambridge University Press.

———. 1997a. The dialogic unconscious: Psychoanalysis, discursive psychology, and the nature of repression. *British Journal of Social Psychology* 36:139–159.

———. 1997b. Keeping the white queen in play. In *Off white*, eds. M. Fine, L. Weis, L. C. Powell, and L. M. Wong. London: Routledge.

———. 1997c. Rhetorical and discursive analysis: How families talk about the royal family. In *Doing qualitative research in psychology*, ed. N. Hayes. Hove: Psychology Press.

———. 1998. Dialogic repression and the Oedipus Complex: Reinterpreting the Little Hans case. *Culture and Psychology* 4:11–47.

———. 1999. *Freudian repression: Conversation creating the unconscious*. Cambridge: Cambridge University Press.

Billig, M., S. Condor, D. Edwards, M. Gane, D. Middleton, and A. R. Radley. 1988. *Ideological dilemmas*. London: Sage.

Buttny, R. 1993. *Social accountability in communication*. London: Sage.

Drew, P. 1995. Conversation analysis. In *Rethinking methods in psychology*, eds. J. A. Smith, R. Harré, and L. Van Langenhove. London: Sage.

Dunn, J. 1988. *The beginnings of social understanding*. Oxford: Blackwell.

Edley, N., and M. Wetherell. 1995. *Men in perspective*. London: Harvester Wheatsheaf.

Edwards, D. 1997. *Discourse and cognition*. London: Sage.

Edwards, D., and D. Middleton. 1988. Conversational remembering and family relationships: How children learn to remember. *Journal of Social and Personal Relationships* 5:3–25.

Edwards, D., and J. Potter. 1992. *Discursive psychology*. London: Sage.

Fivush, R., and J. Kuebli. 1997. Making everyday events emotional: The construal of emotion in parent–child conversations about the past. In *Memory for everyday and emotional events*, eds. N. L. Stein, P. A. Ornstein, B. Tversky, and C. Brainerd. Mahwah, NJ: Lawrence Erlbaum.

Forrester, J. 1990. *The seductions of psychoanalysis*. Cambridge: Cambridge University Press.

Freud, S. [1909] 1991. Notes upon a case of obsessional neurosis. *Penguin Freud library*, vol. 9. Harmondsworth: Penguin.

Freud, S., and J. Breuer. [1895] 1991. Studies on hysteria. *Penguin Freud library*, vol. 3. Harmondsworth: Penguin.

Gergen, K. J. 1994. *Realities and relationships*. Cambridge, MA: Harvard University Press.

Harré, R., and G. Gillett. 1994. *The discursive mind*. London: Sage.

Harré, R., and W. G. Parrott, eds. 1996. *The emotions*. London: Sage.

Heritage, J. 1984. *Garfinkel and ethnomethodology*. Cambridge: Polity Press.

Lynch, M., and D. Bogen. 1996. *The spectacle of history*. Durham, NC: Duke University Press.

Middleton, D., and D. Edwards, eds. 1990. *Collective remembering*. London: Sage.

Nofsinger, R. E. 1991. *Everyday conversation*. Newbury Park, CA: Sage.

Parker, I. 1992. *Discourse dynamics*. London: Sage.

———. 1998a. Discourse analysis and psycho-analysis. *British Journal of Social Psychology* 36:479–495.

———. 1998b. *Psychoanalytic culture*. London: Routledge.

Potter, J. 1996. *Representing reality*. London: Sage.

Potter, J., and M. Wetherell. 1987. *Discourse and social psychology*. London: Sage.

Psathas, G. 1995. *Conversation analysis*. Thousand Oaks, CA: Sage.

Sacks, H. 1987. On the preferences for agreement and contiguity in sequences of conversation. In *Talk and social organisation*, eds. G. Button and J. R. E. Lee. Clevedon: Multilingual Matters.

Sampson, E. E. 1993. *Celebrating the other*. New York: Harvester Wheatsheaf.

Schacter, D. L. 1993. Understanding implicit memory: A cognitive neuroscience approach. In *Theories of memory*, eds. A. F. Collins, S. E. Gathercole, M. A. Conway, and P. E. Morris. Hove: Lawrence Erlbaum.

———. 1996. *Searching for memory*. New York: Basic Books.

Shotter, J. 1993a. *Conversational realities*. London: Sage.

———. 1993b. *Cultural politics of everyday life*. Buckingham: Open University Press.

Silverman, D. 1998. *Harvey Sacks: Social science and conversation analysis*. New York: Oxford University Press.

Tessler, M., and K. Nelson. 1994. Making memories: The influence of joint encoding on later recall by young children. *Consciousness and Cognition* 3: 307–326.

Wetherell, M., and J. Potter. 1993. *Mapping the language of racism.* New York: Harvester Wheatsheaf.

Wittgenstein, L. 1953. *Philosophical investigations.* Oxford: Blackwell.

———. 1980. *Culture and value.* Oxford: Blackwell.

19

• ■ ■ ■ ■ ■ ■ ■ ■

Gatekeepers as Change Agents

What Are Feminist Psychologists Doing in Places Like This?

Abigail J. Stewart and Stephanie A. Shields

IN HER RECENT MEMOIR, Sandra Bem (1998) describes her commitment to do feminist research in 1970 and her early success, followed rapidly by Stanford's denial of tenure to her. That story, unlike some women's of the same generation, ended well, with her appointment as director of Women's Studies at Cornell, and a creative and influential career as a feminist psychologist. Bem mentions that in the ensuing years she committed herself to supporting the development to tenure of younger feminist scholars in women's studies. She saw herself as being in a position to influence the survival of feminist scholars in the academy, and she used that position to make a difference. In short, she became a "feminist gate-keeper"—a feminist scholar who had, however improbably, become one of those in a position to guard, or open, professional gates. In this chapter we focus on the strange "standpoint" of feminist psychologists (like Bem and like us) who began our careers with critiques of our discipline and retain a sense of marginality within it, but who also, by virtue of our own survival and seniority, engage in gatekeeping activities for it. We examine some of the ironies and complexities of that standpoint for the individual and, more importantly, for the project of transforming psychology.

We consider gatekeeping practices that are alive and well in the institutions of psychology and that particularly impinge on the acceptance and evaluation of qualitative methods in the field. The question of gatekeeping highlights the contentiousness of debates about the ownership of psychology and reminds us that gatekeeping, though sometimes involving seemingly minor acts of judgment, is, cumulatively, a powerful tool to shape the larger landscape of the profession. Feminist scholars have been vocal both in articulating the limitations of traditional methods and in advocating use of a wider range of approaches, especially those offering greater voice and control to research participants (see Fine and Gordon [1989] 1992). Therefore, we focus on feminist psychologists' gatekeeping practices in the area of methods.

"Gatekeeping" involves both admitting and barring entrance, and it can bring about or prevent constructive change. Our focus is on two consequences of gatekeeping in the domain of methodology: the way it shapes students' training in psychology, and the way it affects judgments of the work and career potential of our students and junior colleagues. That said, it is important to emphasize that methodology is but a single element of a much larger theme concerning criteria for epistemological voice and authority within established, conventional behavioral science. We are especially concerned with academic psychology, particularly as it is found in major research universities, and the evaluative criteria that define quality and, indeed, academic survival in those settings.

Our business, as researchers, is to create new knowledge. The elite private institutions and large and (relatively) well-funded state-affiliated universities within which we work fiercely guard the threshold of what counts as "new knowledge." Feminist gatekeeping thus occurs within a larger and comparatively inflexible structure devoted to preserving a status quo assumed to be functioning optimally, and monitoring professional performance to be consonant with that status quo.

Debates about quantitative "versus" qualitative methods are often really debates about the ideal position of the researcher vis-à-vis the research participant (see, e.g., Morawski 1994). Debates about quantitative and qualitative methodologies tend to be cast as a contest between innovative, socially responsible methods versus obstinately conservative and narrow-minded methods (if you take the qualitative side), or precise, sophisticated techniques versus mere "common sense" (if you take the quantitative side). We would argue that quantitative methods themselves do not necessarily involve denial of the participants' perspective, nor do qualitative methods by themselves resolve problems such as reductionistic thinking. We suggest, instead, that the quantitative/qualitative debate is really a debate about whether and how contemporary behavioral science should treat research participants' experience and point of view. Are they at the *center* of the research project, or are they ancillary to or even contaminating of the main goals?

Our discussion is based on our own experiences and those of a small sample of other senior feminist psychologists whom we contacted by electronic mail. We began with the Fellows of the Society for the Psychology of Women (Division 35 of the American Psychological Association [APA]) and randomly selected forty names from among those at research institutions.[1] By defining the sample in this way, we hoped to include feminist psychologists who (1) were engaged in the research training of graduate students, and (2) had attained the seniority and recognition in psychology associated with Fellow status within APA, and therefore (3) were likely to have had gatekeeping experiences. We found our sample scholars' e-mail addresses through their institutions and sent them a message explaining our project and asking the following questions:

> As senior feminist psychologists, many of us find ourselves—often to our own surprise—in the position of potential "gatekeepers" of psychology scholarship in general, and feminist psychology scholarship in particular. This comes up particularly in our roles as reviewers and editors; as teachers and mentors; and in hiring.
>
> Have you found this to be true? If yes, in which of these domains—Reviewing/editing? Teaching/mentoring? Hiring? In any other domains?
>
> Please describe one or more situations that strike you as capturing the core of this position, or important features of it.

We received fourteen responses (35 percent). We analyzed these for recurrent themes, so we could focus on the features of our own experience that seemed most widely shared by colleagues in similar positions.

The Personal Is Political Is Professional

Like Sandra Bem, this generation of feminist psychologists has a fund of personal experiences in the discipline that is different from that of pioneering women of earlier generations, and different from that of our students. Like earlier generations, we often faced experiences of exclusion or discrimination without consensual language or concepts (e.g., "sexual harassment"), and often without women teachers and feminist mentors. Like them, we often struggled alone to make sense of particular events. Like our students, however, we eventually benefited from the evolution of concepts and language (like "chilly climate" or "glass ceiling"); they have helped us understand what happened to us at earlier stages of our careers. We have also benefited from each others' survival and the slow but steady growth of a community of feminist psychologists. Our generation, like earlier ones, also carries with it vivid memories of talented women who did not survive in the academy. Our struggles to understand the discrimination we both experienced and observed led many of us not only to an understanding of exactly how various "systems" (admission, hiring, peer review, tenure) operate to exclude, but also a commitment to try to change them. The life experiences of senior feminist psychologists color our understanding of "gatekeeping" and its power to reproduce the discipline of psychology we are trying to change.

Three key issues emerged in our respondents' comments about gatekeeping. First, they stressed the importance of maintaining a critical stance with respect to methodologies even as one becomes accomplished in their practice. Indeed, a sustained critical stance is necessary, regardless of where one's methods fall on the conventional versus innovative, qualitative versus quantitative, "basic" versus "applied," empirical versus theoretically driven, or other dichotomized axes of scientific practice. A few of our respondents mentioned that this critical stance required them to draw a distinction between their "feminist" self and their "scientist" self. For these researchers science and politics felt like competitors. Others argued that "scientific" or quantitative methods are inherently oppressive. However, most of the scholars we heard from described themselves as evaluating critically the quality of all work, and as appreciating a wide range of methodological approaches. This more common view required researchers to articulate criteria for evaluating different kinds of work, rather than viewing certain methods as automatically valid or legitimate (see Morawski 1994). Our challenge as gatekeepers is twofold: to expand the range of methods we have grown comfortable with; and to expand opportunities and rewards for our students and junior colleagues for pursuing methodological innovation.

A second theme speaks especially to our roles as teachers and mentors. How do we best foster a wider and more innovative view of what methods are deemed "worthy," while still providing our students with the depth of competence they need to succeed in the present environment? Whether the technique is log linear analysis or focus groups, there are conventions that our students must master. Beyond these conventions lies another, often covert, level of knowing and practice—the "tricks of the trade" that differentiate skilled and accomplished use of the research technique from its naive, and thus less successful or persuasive, application. To become comfortable and competent as professionals, our students must be conversant with both the explicit rules of research and the implicit, unwritten conventions. If we believe, too, that they need to gain this level of skill in a wide range of methods, we are surely raising the bar, not only above that required for previous generations, but also above that required for contemporary "mainstream" psychology students. Since the next generation also needs to retain the capacity to critique new developments in the field that may replicate previous problems or create new ones, we also must be sure that our students acquire expertise at broader levels of theory and critique. Can feminist gatekeepers help their students meet all of these demands, to create what Naomi Weisstein (quoted in Kitzinger 1993, 191) named "insurgent science"?

A third and related issue concerns the feminist research goal of making a difference in people's lives. Philosopher Lorraine Code depicts "feminist methods as *vigilant* methods, dependent on sensitized hearing, seeing, and reading" (1995, 33; emphasis added). Feminist research differs crucially from "mainstream research" in its conscious, open position of advocacy, even when its aim is knowledge production for its own sake. Beyond simply abandoning the possibility of scientific objectivity, Code observes, feminists "have insisted upon the accountability—the epistemic responsibilities—of knowers to their research and everyday communities, not just to the evidence" (38). How through our gatekeeping practices do feminist psychologists foster accountability to the wider society?

The Focus of the Critical Gaze

The Issue

Though feminist psychologists share many critical views of the discipline of psychology, they differ in epistemological stances. Socialization as a research psychologist is saturated with a quite specific scientific ideology. Indeed, the *APA Style Manual* itself "encapsulates the core values and epistemology of the discipline" (Madigan, Johnson, and Linton 1995, 428). Being an empirical researcher who is a feminist psychologist does not strictly imply choosing quantitative or experimental methods over other investigative strategies, but it does imply choosing methods that enable systematic (albeit imperfect) evaluation of competing truth claims. Some feminist psychologists are drawn to the public definition of what constitutes "evidence"; to the order promised by the replicability of results; and to the magic of the possibility of unraveling cause and effect. These scholars worry about evidence that seems unreproducible or an unsound basis for generalization. Other feminist psychologists emphasize more that the empirical tools we have are just that—tools that allow us to piece together stories of how our social selves are created and maintained. Still others argue that certain tools—tests, experiments, quantification—are inherently dangerous and destructive. Few of our respondents adopted absolute positions; most described participating in the discipline as it is, while maintaining a critical stance toward the scholarship in it and working to transform it from within.

Our Observations, Our Respondents

Some of our respondents were more closely identified with the discipline than with critique of it. One discussed the process of reviewing a journal article from a feminist psychologist:

> This individual takes a position that I think is not supported by the research literature and offers weak evidence for her contrary position. She seems to

be motivated, however, by a political position with which I agree. I think that her politics has gotten in the way of her science, and that, moreover, she has a somewhat superficial political vision. . . . I would provide as cogent and helpful a review as possible. . . . I would probably suggest that the editor ask for a revision.

Most of the respondents, however, were much less identified with the mainstream. For example, one indicated that she reviewed journal articles "with an eye to inclusions of feminist theory, gendered terminology, misrepresentation of feminist principles or theories, appropriate interpretation of data with respect to the 'sex difference' element, interpretations of data that over-estimated sex differences, inclusion of minority representation in the sample description, etc." For these respondents, critical gaze was directed more at the discipline than at feminists working in it. For example, one mentioned her frustration with the practices associated with choosing editors of APA journals:

Unfortunately, the way that the APA Publications and Communications Board is set up, they have only one position open every year that focuses on a specific background (e.g., neuropsychology, children) and never anything related to my background. This in itself is gatekeeping in a major way, as this committee selects editors of APA journals and approves topics for thematic issues.

Strategies

Regardless of how they focus their critical gaze, all of our respondents were aware of the many ways in which they are called on to stand in judgment of students and other colleagues in a diverse area of activities. As we are called to do so, some troubling practices have emerged among feminist psychologist gatekeepers, including a tendency to replicate exclusionary hierarchies among ourselves. As one of our respondents put it:

It's shocking how this works—one is called on to differentiate in a hierarchical manner the contributions of feminists when there are limited gold stars (awards) or space as a person who must judge others' work and achievements. . . . [F]eminists are more like their institutions than not, and we too often play the game. Not only that, we re-construct the same game in our own world.

More positively, though, some feminist social scientists are finding creative new ways to advocate for inclusion, particularly in the methodological domain. For example, on review panels and in journal article reviews, as on dissertation committees, we ask for qualitative methods that are missing, wonder about the over-reliance on conventional indicators, and question the completeness of a research program that depends only on experimental or survey data.

Feminist gatekeepers are aware of the great power they have over some others (particularly their students, junior colleagues, and authors) through specific gatekeeping practices. At the same time, they frequently describe how powerless they feel to bring about systemic changes in institutions—changes that would affect more individuals and in more enduring ways. These institutions include the peer review practices of journals and funding agencies (see Blair, Brown, and Baxter 1994, for a particularly chilling account) and especially hiring and promotion processes within universities. For example, one respondent described feelings that have been an unchanging part of feminist psychologists' experience for many years:

> In hiring, there is sometimes the difficulty of having the top female candidate evaluated as less worthy than a group of several male candidates. Then I wonder if we are being fair or if bias has not crept into our evaluations. I wonder about the value of giving the job to the person with high numbers of publications and an assertive self-presentation. I wonder if women are being excluded for the wrong reasons.

We, too, have had experiences in the graduate student selection process and in faculty hiring in which women with paper qualifications equal to those of men in the pool are repeatedly passed over because they don't "look" as strong. (See Valian 1998, for a discussion of the cumulative effects of subtle bias.)

What Does a Mentor Want: A Mile Wide and an Inch Deep?

The Issue

The advice that we feel compelled to give our students today is not that different from the advice given to us. As young entrants into the profession we were advised that it was OK to be interested in "women's concerns," but that this would never get us tenure or respectability. This has changed over the years. Some topics then disparaged as unworthy of scientific study, such as women's reproductive health or violence against women, are now acceptable. Many feminist psychologists are disturbed that nevertheless we feel compelled to counsel students and junior colleagues to "balance" their practice of innovative, interdisciplinary, and feminist research with expertise in conventional methods, aiming to place their work in the "flagship" conventional journals. It is the academic version of having to be twice as good to get and keep the job.

In many respects, the "how" of doing research has been more resistant to change than the questions or problems considered legitimate for study (Lykes and Stewart 1986). Furthermore, with more informational and computational resources available to junior faculty, and postdoctoral experience becoming the norm, the productivity bar for tenure has been raised considerably. Junior colleagues who hope to create a career that crosses the boundaries between psychology and women's studies, for example, must be conversant in both the increasingly sophisticated language and form of psychological statistics and the increasingly sophisticated language and form of feminist theory.

The dilemma for senior feminist psychologists, then, is to figure out how we can help our students and junior colleagues survive with their values intact. We search for ways to help them be planful and career-smart, without encouraging them to become self-promoting careerists; to draw sustenance from work that is personally meaningful, but also ensure survival with work that is acceptable to the powers that be. Many of us had hoped that—decades after we were making similar decisions—more would have changed. We hoped we could encourage our students to embrace the methods that suit their talents and the problems under study. We hoped they would be freer than we were from the need to "do it all." But they are not. So we find ourselves policing their training not so much in accord with our private views, but with full attention to the demands that will be made on them by people with very different views. Moreover, we may have difficulty finding both the will and the time to explain ourselves fully to them. Senior women are under-represented in both faculty and administrative positions; for just that reason, they are often proportionally over-represented in service positions when the administration attempts to bring women to decision-making tables (Shields 1999). As senior women advance the general cause of gender equity through this time-consuming service, junior colleagues and students may feel that their mentoring needs are not met because senior women are not available.

Our Observations, Our Respondents

Our respondents were concerned with the difficult balance between being supportive and open to new ideas, and being expected or required to identify and police "quality," particularly when they perceive that the criteria for quality are contentious or arbitrary. For example, universities increasingly tout the importance of interdisciplinarity, but they often still evaluate tenurability on the basis of publication in major disciplinary journals. One of our junior colleagues who participates in a large-scale multidisciplinary research interest group reluctantly has decided not to place her work in *the* leading journal in physiology because at her mid-stream review she was urged to publish instead in psychology journals.

Our respondents' unease with the expectation that they will, as senior colleagues, be pressured to implement standards that they do not endorse, is reflected in the way many think about gatekeeping. One suggested that the name "gatekeeping" itself implies exclusion: "Isn't there a better way to say that? How about monitors? Monitors keep an open eye without necessarily slamming the gate shut." Another respondent discussed her role as journal editor as involving "values conflicts—excellence, inclusion . . . issues of trust and responsibility vs. use of power and hierarchy."

Adopting the stance of inclusiveness and support, however, does not by itself resolve the monitor's dilemmas. For example,

> In teaching the psychology of gender, there is the dilemma of having some highly feminist and committed students turn in work that is not academically strong. Their heartfelt writing and passionate politics do not happen to produce a coherent term paper, for example. There is no alternative except to grade on academic merit, but I think that I may have dampened the student's feminism, to say nothing of her enthusiasm for psychology.

Strategies

The frustration our respondents experience as they juggle the demands of gatekeeping and a commitment to inclusiveness serves as a continual reminder of the need to be vigilant in these tasks. There are numerous, predictable situations in which we know that if we do not speak up, no one will. Often we are called on to be *the* "feminist monitor" when we least expect it, and even those senior to us may depend on us as monitors/gatekeepers. One of our respondents described serving on a selection committee for an award no woman had ever won. The male chair of the committee was a strong proponent of a particular male recipient, and one of the others under consideration was a well-established woman. A heated debate about each candidate's merits ensued. As the debate progressed, our respondent felt that this needed be one of those situations where she pressed forward in the interests of gender equity. That qualified women had been nominated but had never won this prestigious award suggested a subtle pattern of bias in selection practices, a pattern that must be broken in order to be revealed and corrected. Our respondent noted, "In truth, Dr Male might have been the one I would have chosen myself were it not for the gender issue. . . . I thought that I had to practice what I preach."

Accountability: Scholarship That Makes a Difference

The Issue

The quantitative-qualitative debates stimulate thinking about what constitute the appropriate tools of scientific psychology. Once one admits the reflexive and often political nature of the enterprise of scientific psychology, it becomes less tenable to assert scientific objectivity or to privilege truth claims that presume data have self-evident meanings, and thus a life of their own. In other words, questions about "appropriate" methods lead to questions about foundational constructs: "What is offered as evidence?" and "Who needs this construct and for what ends?"

Second-wave feminist psychologists set out to challenge the operation of sexism in the field and make the field accountable to women's experience (e.g., Sherif 1979). We hoped to transform not only the discipline, but also the institutions and institutional practices that define and shape the discipline: universities (particularly in the areas of hiring and promotion), publication, and research funding. We hoped to make the discipline and the institutions open to feminist analysis and thereby more accountable.

Our Observations, Our Respondents

We find ourselves tired after some thirty years of struggle as feminist psychologists. There are many improvements to celebrate: new journals, increased openness to long-ignored or marginalized topics of study, more recognition for women psychologists. Even so, we are frustrated by lack of change in the terms of the discourse—for example, about the impact of values and "politics" on all scholarship or about the value of studying women and women's issues.

Strategies

In certain areas our respondents were optimistic about the eventual payoff of efforts to alter psychology's practices. Many of our respondents believed they could make a substantial difference in the arena of editing and reviewing—areas, we note, where there is no money, little glory, vulnerability to guilt and doubt, exposure to colleagues' hostility, and distraction from one's "own" research, teaching, and students. One respondent disparaged peer review as it is presently practiced, pointing out how much power editors have to select reviewers and then accept or reject their recommendations. On the other hand, she noted that as editor she has "wonderful opportunities . . . of publishing material on completely new topics. I can invite authors to submit work. I can encourage students to submit their work. I have told junior colleagues that if they have trouble finding journals that publish their work, it's much easier to start their own journal!" Another respondent described how her work as an editor harmonized with her identity as a feminist psychologist: "I think that my 'scientific' training becomes interwoven with my feminist understandings. . . . [As an editor] I attempted to translate feminist principles that I endorse to the way in which research was conducted, described, and represented to the public. In such a manner, we can help frame or reframe the perception of women's lives to the public and to the field of psychology."

In contrast to the sense of efficacy obtained in editorial work, our respondents felt *least* able to make a difference in established bureaucratic structures (in which money, prestige, and obvious power reside). For example, one respondent bluntly noted, "I do not feel I have been able to have much impact at all on hiring." Another described the intractability of the tenure procedure: "I recently had to defend to the teeth the quality of an assistant professor's feminist scholarship before our college [decision-making] committee. We lost the case in part because the committee would not recognize the difficulty of doing interdisciplinary feminist scholarship."

Psychology's Next Hundred Years

We began this chapter drawing on the recollections of an eminent contemporary feminist psychologist; it is fitting to conclude with a view to psychology's past. Laurel Furumoto (1996) included the story of Miriam Van Waters (Freedman 1996) in her presidential address to APA's Division 26 (History of Psychology). The story shows how gender ideologies shaped the definition of American psychology in the early 1900s.

Van Waters entered Clark University's graduate program in the fall of 1910 to work with one of the guiding lights of American psychology, G. Stanley Hall. Furumoto notes that at first, Van Waters was very enthusiastic about her mentor, describing him in a letter as "that clear-thinking, logical man of science" (quoted in Freedman 1996, 37). As she became aware of discrimination at Clark she joined other university women who came together in response to the hostile climate, "sharing both horror stories and moments of triumph" (41). By winter of her first year she was discouraged by Hall's demands for intellectual conformity, lamenting in letters home that if a student did not elect to work on "one of *Dr. Hall's* problems— one got nothing out of him" (46).

Van Waters also found herself at odds with the new scientific psychology—especially its emphasis on objectivity. She preferred the older philosophical psychology with its broad, humanistic approach. Like many feminist psychologists today, she was "dejected by the knowledge that 'a trained psychologist measuring heartbeats in a laboratory experiment in attention, memory, fatigue etc. is rated higher in the modern academic world than the most oracular of living philosophers'" and was "convinced that doing a dissertation in psychology depended too much 'on one's ability to dissect thoroughly one inch of reality'" (Furumoto 1996, 68–69, citing Freedman 1996, 46). Summing up her qualms, she questioned the wisdom of harnessing herself "to some sort of mental peanut, and by much straining and groaning—lift it from the ground" (Freedman 1996, 47). Van Waters eventually switched advisors and fields and went on to a long and distinguished career devoted to social service, first in the juvenile court system and later as a prison superintendent.

Van Waters' simultaneous disenchantment with the prevailing scientific psychology and de facto exclusion from it is not an uncommon story. Although many of them made fulfilling and productive professional lives, these first-wave feminists did not have a lasting impact on psychology's development as a field of study. Employment discrimination shifted many out of the academic market into applied fields. Both those working outside of universities and those who did find positions within academe, moreover, generally were not in positions to have the direct, major impact on graduate training that is necessary to establishing a professional legacy. Their legacies as feminist researchers were more subtle, often needing to be "rediscovered" by feminists of the second wave. Leta Stetter Hollingworth, for example, is one such noteworthy "lost feminist" (Shields 1975). Some second-wave feminist psychologists experienced similar exclusions from academic psychology, but others have found uneasy positions within it— positions that include a simultaneous sense of marginality and gatekeeping authority.

The current academic job market in psychology is the best it has been since the early 1970s, and the time is ripe to bring innovative methods and a participant-centered research ethos to (so-called) mainstream research psychology. If the "third wave" of feminists is going to succeed in creating visible, central, and lasting changes in the scientific practice of psychology, they must be in positions that make that influence possible. Getting those positions and advancing in them takes more than the assistance of supportive and welcoming feminist gatekeepers, particularly when the gatekeepers themselves are few, stretched thin, and often needing to work from the margin to the center. Feminist researchers begin today with the advantages of a greater feminist presence within psychology and more widespread acceptance of feminist theory's validity as a research framework. The issues they face necessarily will differ from those that characterize the current climate. That said, it is imperative that feminists who are in a position to lead do so with confidence and healthy skepticism and keep the goal of transforming psychology front and center in our collaborative undertakings.

Note

1. We are grateful to Pamela S. Hartman at the University of Michigan for her assistance in creating the sample.

References

Bem, S. 1998. *An unconventional family.* New Haven, CT: Yale University Press.

Blair, C., J. R. Brown, and L. A. Baxter. 1994. Disciplining the feminine. *Quarterly Journal of Speech* 80:383–409.

Code, L. 1995. How do we know? Questions of method in feminist practice. In *Changing methods: Feminists transforming practice*, eds. S. Burt and L. Code, 13–44. Peterborough, Ontario: Broadview Press.

Fine, M., and S. M. Gordon. [1989] 1992. Feminist transformations of/despite psychology. In *Disruptive voices*, ed. M. Fine, 1–26. Ann Arbor: University of Michigan Press.

Freedman, E. B. 1996. *Maternal justice: Miriam Van Waters and the female reform tradition.* Chicago: University of Chicago Press.

Furumoto, L. 1996. Reflections on gender and the character of American psychology. *History of Psychology Newsletter* 28:63–71.

Kitzinger, C., ed. 1993. "Psychology constructs the female": A reappraisal. *Feminism and Psychology* 3:189–193.

Lykes, M. B., and A. J. Stewart. 1986. Evaluating the feminist challenge to research in personality and social psychology: 1963–1983. *Psychology of Women Quarterly* 10:393–412.

Madigan, R., S. Johnson, and P. Linton. 1995. The language of psychology: APA style as epistemology. *American Psychologist* 50:428–436.

Morawski, J. 1994. *Practicing feminisms, reconstructing psychology: Notes on a liminal science.* Ann Arbor: University of Michigan Press.

Sherif, C. 1979. Bias in psychology. In *The prism of sex*, eds. J. A. Sherman and E. T. Beck. Madison: University of Wisconsin Press.

Shields, S. A. 1975. Ms. Pilgrim's Progress: The contributions of Leta Stetter Hollingworth to the psychology of women. *American Psychologist* 30:852–857.

———. 1999. Ethical issues for women's leadership in the university. In *Ethics in academia*, eds. S. K. Majumdar, H. S. Pitkow, L. Bird, and E. W. Miller. University Park: Pennsylvania Academy of Science.

Valian, V. 1998. *Why so slow? The advancement of women.* Cambridge, MA: MIT Press.

■ ■ ■ ■ ■ ■ ■ ■ ■

20

Making Room for Subjectivities

Remedies for the Discipline of Psychology

Mary Brydon-Miller and Deborah L. Tolman

THE CONTRIBUTIONS MADE TO THE FIELD of psychology by the researchers included in this volume demonstrate the vibrant, vital, and socially significant knowledge that interpretive and participatory methods can generate. In chapter 1, we observed that transformation can be both personal and political. The contributors to this volume articulate specific links among their personal experiences, their political perspectives and goals for social change, and their research. In most areas of psychology, such linkages—or at least the articulation of them—continue to be anathema. Those who employ interpretive and participatory methods, however, realize fundamentally that not only is our research political in nature, but all research in the social sciences has political contours. As this volume demonstrates, researchers using interpretive and participatory methods are making unique contributions that not only generate new knowledge, but also benefit participants through increased self-knowledge, empathic relationships, and positive social change.

The exemplars included in this volume demonstrate the quality and usefulness of these methods and the variety of ways in which they can be adapted to different situations. The work of Larry Davidson and his colleagues is both informative and practical, illustrating the very different sets of priorities and interpretations used by individuals with schizophrenia to define the experience of institutionalization. Until researchers can understand what role institutionalization plays in the lives of these individuals, effective alternatives to institutionalization will continue to be elusive.

Niobe Way's research with adolescent boys provides another example of the way in which different methods present participants' lives in very different ways. This research is particularly important because many of us have come to understand the experience of boys through more traditional research, while the experience of girls has been presented through the work of researchers such as Lyn Mikel Brown, whose interpretive methods have yielded a very different image of adolescence. To know boys through this same interpretive lens gives us a richer image of their experience; as two mothers of sons, we know the immediate impact such information can have on our lives and on our relationships with our children.

Similarly, as M. Brinton Lykes's work in Guatemala and Cynthia Chataway's work with Native Canadian populations demonstrate, when research participants are allowed to define their own concerns, not only are concrete issues addressed, but researchers and community members alike develop a more complex understanding of their experience, especially when that experience is culturally and socially very different from that of the researcher.

The theory and research included in this volume represent many of the issues, approaches, and contributions that are possible through the use of participatory and interpretive research methods. Nonetheless, questions regarding the basic nature of psychological research and its practice remain unresolved and divisive. How can we build conceptual bridges by which researchers can tolerate, and hopefully embrace, the full range of systematic ways of understanding psychological phenomena at our disposal—or at least stand on one side of the bridge and respectfully, if adamantly, disagree with our colleagues on the other side? While we cannot address here the full range of issues that must constitute this ongoing debate, we note three pressing concerns.

First, we suggest a simple transformation that could prove useful in such a building process: the rehabilitation and reclamation of "empirical." In psychology, the term "empirical" has somehow become equated with "measurable," and thus is associated solely with research conducted within a positivist paradigm. Carol Gilligan (personal communication) has observed that the word "empirical" does not in fact mean quantitative; this common misuse of the word is the habit of psychologists. Rather, empirical means "from experience"; empirical knowledge is what we know through our senses. If we return to this original meaning of "empirical," we can no longer privilege experimental and survey methods as "the" empirical methods. Instead, we redirect our consideration toward what methods of research enable us to know through different sorts of experiences. All such methods should comprise psychologists' repertoire.

This then leads to the question of validity. What does validity mean for psychologists using interpretive and participatory methods? The question of how to judge the quality of information that emerges through interpretive and participatory methods is a very challenging one for the field of psychology. While we all agree that standards regarding the rigor and applicability of this kind of knowledge are crucial, we also recognize that the currently accepted criteria for establishing validity in psychology are not necessarily appropriate for these methods. Validity as correspondence with "reality," as assessed by specific techniques, does not make sense in the context of a practice of research in which multiple, contradictory realities are recognized. Given this epistemological challenge, researchers using these methods have reappraised validity. As Brinberg and McGrath observe, "Validity is not a commodity that can be purchased with techniques. . . . Rather, validity is like integrity, character, and quality, to be assessed relative to purposes and circumstances" (1985, 13, cited in Maxwell 1992). Perhaps the greatest hurdle in initiating a reasoned discussion of validity across epistemological divides is understanding that validity—an evaluation of whether data are what a researcher claims they are and are thus credible—may "look different," depending on what criteria and assumptions make sense from a given epistemological perspective.

How to think about validity is currently a lively conversation among qualitative researchers. Central to this discussion is the question of how to evaluate our data in the context of acknowledging multiple, equally valid perspectives on the phenomena we study (see, e.g., Altheide and Johnson 1994; Lather 1993). Maxwell (1992) suggests that validity in qualitative research is about the kinds of understanding that an account of a phenomenon can embody and suggests a typology of five forms of validity:

descriptive validity, interpretive validity, theoretical validity, generalizablity, and evaluative validity. Mishler suggests using exemplars or concrete models of research practice that can reflect "the criteria and procedures for evaluating the 'trustworthiness' of studies" (1990, 422). As an alternative to searching for a correspondence with an absolute truth or reality, we can use another form of correspondence to assess the validity of interpretive and participatory action research: The resonance of our findings for those who have participated in our research. Does what we come to know "ring true" to them? Validity in participatory research can also include a consideration of its impact on people's lives and social conditions: How can the new information produced by our research be put to use in addressing important social concerns? These questions about validity inspired and incited by qualitative research can offer new strategies for evaluating the validity of any type of psychological research.

The work showcased in this volume also presses us to consider not only what we learn, but who learns what and who profits in what ways from that learning. Perhaps the most central, and certainly the most radical, contribution made by interpretive and participatory research methods is in the democratization of knowledge generation and information ownership. Typically, the knowledge generated through psychological research is "owned" by the academic researchers who have conducted a study and those who have provided the funding for the work. How information is selected and presented is entirely within their control. Secondarily, the knowledge is owned by the fairly select group of researchers who share an interest in the issues under examination. Any translation of the information into more widely useable form, such as press coverage or congressional hearings, is usually at the sole discretion of the "original owners." In interpretive and participatory research, ownership is not so exclusive.

In interpretive research those participating in the research do, in some sense, "speak for themselves." Rather than forcing subjects to choose among a range of responses defined by the researcher in predetermined interview probes or survey questions with a discrete set of choices, interpretive studies generally ask participants to "tell stories" about their experience with varying degrees of freedom, depending on the research questions and specific interview techniques used. When these studies are published, participants are usually quoted extensively, giving them a chance to express their feelings and thoughts at length, in their own words, and with the individuality of their experience preserved in the process. Although questions of power still loom large in such moves to "empower" research participants (Fine 1994), staying in connection with participants by listening to, respecting, and representing their voices shifts at least some authority away from the monolithic voice of the psychologist-expert. However, as Erica Burman points out, we need to avoid seeing the use of these methods as simply a more convenient or more compelling way of convincing people to divulge important aspects of their lives to us. When the researcher is able to engage with participants in a more genuine relationship, the research questions themselves are often transformed, as the researcher grows to understand the experience of the participants more fully. Furthermore, the researcher is often transformed through the process of listening to others.

Participatory research, which utilizes both quantitative and qualitative methods as needed, makes the issue of ownership even more explicit. Research within this model is generated and owned by participants and researchers acting together to address issues raised by the participants themselves. From the initial identification of community concerns, through the use of the information generated in the research process to address specific community-based issues, the process remains under the control of the community. While academic researchers working within this model help to shape the process and outcomes of the research, any use of the results is negotiated with members of the community rather than simply imposed.

Both interpretive and participatory methods of research in psychology acknowledge the relationships between researchers and participants and view these relationships as adding power to, rather than contaminating or detracting from, the research process. This grounding in relationship puts the issue of the ethical nature of research practices into high relief. Based on the theory and practice of interpretive and participatory methods, we suggest the following criteria as an alternative way to shape a general debate about the ethics of various research methods.

1. Conduct research that is important to addressing the immediate and concrete problems facing communities. This goal entails spending time in our communities in relationship with community members to determine what those issues are, and it requires us to take an active role in finding the resources to address those issues. Special emphasis should be placed on

expanding work with minority communities and with other politically and economically disadvantaged groups.

2. Accept—even embrace—the inherently political nature of any research activity and identify clearly the political and economic position and interests of both researcher and funding source. We cannot deny responsibility by saying that policymaking is "someone else's department." If our research is to have a concrete impact on important social issues, we must take part in the process of shaping these policies and insist that the people affected by them are included in the process as well.

3. Make the knowledge generated from the research more readily available, especially to those immediately affected by the work. We must be committed to disseminating information in a variety of forms and to making ourselves more available to communities and groups who wish to be informed about the nature of our work. We draw our livelihoods and our recognition from the results of our research in communities, and we need to offer our services back to the community, whenever possible.

4. Agree to stop using deception in any form in psychological research. The current APA guidelines advise against the use of deception, but accept the notion that under some circumstances we can still justify misleading participants regarding the nature of our work. This practice has led to a climate of suspicion that undermines the development of trust and open communication demanded in interpretive and participatory research.

5. Focus on the broader cultural implications of psychological research and work to make psychological research more relevant to addressing issues of economic and social equity worldwide. To accomplish this goal, we must encourage psychologists from developing countries by providing support for education, training, and research. In addition, we need to seek out ways to draw on indigenous approaches to understanding psychological phenomena, avoiding the hubris of believing in the superiority of our own theories and methods.

Clearly, many researchers in psychology are already working in ways that address critical social issues in a responsible and open manner, and we can draw on a legacy of psychological researchers who have made significant personal and professional commitments to social change. We offer these guidelines not to chastise researchers but to frame some of the concerns we have heard raised about the current state of psychological research in a way that might generate further reflection and discussion.

We conclude by outlining some of the structural changes in training and employment that will enable the transformative innovations represented in this volume to find broader acceptance in the field. The psychology curriculum is a good place to begin serious evaluation and change. The positivist paradigm is so deeply embedded in our discipline that we tend not to acknowledge its existence, nor do we provide sufficient training to students, undergraduate or graduate, in other theoretical frameworks. Research methods courses can examine the advantages and disadvantages of all methods more critically by providing equal weight to interpretive and participatory methods. Jeanne Maracek, Michelle Fine, and Louise Kidder's chapter illustrates that, at present, the answer to the question, "Can I do a qualitative dissertation?" is, at best, "Yes, as long as there is a quantitative component." Using our own experiences as exemplars, Deb was able to use interpretive methods in her dissertation research because she was working with faculty already committed to these approaches and to supporting their use in her institution. Mary was able to use participatory methods because she had taught statistics for so long that she had already established her credibility as a researcher. As one member of her committee said, "It's so nice to have someone actually choose to use this method, rather than doing it only because they can't handle the statistics." To strengthen everyone's appreciation for both the usefulness and the vulnerabilities of all methods available to us, we need to shift away from the assumption that experimental and survey methods are always acceptable and that interpretive, participatory, and other qualitative methods are always suspect. Rather, we can focus our training efforts on how to ask and answer compelling, socially significant research questions using the most appropriate methods for answering those questions.

Even where education is more amenable to these methods, faculty must be concerned about the future employability of their students. It is relatively easy for those well established in the field and in their departments to make the leap of faith necessary in the current climate to engage in research using interpretive and participatory methods. But having done so, and having communicated to our students the relative merits of these new ways of working, those of us with the power to shape curricula, pass proposals, evaluate research, and hire new faculty need to work together with our colleagues to demand that these approaches be accepted and valued within the academic world our students will be entering.

Valuing these methods takes many forms. In part it means expanding the opportunities for publishing and presenting this research. We are grateful to the editors and reviewers of the *Journal of Social Issues* for giving us the initial opportunity to present much of the work included in this volume, and we look to that publication in particular to set a new standard for incorporating interpretive and participatory research into the field. Similarly, we appreciate the support of New York University Press in bringing this volume to a broader audience and to making it possible for us to include a wider range of authors. The role of such progressive publishers and editors in supporting this work is vital to its success.

In some ways interpretive and participatory research are akin to longitudinal research in that they require a long-term commitment of time and resources. These increased demands and the greater levels of community and political involvement such research entails can be acknowledged by changing expectations for employment and promotion. These types of activities could be considered important contributions to one's vita, just as publications and conference presentations now are. The types and numbers of publications that emerge from these methodological practices are not meaningfully measured by the criteria currently in place in the field. A shift away from number of publications in peer-reviewed journals (though interpretive and participatory research are infrequently reviewed in such contexts by true "peers") and toward a consideration of the importance and depth of work published would be more appropriate. Traditional sources of funding for psychological research are beginning to consider the unique contributions that might be made by interpretive and participatory research. While many of us have learned to be quite resourceful in finding support for our work, engaging our funders in this process of change will make it possible to pursue interpretive and participatory research in more focused and more tangible ways.

Finally, we want to suggest that the time has come for all of us to engage in an open—and open-minded—debate about the future of psychology. Some of the authors in this volume would advocate a peaceful coexistence with positivist psychology, while others would call for a fundamental paradigm shift in the field, a specific rejection of positivism (though not of empiricism or quantitative research) in favor of an array of theoretical frameworks that would fundamentally reshape the discipline. We should resist the urge to flee from this highly charged debate, in which careers, reputations, and psyches are at stake, and strive not to create combatants out of colleagues. We hope that the idea of transformation that permeates the work included in this volume can be of use in this project, and that we can redirect our energy to exploring ways in which the discipline of psychology might be transformed into a more powerful force for change and social justice.

References

Altheide, D., and J. Johnson. 1994. Criteria for assessing interpretive validity in qualitative research. In *Handbook of qualitative research*, eds. N. Denzin and Y. Lincoln, 485–509. Thousand Oaks, CA: Sage.

Fine, M. 1994. Working the hyphens: Reinventing self and other in qualitative research. In *Handbook of qualitative research*, eds. N. Denzin and Y. Lincoln, 70–82. Thousand Oaks, CA: Sage.

Lather, P. 1993. Fertile obsession: Validity after poststructuralism. *Sociological Quarterly* 34 (4): 673–693.

Maxwell, J. 1992. Understanding and validity in qualitative research. *Harvard Educational Review* 62 (3): 279–200.

Mishler, E. 1990. Validation in inquiry-guided research: The role of exemplars in narrative studies. *Harvard Educational Review* 60 (4): 415–442.

Contributors

Michael Billig is Professor of Social Sciences at Loughborough University. His recent books include *Banal Nationalism* (Sage) and *Freudian Repression* (Cambridge). He is currently completing a book on the history of rock'n'roll.

Lyn Mikel Brown is Associate Professor of Education, Human Development, and Women's Studies at Colby College. She is co-author (with Carol Gilligan) of *Meeting at the Crossroads: Women's Psychology and Girls' Development* (1992) and author of *Raising Their Voices: The Politics of Girls' Anger* (1998), as well as numerous articles on girls' development and education and feminist research methods.

Mary Brydon-Miller is Assistant Professor, College of Education, University of Cincinnati. She is co-editor of *Voices of Change: Participatory Research in the United States and Canada* and is currently working on research in the area of cross-cultural psychology dealing especially with issues facing immigrant women and their families.

Erica Burman is Professor of Psychology and Women's Studies at the Manchester Metropolitan University. She is the editor and author of a number of publications, most recently *Culture, Power and Difference* (Zed Press, 1997), *Deconstructing Feminist Psychology* (Sage, 1998), *Qualitative*

Methods in Psychology (Open University Press, 1994), *Deconstructing Developmental Psychology* (Routledge, 1994), and *Psychology Discourse Practice: From Regulation to Resistance* (Taylor and Francis, 1996).

Cynthia J. Chataway is Assistant Professor of Psychology at York University. She works on the practice and theory of conflict resolution, specializing in interactive problem-solving and participatory research processes with groups in conflict. With a primarily indigenous committee, she is currently designing a research program for understanding strong indigenous community systems.

Larry Davidson is Associate Professor of Psychiatry, Yale University School of Medicine, and Director of Clinical Services, Connecticut Mental Health Center, New Haven, Connecticut.

Michelle Fine is Professor of Psychology at the Graduate Center of the City University of New York. Her recent publications include *Unknown City* (with Lois Weis, 1998); *Off White: Essays on Race, Power and Society* (with Lois Weis, Linda Powell, and Mun Wong, 1997), and *Becoming Gentlemen: Women, Law School, and Institutional Change* (with Lani Guinier and Jane Balin, 1995).

Sandra J. Jones is a Visiting Research Scholar at the Wellesley College Center for Research on Women and a lecturer at the University of Massachusetts, Boston. Her research interests include the psychology of women, self and identity, and qualitative research methods.

James G. Kelly is Professor Emeritus at the University of Illinois at Chicago and a Visiting Scholar at the University of California (Berkeley and Davis). He is the author of several articles and books in the field of community psychology and past president of Division 27 of the American Psychological Association. He is the 1999 recipient of APA's award for Distinguished Contribution for Psychology in the Public Interest.

Louise Kidder is Professor of Psychology and Women's Studies at Temple University. She co-authored the text *Research Methods in Social Relations* and co-edited *New Directions for Methodology of Social and Behavioral Science: Forms of Validity*. Her interests in qualitative methods were formed more than twenty-five years ago during her graduate studies when she combined participant research observations with quasi-experimental research.

Stacey Lambert is Assistant Professor of Psychology, Nova Southeastern University, Ft. Lauderdale, Florida.

M. Brinton Lykes is Professor and Chair of Community/Social Psychology at the University of the Witwatersrand in Johannesburg, South Africa, and is on leave from the School of Education at Boston College. She teaches courses in culture and psychology, participatory action research, and social and community psychology and has published extensively in journals and co-edited several books, including *Myths about the Powerless: Contesting Social Inequalities* (1996) and *Gender and Personality* (1985).

Patricia Maguire is Associate Professor of Education and Chair of the Gallup Graduate Studies Center at Western New Mexico University. She is an educator and community activist and works on issues of educational equity, violence against women, child sexual assault, and the equitable integration of and access to web-based communication technologies in support of learning and knowledge production.

Jeanne Marecek is Professor of Psychology and Coordinator of the Women's Studies Program at Swarthmore College. She is co-author (with Rachel Hare-Mustin) of *Making a Difference: Psychology and the Construction of Gender*. She is currently engaged in a discursive study of feminist therapists and a study of the social meanings and consequences of suicidal behavior in rural Sri Lanka.

Lynne O. Mock is a Research Specialist at the Community Mental Health Council in Chicago. Her work examines the processes by which community leaders create personal visions aimed at producing community change, as well as the connections between spirituality and psychology.

Jill Morawski is Professor of Psychology at Wesleyan University, where she also has appointments to the Women's Studies Program and Science and Society Program. Her work on feminist theory in psychology includes a book, *Practicing Feminism, Reconstructing Psychology: Notes on a Liminal Science*. She is currently engaged in examining concepts of agency in psychological theories and a study of the history of male reproduction.

Niva Piran is a clinical psychologist and Professor of Education at the University of Toronto. She has published widely in the area of women, body image, and health promotion and is the co-editor of two books in the area of eating disorders. Dr. Piran consults to schools in the area of body image and self esteem.

Vita Carulli Rabinowitz is Professor and Chair of the Department of Psychology at Hunter College and Professor at the Graduate Center of the City University of New York. Her current work is in the areas of methodological issues in the study of gender and gender issues in health and coping research. Her recent publications include the book *Engendering Psychology*, co-authored with Florence L. Denmark and Jeri A. Sechzer.

Stephanie A. Shields is Professor of Psychology and Women's Studies at the Pennsylvania State University. Previously, she was on the faculty at the University of California, Davis. She has served as Director of Women's Studies at both universities. She was founding director of the U.C. Davis Consortium for Research on Women.

William H. Sledge is Professor of Psychiatry, Yale University School of Medicine, and Assistant Chief of Psychiatry, Yale New Haven Hospital, New Haven, Connecticut.

Peter Smith is a doctoral candidate in clinical psychology at Curtin University in Perth, Australia.

David A. Stayner is Assistant Professor of Psychiatry, Yale University School of Medicine, and Associate Director of Clinical Services, Connecticut Mental Health Center, New Haven, Connecticut.

Abigail J. Stewart is Professor of Psychology and Women's Studies at the University of Michigan and Director of the Institute for Research on Women and Gender. Her research has focused on the intersection of individual personality development and social history and social structure. Her latest book (with Mary Romero) is *Women's Untold Stories* (1999).

S. Darius Tandon is a doctoral candidate in community psychology/prevention research and National Institute of Mental Health Predoctoral Fellow in urban children's mental health and AIDS prevention at the University of Illinois at Chicago. His research focuses on community leadership development, community capacity building, and adolescent mental health and educational achievement.

Mark B. Tappan is Associate Professor and Co-Chair of the Education and Human Development Program at Colby College. He is the co-editor (with Martin Packer) of *Narrative and Storytelling: Implications for Understanding Moral Development* (Jossey-Bass, 1991) and *Cultural and Critical Perspectives on Human Development: Implications for Theory, Research, and Practice* (SUNY Press, in press). He has published numerous articles and book chapters in the areas of moral development, moral education, narrative, hermeneutics, gender differences, and adult development.

Deborah L. Tolman is Senior Research Scientist and Director of the Gender and Sexuality Project at the Center for Research on Women at Wellesley College. She is the author of *Dilemma of Desire: Portraits of Adolescent Girls' Struggles with/for Sexuality* (Harvard University Press, in press) and numerous articles and book chapters on female adolescence, adolescent sexuality, and research methods, and co-editor (with Carol Gilligan and Annie Rogers) of *Women, Girls, and Psychotherapy: Reframing Resistance.*

Niobe Way is Assistant Professor in the Department of Applied Psychology in the School of Education at New York University. She is co-editor of *Urban Girls: Resisting Stereotypes, Creating Identities* (NYU Press, 1996) and author of *Everyday Courage: The Lives and Stories of Urban Adolescents* (NYU Press, 1998).

Susan Weseen is an advanced doctoral student in social-personality psychology at the Graduate Center of the City University of New York. She is completing a study on first-time mothers' negotiations of cultural constructions of motherhood. She has published articles on issues related to qualitative research.

Permissions

We gratefully acknowledge Blackwell Publishers for granting permission to reprint revised versions of the following essays from *Journal of Social Issues*, Vol. 53, No. 4, 1997: "Transforming Psychology: Interpretive and Participatory Research Methods," Deborah L. Tolman and Mary Brydon-Miller (chapter 1); "Elu(ci)d(at)ing Epistemological Impasses: Re-Viewing the Qualitative/Quantitative Debates in Psychology," Vita Carulli Rabinowitz and Susan Weeson (chapter 2); "Working Between Worlds: Qualitative Methods and Social Psychology," Jeanne Marecek, Michelle Fine, and Louise Kidder (chapter 3); "Interpretive Psychology: Stories, Circles, and Understanding Lived Experience," Mark B. Tappan (chapter 4); "Participatory Action Research: Psychology and Social Change," Mary Brydon-Miller (chapter 6); "The Science behind Feminist Research Methods," Jill Morawski (chapter 5); "Performing Femininities: Listening to White Working-Class Girls in Rural Maine," Lyn Mikel Brown (chapter 7); "Using Feminist Research Methods to Understand the Friendships of Adolescent Boys," Niobe Way (chapter 8); "Activist Participatory Research among the Maya of Guatemala: Constructing Meanings from Situated Knowledge," M. Brinton Lykes (chapter 12); "An Examination of the Constraints on Mutual Inquiry in a Participatory Action Research Project," Cynthia J. Chataway (chapter 15); "Phenomenological and Participatory Action Research on Schizophrenia: Recovering the

Person in Theory and Practice," Larry Davidson, David A. Stayner, Stacey Lambert, Peter Smith, and William H. Sledge (chapter 11); "Minding the Gap: Positivism, Psychology, and the Politics of Qualitative Methods," Erica Burman (chapter 16); and "Engaging the Process of Transformation," Mary Brydon-Miller and Deborah L. Tolman (chapter 20)

Index